The Backcountry and the City

The Backcountry and the City

Colonization and Conflict in Early America

Ed White

University of Minnesota Press
Minneapolis
London

An abbreviated version of the Conclusion appeared in "Urbane Bifocals: The Federalist Sociology of Franklin's *Autobiography*," *American Literary History* 11, no. 1 (1999): 1–33; reprinted by permission of Oxford University Press.

Published by the University of Minnesota Press
111 Third Avenue South, Suite 290
Minneapolis, MN 55401-2520
http://www.upress.umn.edu

Library of Congress Cataloging-in-Publication Data

White, Ed, 1965–
    The backcountry and the city : colonization and conflict in early America / Ed White.
        p.   cm.
    Includes bibliographical references and index.
    ISBN 0-8166-4558-2 (acid-free paper) — ISBN 0-8166-4559-0 (pbk. : acid-free paper)
    1. North America—History—Colonial period, ca. 1600–1775.   2. North America—History—Colonial period, ca. 1600–1775—Historiography.
3. North America—Colonization.   4. North America—Rural conditions.
5. Frontier and pioneer life—North America.   6. City and town life—North America—History—18th century.   7. Political culture—North America—History—18th century.   8. Federal government—North America—History—18th century.   9. Social conflict—North America—History—18th century.
10. American literature—Colonial period, ca. 1600–1775—History and criticism.   I. Title.
    E46.W47   2005
    320.973'09'033—dc22   2005007996

Printed in the United States of America on acid-free paper

The University of Minnesota is an equal-opportunity educator and employer.

12   11   10   09   08   07   06   10   9   8   7   6   5   4   3   2

In memory of

Frederic M. Howland (1905–1982)
M. Ruth Howland (1904–1989)
Cornelia B. White (1912–1994)
Homer G. White (1905–2001)

What has excitement got to do with geography and how does the land the American land look from above from below and from custom and from habit.

—*Gertrude Stein*, "*The Geographical History of America*"

Barely tolerated on the threshold of the national life, the peasant stands essentially outside the threshold of science. The historian is ordinarily as little interested in him as the dramatic critic is in those gray figures who shift the scenery, carrying the heavens and earth on their backs, and scrub the dressing-rooms of the actors. The part played by the peasantry in past revolutions remains hardly cleared up to this day.

—*Leon Trotsky*, A History of the Russian Revolution

Contents

Preface

Feelings of Structure in Early America

When I began this project a decade ago, I set out to write a case study of the public sphere as it operated in that eighteenth-century center of publication, Philadelphia. I wanted to engage Habermas's account of the English, French, and German public spheres, the streamlined adoption of that framework for the American context, and the updated but still deeply traditional celebration of the Franklinian printer and the Zengerian free press. Early in my reading, however, I started grappling with Philadelphia's first major pamphlet war, the sixty-odd publications responding to the Paxton Riots of 1763–64. The Paxton controversy soon raised a number of historical and theoretical problems that rapidly eroded my tidy project. There were clear narratives of the riots, yes, but what did the two grotesque massacres of Indians and the threatened but aborted march on Philadelphia have to do with the circulation of public discourse? Were they simple topics of discussion? Clearly not. Did they influence the functioning of the public sphere itself? Probably, but how? How did the rioters come to be labeled "*Boys*"? How did Native Americans influence this debate? Was it even a *debate?* It seemed, rather, an anxious discussion about rural and religious culture, or about the legal status of Native Americans, not to mention a surprising moment of literary experimentation not normally associated with the rational exchange of ideas. From there the questions became bigger and bigger. What was the role of an urban public sphere in a largely rural society? A more troubling variant of this question: what did it mean to focus on urban literate culture in making claims about eighteenth-century Pennsylvania? And a related thought experiment: what would an account of the public political culture look like if one started with rural insurrections or Native American politics?

Around this time I reread Charles Brockden Brown's *Wieland* and realized that this novel, in plot, setting, and problem, was directly concerned with the Paxton Riots; the riots, in fact, had been a critical touchstone for Brown's teacher, Robert Proud, in his *History of Pennsylvania*. Why, I wondered, was a novelist of the 1790s still interested in these seemingly minor riots of the 1760s? What were the connections between literary texts (especially novels) and rural rebellions? Why didn't literary critics have much to say about rural life, and how would they say it if they did? And then another series of questions arose, inspired by Brown's chronological leapfrogging. Having naturally assumed a heavy focus on the public sphere of the American Revolution, but having started in the very different world of the Seven Years' War, I began to rethink conventional periodization and the categories of "colonial" and "national." From a backcountry perspective, what had actually changed with the American Revolution? How, for instance, was the post-revolutionary Whiskey Rebellion different from the Paxton Riots? In what sense were the earlier events "colonial"? There followed some related questions of the political terminology we take for granted: assuming continuities across the eighteenth century, was there a colonial version of federalism? How about *anti*federalism? Or, counterintuitively, a colonial nationalism?

As the original project happily fell apart, and a new project exploring the relation between backcountry and city took shape, I naturally turned to Raymond Williams's *The Country and the City*. Williams drove home for me a greatly unappreciated paradox of American literary development. Writing of the English context, he noted that "English attitudes to the country, and to ideas of rural life, persisted with extraordinary power, so that even after the society was predominantly urban its literature, for a generation, was still predominantly rural; and even in the twentieth century, in an urban and industrial land, forms of the older ideas and experiences still remarkably persist."[1] English literature, in other words, was profoundly grounded in a rural culture that persisted after its diminishment. But the *opposite* holds true for early America, where, in an overwhelmingly agrarian culture, the literary production, from the sermons and tracts all the way to the earliest newspapers and novels, is predominantly urban. Further, the North American "country," and specifically the backcountry, was a different thing altogether from the English country. Williams rightly stressed the need to explore the variegated practices of rural modes of production, from "the tribe and the manor to the feudal estate, from the small peasantry and tenant farmers to the rural commune, from the *latifundia* and the plantation to the large capitalist enterprise and the state farm" (1). Accordingly I have tried to consider the various connotations of the American prefix *back-*: from retreat, reversal, informality, abandonment, and failure, to distance, opposition, past, support, or even core. All of these undertones point to the political, organizational, and cultural distance between the agrarian regions and the Atlantic littoral. The Indian nations, the breakaway pan-Native communities, the squatters, the emigrants in their resettlement, the populace of the military buffer zone, the self-organizing rebel posses—all of these are "back" in the country, beyond the confident planning and steady management of the coastal authorities. In this sense, the backcountry is what the American "country" (the incorporated counties surrounding the cities) used to be; it is the ongoing problem of conquest and agrarian colonization, the continuing imperative to organize and administer.

But such a different American context foregrounded some limitations in Williams's approach to his subject, an approach that hinges on "certain images and associations that persist" in the English sense of the country–city opposition. Williams's goal was "to describe and analyze them, to see them in relation to the historically varied experience" (1–2)—in other words, to focus on the responsive and reactive "images and associations" that comprise a culture's "structures of feeling," in his famous formulation. Speaking of the common English trope linking the country with a "traditional" society, he writes that the "structure of feeling within which this backward reference is to be understood is then *not primarily a matter of historical explanation and analysis. What is really significant is this particular kind of reaction* to the fact of change, and this has more real and more interesting social causes" (35, emphasis added). In this analytical framework, cultural explanation can be dissociated, if not quite cut loose, from "historical explanation and analysis," and the crucial problem is one of perception, of *our* structures of feeling. There is a logic, then, to *The Country and the City*'s concluding romantic call for cultural revolution: "This *change of basic ideas and questions*, especially in the socialist and revolutionary movements, has been for me the connection which I have been seeking for so long, through the local forms of a particular and personal crisis, and through the extended inquiry which has taken many forms but which has come through as this inquiry into the country and the city" (305, emphasis added). We will change our ideas and *then* tackle "the problem of overcoming the division of labour . . . in new forms of cooperative effort" (306). It seemed to me, however, that a more useful approach would reverse the terms, focusing instead on the *feelings of structure* along the country–city divide. By this I mean the vernacular phenomenology of practical ensembles, the collectives in, from, against, and through which people sought to understand, initiate, sidestep, win, co-opt, or manipulate the antagonisms or projects of the time. Rather than separate "historical explanation and analysis" from a "particular kind of reaction," we instead find the two inseparable, with reactions assuming their particularity from historical explanation. It follows, I think, that "new forms of cooperative effort" will best be realized by the study of collective life and its cultural intricacies; we need less to change our attitudes in order to take up new practices, than to understand the established practices in order to achieve new attitudes. As a new project took shape, then, I tried to discern what might be called a *structural analysis from below*, a sense of the backcountry–city split articulated in diverse and contradictory ways and forms by the eighteenth century's everyday intellectuals, as Gramsci put it in his prison notebooks.

All of this is to say that, for better or worse, I've reconstructed a project that foregrounds its own theoretical hurdles. These most obviously concern the relationship between the backcountry and the city, a relationship most sensationally illustrated by the agrarian insurrections, white and Native American, that punctuate the eighteenth century. Equally important, was the problem of periodization or, more generally, the conceptualization of early America as a field of study. Scholarship of British North America, for instance, tended to emphasize colonization, contact, and Puritanism in the seventeenth century, but work on the eighteenth century seemed heavily tilted toward the revolutionary period and the postrevolutionary or "early national" moment. Implicit in this division of labor was a common-sensical narrative of modernity, with Native Americans, yeoman farming, literary crudity, and a vague "American simplicity" contrasted with the spectacular political, cultural, and economic development triggered by the American Revolution and based in the cities of the United States. In foregrounding historical categories, I wanted to defamiliarize concepts like the "nation," and consider the possibility of a properly colonial modernity in which backcountry culture played a definitive role. Finally, and perhaps most elusively, I have tried to reconsider the political concepts—nation, citizen, federalism, antifederalism, republicanism—that so dominate early American studies and make it such a fascinating field of study. Here I have been inspired by the recent work of Antonio Negri and Michael Hardt, among whose virtues has been to draw the insular terms of an American political tradition into the contemporary discussions of political theory so long dominated by Euro-centric traditions. My more modest aim has been to reconsider federalism as a broader project of eighteenth-century colonization, from which U.S. nationalism emerged.

This book cannot adequately address all of these questions, some small lines of which have been developed elsewhere.[2] I should stress at the outset the speculative nature of this study; my hope is that it will offer a rural elec-trification of Early American Studies, expanding the range of study beyond what has emerged in the past decade of "early America" scholarship. For, despite the great strengths of that scholarship, particularly in exploring the importance of race and gender for early American subjectivity, it nonethe-less suffers from an overemphasis on elite discourses as discourse, an exagger-ated focus on nationalism, and a neglect of recent ethnohistorical work. I have thought useful, as a result, to connect historical explication with literary analysis, sociological theory, and historiographic discussion. One cannot con-sider backcountry culture without simultaneously addressing such interpre-tive frameworks as the republican synthesis, social history, Benedict Ander-son's account of "imagined communities," or the canonical weight of such texts as the *Federalist Papers* and Benjamin Franklin's *Autobiography*. To that end, the central chapters, which seek to piece together a vernacular sociology of three recurrent practical ensembles of early American life, weave together instances that illustrate historical projects, literary texts, historiographic methods, and theoretical programs. For instance, chapter 2, "Seriality," dis-cusses such vernacular expressions as dispersal, flight, freeholding, and squat-ting, as well as "woman," with reference to specific projects of the time: the forced relocation of the Acadian refugees, the emergence of a culture of squatting, the operation of Pennsylvania's Land Office, and certain legal and commercial dimensions of Indian policy. Each of these projects pro-duced a body of texts worthy of analysis, but expressions of seriality are evident in more conventionally literary texts as well. Jean de Crèvecoeur's *Letters from an American Farmer*, for instance, imaginatively reconstructs a seriality in multiple valences—comic-heroic (in the celebratory portrait of free-holding), tragic (in the account of wartime flight), and utopic (in the fantasy of Indianization). But my treatment of these practical and imaginative mani-festations of seriality aims at more than description, and thus explores the role of seriality in today's "social history" of statistics, averages, and representatives.

A similar range of analyses is attempted in chapters 3 and 4. The third chapter looks at the fused group—whose more familiar colonial synonyms include mob, riot, and tribe—and focuses on the infamous Paxton Riots. The

theory of fusion was likewise central to eighteenth-century theories of warfare emergent from white–Indian conflicts, while conversely it informed the
Native American revival movements from the 1740s on. My primary literary
guide here is James Smith, whose 1799 captivity narrative opens up a different tradition of subject-formation from that now associated with the
canonical narrative of Mary Rowlandson. I also address contemporary historiography's hollow treatment of rural insurrections, whereby group actions
like those of the Paxton Boys are squeezed into an hourglass separating causal
aggravations from long-term effects, before I conclude with a brief reading
of the Paxton Riots' pamphlet war. In chapter 4, I turn to colonial theories
of the *institution*, which extend and build on vernacular accounts of seriality
and fusion. Here my emphasis is on the related projects of Indian diplomacy,
missionary work, and constitution-building. Thomas Paine's "Agrarian Justice"
and Publius's famous *Federalist No. 10* are treated as expressions of federalist
cultural theory in the eighteenth century, joined with an account of David
Brainerd's Delaware Valley mission. I conclude this chapter with an overview
of the play of practical ensembles in greater Pennsylvania, in what I call a
"federalist counter-synthesis."

Chapter 1 and the Conclusion frame this discussion between two hegemonic myths: the republican synthesis, which dominates contemporary interpretation of eighteenth-century American writing, and Franklin's *Autobiography*, that most canonical of critical touchstones. If chapter 1 begins by
suggesting shortcomings of elite discourse analysis—above all, the over-
inflation of metalanguage at the expense of the vocabulary of *praxis*—the
Conclusion posits an alternative critical mode highlighting clashing feelings of structure. If chapter 1 sketches the rudiments of the cultural field of
eighteenth-century Pennsylvania, the Conclusion seeks to locate Franklin's
writing within that situation. If chapter 1 broaches some basic questions of
periodization and modernity, the Conclusion ventures a response through
thick description.

Acknowledgments

There are many people I would like to thank for encouragement, advice, time, and patience.

Jim Holstun and I first met when I was an employee at the University of Vermont, he the director of graduate studies there. Since his first bit of advice (a crafty piece of reverse psychology recommending that I stay away from graduate work in English), and his Milton seminar of 1988 (which remains fresh and exciting in my memory), Jim has been my teacher, giving me a sense of what grounded intellectual work should be. He has endured hundreds of pages of my writing, always responding with patience, sharp insight, good humor, and a rare intellectual integrity. At Louisiana State University, Rick Moreland has been mentor, neighbor, and best man. He gave an early, sharp reading of chapter 2, warning me that in writing solely to historical materialist farmers I was perhaps limiting my audience to three. Rick, too, has endured hundreds of pages of exploratory ideas and has responded with grace, insight, and puns. Michael Drexler has been a friend, intellectual comrade, and sometime coauthor since shared days at the Cornell Writing Center. For more than a decade, he has generously shared his wit about our common field of study, and I'm sure that many of the ideas expressed here are clumsy approximations of his insights.

My parents and late grandparents gave me the gift of a joy in labor: only as an adult did I appreciate how wonderful loving one's work can be. I'm grateful that Fred and Ruth Howland introduced their daughter to the son of Homer and Cornelia White, who lived cross-lots. They also offered their grandchildren four richly different ways of looking at the same place. As for my parents, Pat and Dave White, they probably understand better than I do how this book comes from them, a teacher and a farmer.

At Cornell University, my dissertation committee—Satya Mohanty, Peter Hohendahl, Shelly Wong, and Joel Porte—allowed me to pursue an odd project, and gave me their support. Walter Cohen introduced me to Sartre's work and gave me encouragement to read on. Barry Maxwell provided a similar introduction to Randolph Bourne. Although I never took a class with Pete Wetherbee, I learned much from our occasional drives to Auburn. The members of the graduate students' Radical Caucus provided a community that reinforced my sense that no scholarship can neglect reflection on its institutional location. Together we produced an eighty-page analysis of Cornell's English department, which, for all its flaws and its remarkably hostile reception, was offered to make the department better.

At Louisiana State University, I have appreciated the friendliness and support of a large and generous department. My special thanks go to Carl Freedman, Pat McGee, Jerry Kennedy, Peggy Prenshaw, Katy Powell, Malcolm Richardson, Michelle Massé, Jim Catano, Debbie Normand, and Elsie Michie. A departmental course-relief award in 2002 allowed me to finish this book.

Naresh and Chandan Sharma provided many meals and words of support—and hosted the best party I ever expect to attend. The generous families of Nuevo San Jose and Fatima have given me a richer understanding of what I'm trying to do and how it falls short. To them, to Lynn Haanen, and to the amazing teachers at the Escuela: *muchísimas gracias*.

Special thanks are due Dana Nelson, without whom this book would not be possible. Gordon Hutner offered generous criticism from his position as editor of *American Literary History*. George Justice and Devoney Looser gave many hours of stories and laughter that made it possible to finish this project. Gordon Sayre and Timothy Sweet gave generous and helpful readings of the manuscript. June English helped me find this cover photograph. I also thank Richard Morrison at the University of Minnesota Press, and Paula Friedman for her kind and insightful work on the manuscript.

Finally, it is difficult even to begin to thank Amisha Sharma. This book has been my volcán Pacaya: at times lush, easy, and green; at others, a barren and rusty ascent through loose rock—two steps up and one slide down; at still others, a terrifying plunge through the clouds, shoes full of rock. Now the amazing view of fields and pueblos, now the blinding cloud of azufre, and, here as the air thins, you the *guía* shouting and whispering *tú puedes hacerlo. Lo pude, pero sólo contigo.* Thank you.

1

Divides

Back Rows

Getting out of the city and into the country requires more than simply hitting the road, particularly if the roads are laid out by the urban planners. We need to be aware, somehow, of which of our analytical categories pledge allegiance to urban federalism. This would be a less intimidating chore were it simply a matter of pointing out the city bias of much criticism—the urban writers and institutions, the constant location of culture in cities, and so on. There's an initial defamiliarizing value to such a crude identification of adversaries, and a correspondingly brute insistence on competing contexts. In such a fashion we might begin with that most obvious index of the back-country–city divide, the series of insurrections that occurred from the late seventeenth century to the end of the eighteenth: Metacom's War (1675–76), Bacon's Rebellion (1676), Virginia's Plant-Cutter Riots (1681–83), the Yamasee War (1715–17), the Conojacular War (1732–37), the Jersey Land Riots (1745–55), the New York anti-rent riots (1753–66), the Cherokee War (1759–61), Pontiac's Uprising (1763), the Paxton Riots (1763–64), the North Carolina Regulation (1764–71), the South Carolina Regulation (1767–69), the Yankee–Pennamite Wars (1769–84), the Vermont insurgency (1770–75), the Massachusetts Regulation (1786–87), Little Turtle's War (1790–95), the Whiskey Rebellion (1794), and the Fries Rebellion (1799), among others.[1] Although such eruptions syncopate colonial history, disrupting the beat of the established seaport melodies, they often sound as remote, decultured, and geological as the Watchung Lava Flow or the Taconic Orogeny.

Nonetheless these episodes have generally been cast by historians as either localized versions of national phenomena or, worse, as so many *symptoms* of a broad unrest to be registered by the urban centers. One contemporary textbook, for instance, summarizes the upheavals of 1763–64 as a sign of the challenges posed for the imperial metropolitan center: "Pontiac's uprising and the march of the Paxton Boys showed that Great Britain would not find it easy to govern the huge territory it had just acquired from France." Another characterizes white rural actions as local foreshadowings of the American Revolution, so many "rivulets that fed the main stream of revolutionary consciousness."[2] Still another textbook suggests that "the failure to give representation or consideration to the rapidly growing frontier settlements led to sporadic tensions and occasional outbreaks of violence." The authors quickly sum up the Bacon and Leisler Rebellions, the tenants' riots of New York and New Jersey, the Massachusetts Land Bank conflict, the Paxton Riots, and the Carolina Regulators in seven sentences, before offering a characteristically mixed conclusion. "The tension between the old and new settlements was only a phase of a more general tension that accompanied the emergence of somewhat sharper class distinctions in the eighteenth century," they note, before adding, "Too much can be made of socioeconomic conflict in eighteenth-century America. . . . Certainly, few historians would argue today that class tension was a principal, or even an important, cause of the Revolution."[3] Imperial headaches, Minute Men in training, rural extremities to the complex urban organs—in most cases, the historiographic pattern is that outlined by Ranajit Guha, in which insurrectionary events are reduced to "the middle term between a beginning that serves as a context and an end which is at the same time a perspective linked to the next sequence." He concludes, "The rebel has no place in this history as the subject of rebellion," and we might add that rebellions themselves have no place in the larger history as objects of culture.[4] So one of the most stunning manifestations of early American culture is frequently evacuated of meaning.

If we have trouble knowing what to say about the insurrectionary backcountry, we are equally flummoxed when faced with that slumbering silent realm. Set against the well-documented and articulate culture of the urban seaports, the backcountry lolls like a massive negation, a cultural nonbeing. One recent study of early American farming wishfully assumes that "the profusion of specialized studies and new fields—women's history, African American history, Indian history, and rural history" means that "the center of historical understanding has collapsed."[5] But this result depends on which center you're talking about, for the *cultural center* remains firmly focused on the elite white men of the cities: the Founding Fathers, the merchants, the professional classes, the intellectuals. The loci of culture remain the statehouse, the office, the printer's shop, and the library, not the hearth, the council fire, the slave quarters, or the field. This leaves the country as either an undeveloped city-in-the-making or, better yet, a theme (the Pastoral, the Wilderness, the Frontier, the Land) for the usual urban suspects.[6] In the anthologies, either the urban writers are ruralized (as in Vernon Parrington's insistence upon Ben Franklin's commitment to "agrarian democracy"[7]), or the agrarians, like Crèvecoeur and Jefferson, are read for their assessments of a broadly "American" citizenship. By the time of the early republican period, the well-worn Jeffersonian and Jacksonian pairing of "farmers and workers" seemingly confirms that the rural–urban distinction simply doesn't hold water in the whiggish progression of antebellum history, and the backcountry is gradually buried beneath the equation of urbanity with modernity. In spite of any number of critiques of the crude stagism of the Frederick Jackson Turners of American historiography, the bias remains: cities are our present and obviously our future, and the agrarian, whether white or (especially) indigenous, must always be the mewling premodern, if not reactionary, resistance to the future. We most comfortably read the colonials, at least those of the eighteenth century, as anticipators: of the new subjectivity, of the new economy, of the new social systems, of the new conflicts. So, in many anthologies, the eighteenth century is the urbane Age of Enlightenment, in contrast to the seventeenth-century Age of Wilderness and Frontiers.

In both cases, the geopolitical divide between country and city is narrativized, resolved in an urban-centered national narrative more often than not anchored around the American Revolution. As endless critics have pointed out, the Revolution has long functioned historiographically as a teleological black hole toward which the early eighteenth century was inevitably being pulled, and, on the flip side, as the originary Big Bang from which all subsequent American history flowed. All conflicts prior to the Revolution are anticipatory rehearsals, all ensuing conflicts so many haunted reprises or logical extensions. But to insist that the Revolution wasn't inevitable is now too obvious to be helpful: what does it mean to deny the Revolution its centrality? Even for the many critics challenging the revolutionary juggernaut, the Spirit of '76 serves up the crucial cultural categories of contemporary scholarship (nation, citizen, republic, constitution), the figures to study (the Founding Fathers, who establish the framework for all subsequent thought), the important cultural battles (freedom, independence, debate, liberty, republicanism), the modes of communication (newspaper, political oration, novel), and the arena (the nascent nation-state known as the United States). It's as if the Revolution can be gesturally put aside provided we can substitute its darling end product, the nation. But we're still talking about those grand, revolutionary cultural systems understood to embody, exemplify, and manifest the national culture. Nancy Armstrong and Leonard Tennenhouse's formula of "Anderson and Foucault"—a joining of Benedict Anderson's celebrated account of nations as "imagined communities" with Foucault's account of transcendent discursive horizons—tidily captures the grand dimensions of this approach, in which the Revolution lives on as silent partner.[8] With such a perennial critical linkage among Revolution, nation, and culture, it's not surprising that Jay Fliegelman's attempt to explore "the world of eighteenth-century theories and practices of rhetoric" begins by "recovering the conditions of speaking and writing operative in 1776," though we might suggest that the attempt to explore speaking and writing in 1776 rather allows him to speak confidently of eighteenth-century theories and practices. Likewise, we may not think twice when Michael Warner's *Letters of the Republic* speaks of "a broad change in social and cultural systems" resulting from print culture, and then moves to generalize about "citizen-individual and national people."[9] There's the Revolution coming in again through the back door.

There are larger stakes as well, for underlying the Revolution-to-nation is the very idea of modernity, which has been long associated with metropolitan speed, population density, administrative complexity, concentrated power, cultural and artistic flowering, dynamic capitalist growth, heterogeneity, emancipation. The sites of our revolutionary legends are Boston, Philadelphia, New York, perhaps New Haven and Charleston, and it is in those centers of market activity, printing, publishing, novel writing, and coffeehouse and belle-lettristic societies that we expect to find modernity taking shape. "The cities," historian Gary Nash insists, "predicted the future," as "dynamic loci of change."[10] It is *there*, not in Onondaga, Chillicothe, Alamance, Paxton township, or the Wyoming Valley, that all that is solid melts into air. Even the recent challenges to this account of modernity seem easily subsumed— erroneously—in this urban tradition. Where do we locate Paul Gilroy's Black Atlantic, if not lapping on the piers of the seaports? Where do we find Enrique

Dussel's modernity of colonial conquest, if not in the metropolitan writings that documented it? Yet the challenges posed by Gilroy and Dussel invite us to find a New World modernity beyond the cities, and to resist the backwards projection of Old World industrialism into the colonies.[11] They invite us to think about a colonial modernity, and in so doing to reconsider the seemingly simple question, "What's Colonial about Colonial America?"[12] Here we find that the biases toward the city, the nation, and the modern will not be remedied simply by examination of backcountry contexts, however valuable these may be. If the spatial and temporal contours of Colonial Studies pose nearly mythical barriers between the backcountry and the city, a more profound division is enforced by the interpretive lay of the land.

The Republican Megasynthesis

A useful starting point is the well-known "republican synthesis," which, for more than three decades, has exerted tremendous influence on our understanding of early America, and which, despite any number of divergent historiographic projects, remains firmly at the center of cultural criticism. The synthesis has been extensively summarized and its major tenets outlined, with the industry appropriate to a hegemonic interpretation. Its masterpieces—generally considered to be Bernard Bailyn's *Ideological Origins of the American Revolution* (1967, an expansion of the 1965 introduction to *Pamphlets of the American Revolution*), Gordon Wood's *The Creation of the American Republic* (1969) and *The Radicalism of the American Revolution* (1992), and J.G.A. Pocock's *The Machiavellian Moment* (1975)—set out to explain eighteenth-century Anglo-American political culture, and above all the American Revolution, through the guided unfolding of ideas.[13] Bailyn, for instance, cast the Revolution as a "great, transforming debate" over "intellectual problems," a debate that made it possible for the colonists to "probe and alter their inheritance of thought concerning liberty and its preservation" (*Ideological Origins* 21, 198, 230). As Wood put it, the great accomplishment of the revolutionaries was that they had "broken through the conception of political theory that had imprisoned men's minds for centuries and brilliantly reconstructed the framework for a new republican polity, a reconstruction that radically changed the future discussion of politics" (*Creation of the American Republic*, 614). More precisely, the synthesizers catalogued a constellation of shared notions and values of "Americans" who, as Robert Shalhope summarized,

believed that what made republics great or ultimately destroyed them was
not the force of arms but the character and spirit of the people. Public virtue,
as the essential prerequisite for good government, was all-important. A
people practicing frugality, industry, temperance, and simplicity were sound
republican stock, while those who wallowed in luxury were corrupt and would
corrupt others. Since furthering the public good—the exclusive purpose of
republican government—required the constant sacrifice of individual interests to the greater needs of the whole, the people, conceived of as a homogeneous body (especially when set against their rulers), became the great
determinant of whether a republic lived or died. Thus republicanism meant
maintaining public and private virtue, internal unity, social solidarity, and
vigilance against the corruptions of power.[14]

Republicanism thus amounted to a constellation of whiggish values and
virtues that combined to form an all-encompassing "form of life" in which
events and institutions—any "mere form of government"—were of secondary importance (*Radicalism*, 96).

Further descriptive summary of the republican synthesis risks retracing
well-worn paths, and we're better served by trying to understand its theoretical underpinnings and political appeal. We may start by noting the persistent adversary of the synthesizers, the Progressive historians and their
heirs, who repeatedly stressed two related fractures in early America: a *hori-
zontal*, social division between classes and competing groups, and a *vertical*,
discursive division between public expression and private intention.[15] The
latter split was necessitated by the former: to downplay, dismiss, or deny
class conflict, elite revolutionary discourse frequently distorted, diverged,
and directed expression and meaning; the Progressive examination of revolutionary propaganda (a less loaded term in the era of Walter Lippman and
Edward Bernays) was surely inspired by study of the maneuvers of the
Founders. What is less appreciated is the reverse move made by the republican synthesizers: that is, their bypassing of the problem of social division by
denying the vertical divisions of political discourse. In fact, an insistence
upon a cohesive, unified, republican discourse has been the decisive and
underappreciated dimension of the synthesis, almost too obvious for comment. Gordon Wood, for instance, complained that the Progressives had
shriveled ideas to so many "rationalizations" or "masks obscuring the underlying interests and drives that actually determine social behavior."[16] Bailyn
similarly bemoaned the deployment of the "propaganda" concept, declaring
that for the Progressives, "ideas have never played an important role in
American public life, in the eighteenth century or after" (*Political Experience*, 211), while insisting that "there were real fears, real anxieties, a sense

of real danger behind these phrases, and not merely the desire to influence by rhetoric and propaganda" *(Ideological Origins)*. In a 1994 retrospective interview, Bailyn further insisted "There's nothing 'idealist' about this [approach]. All of this is merely to say that people had in mind a group of ideas and attitudes and fears that led them to behave a certain way in a political and constitutional crisis. Ideas are real, beliefs are real, fears are real" ("Conversation," 647).

Fair enough. But this refusal to reduce revolutionary language to some hidden subtext was merely a point of departure for a larger reformulation of revolutionary discourse, one that hinged on the synthesizers' own distinction between random ideas and ideological systems. Ideology, Bailyn insisted, "is not autonomous. It can only formulate, reshape, and direct forward moods, attitudes, ideas, and aspirations that in some form, however crude or incomplete, already exist" *(Ideological Origins, 11)*. To give a specific example, "the revolutionary leaders undertook to complete, formalize, systematize, and symbolize what previously had been only partially realized, confused, and disputed matters of fact." Consequently,

> Enlightenment ideas were not instruments of a particular social group, nor did they destroy a social order. They did not create new social and political forces in America. They released those that had long existed, and vastly increased their power. This completion, this rationalization, this symbolization, this lifting into consciousness and endowing with high moral purpose inchoate confused elements of social and political change—this was the American Revolution. *(Political Experience, 220)*

Citing Clifford Geertz as early as 1973, Bailyn developed this formula more abstractly to emphasize the synthesizing power of ideology. "Formal discourse becomes politically powerful when it becomes ideology," he wrote:

> when it articulates and fuses into effective formulations opinions and attitudes that are otherwise too scattered and vague to be acted upon; when it mobilizes a general mood, a set of disconnected, unrealized private emotions," into "a public possession, a social fact"; when it crystallizes otherwise inchoate social and political discontent and thereby shapes what is otherwise instinctive and directs it to attainable goals; when it clarifies, symbolizes, and elevates to structured consciousness the mingled urges that stir within us. ("Central Themes," 11)

We find a similar argument in Pocock's claim that "patterns of language and thought" are "kinetic and paradigmatic structures, which act upon the intention using them and the consciousness which they express, and modify the world just as the world modifies them" *(Machiavellian, 51–52)*. And again, in this assessment of revolution by Bailyn: "What was essentially involved in the American Revolution was not the disruption of society, with all the fear, despair, and hatred that that entails, but the realization, the comprehension and fulfillment, of the inheritance of liberty and of what was taken to be America's destiny in the context of the world" (*Ideological Origins*, 19).

We might well ask: why *not* include the violent disruption, the messiness, the fear and despair and hatred? In seeing the Revolution as a matter of words, not struggle, the synthesizers give yet another answer to the old riddle, "What is black and white, but never red?" But what we should note among these theoretical and methodological claims is the elusive, double meaning of the term "synthesis." For the term denotes not simply the historiographic perspective of our moment, as textual materials are pieced together in some new panoramic account of the Revolution; *it refers first and foremost to the synthesis undertaken by the revolutionary elites*, the formulators of ideology who pieced together and made sense of the ideas of the masses. This should be evident from the verbs used again and again to describe the Founders—formulate, reshape, direct, give form, formalize, complete, systematize, symbolize, create, release, endow, lift, articulate, fuse, mobilize, crystallize, attain, clarify, structure, modify, comprehend, fulfill—so that we see that we're fundamentally speaking of the "Founding Synthesizers" who made sense of the inchoate, the crude, the unrealized, the confused, the disparate, the scattered, the instinctive, the mingled. If we simply catalogue the whiggish components of the republican synthesis, we will miss this basic *formal* argument: the defining feature of the eighteenth-century and specifically of the revolutionary period was the synthesizing of values and beliefs in a political and discursive *system*.

This point becomes clearer when we note the occasional Progressive ruptures in the synthesizers' argument, as in Gordon Wood's overview of the Federalist program in the postrevolutionary years:

> By using the most popular and democratic rhetoric available to explain and justify their aristocratic system, the Federalists helped to foreclose the development of an American intellectual tradition in which differing ideas of politics would be intimately and genuinely related to differing social interests. In other words, the Federalists in 1787 hastened the destruction of whatever chance there was in America for the growth of an avowedly aristocratic conception of politics and thereby contributed to the creation of that encompassing liberal tradition which has mitigated and so often obscured the real social antagonisms of American politics. By attempting to confront and retard the thrust of the Revolution with the rhetoric of the Revolution,

the Federalists fixed the terms for the future discussion of American politics. They thus brought the ideology of the Revolution to consummation and created a distinctly American political theory but only at the cost of eventually impoverishing later American political thought. (*Creation*, 562)

An "aristocratic system" suppressing "differing social interests" by appropriating "popular and democratic rhetoric": this is certainly a fascinating diagnosis from the same author who began his career lamenting how Progressive historians "dissolve the distinction . . . between the Revolutionaries' stated intentions and their supposedly hidden needs and desires."[17] How did Wood split the difference between these two interpretations? Well, the Federalists "had little choice in the matter"; faced with the flood of democratic rhetoric and critiques of aristocracy, they could not articulate an aristocratic counter-vocabulary. Their resulting "achievement" rested in "their ability to bring together into a comprehensive whole diffuse and rudimentary lines of thought, to make intelligible and consistent the tangles and confusions of previous American ideas" (563–64). In short, the Federalists synthesized, at the discursive level, the conflicts and confusions of popular forces: what they could not solve socially or politically, they solved rhetorically. Federalism thus amounted not to a masking of reality with rhetoric (the old Progressive view) but to a *systematizing of rhetoric and reality*, as the concepts and practices of democracy were put into a more controlled, controllable, and controlling order.

It is with such insights that we find the strengths and weaknesses, the truths and falsities, of the republican synthesis. For the synthesizers are correct in stressing the constructive project of the Founders, and even in the historians' neglect of social divisions and focus on elite discursive elaborations, they draw our attention to one of the central sites of revolutionary class struggle—the battle to control, fuse, and systematize not only discourse but, more importantly, practical ensembles, to manage, direct, and structure the divisions of the time. In Roland Barthes' terms, federalism became a mythic form, taking the conflicted signs of everyday language and rendering them a second-order signification. The most obvious metonymy here is the Constitution, which in its structuring, crystallizing, and mobilizing attempted to comprehend and reshape the social antagonisms of the moment. What is most striking about the synthesis, then, is the un-ironic identification of the historians with the Federalist Founders. Today synthesizers take up, two centuries later, the very same intellectual project they've correctly identified in the past. This identification becomes clearer when we revise the synthesizers' theoretical formulations by substituting eighteenth-century actors for their idealized metonymies. To paraphrase Bailyn, the Founders could only formulate, reshape, and direct forward the yeomen, the women, the Native Americans, and the slaves that in some form, however crude or incomplete, already existed. Or again: the original synthesizers become politically powerful when they fuse into effective formations the groups and classes that are otherwise too scattered and vague to be acted upon; they mobilize a general mood, a set of disconnected, unrealized private citizens; they crystallize inchoate social forces and direct them toward attainable goals; they clarify, symbolize, and elevate into practical structures the mingled groups that stir within the society. The synthesis is an idealized federalism, and like the federalists the synthesizers overestimate their achievements; like the federalists, they betray a deep theoretical hostility for that which cannot be easily synthesized; like the federalists, they realize that an important part of the battle for order is simply to keep insisting that order exists.

Reading the synthesis against the grain, we might suggest that it outlines the cultural dimensions of a federalist political and cultural praxis in which the vocabulary of republicanism plays an important role. We can begin to move beyond the capitalized Federalists of the ratification battles of the late 1780s and the party factionalism of the 1790s, for which "Federalist" is always a subset of "republican," and identify a grander American project of systematizing culture and society, a project with its early roots in the nature of the colonial enterprise and its greatest flourishing in the mid-eighteenth-century conflicts surrounding the imperial Seven Years' War. In this broader context, in which federalism has profoundly *colonial* rather than postrevolutionary roots, the American Revolution may be read as another moment in the project to consolidate or resist consolidation, to be followed by the Indian wars and yeoman insurrections of the 1790s and beyond. The periodization of the eighteenth century into the Before and After of the Revolution speaks to the power of a federalist feeling of structure: of wanting and finding a clear moment when the organization of culture commences. A critical lexicon stressing nation, citizenship, speaking, writing, the public sphere, the republic, the constitution, and so on, is deeply faithful to the federalist project and already accepts the need for concepts to organize the unruly within an overarching *critical* system. Methodological and political commitments blur here, as scholars privilege a host of federalist maxims (*culture is a unified structure, it operates with certain checks and balances, it implies a regular state of equilibrium, tradition, and continuity that allows for dissent,* etc.) over a sense of culture's fundamental divisions. This is not to insist upon or celebrate an anarchic fragmentation of culture, nor is this an attack through the back door on nationalism. Although what has become American nationalism is inextrica-bly tied to federalism, I will be arguing that "nationness" was a profoundly colonial development of a racialized backcountry, in which the "nation" was the Other marked by cultural fusion. In this context, federalism, far from being a postrevolutionary movement *within* the new nation, was a colonial movement with strongly para- and anti-national tendencies, seeking (with success) to subsume and control expressions of colonial nationality. To put it crudely, federalism is not an historical subset of the "nation": the (U.S.) "nation" is a development within a federalism with roots in the top-down managerial project of colonization. In this framework, federalism is a move-ment of a long eighteenth century, a movement of colonial origins and a movement extending beyond the Revolution.[18]

Now this discussion of the republican synthesis may strike some as mis-directed, given the neglect and criticism the synthesis has received from historians in recent years. Many historians have left the republican synthesis behind, and, a full decade ago, a historians' roundtable in *The William and Mary Quarterly* took Wood's *The Radicalism of the American Revolution* to task for its: overemphasis on elites at the neglect of "those at the bottom"; dismissal of "the complexity and contrariety, the very grain, of history and life"; argumentation through "sheer rhetorical affirmation"; and implicit as-sumption that the "country and the culture are homogeneous, and its homo-geneity is expressed by affluent white northeastern males."[19] These criti-cisms, which closely echo the canon wars of literature departments, only highlight an irony of the staying power of the synthesis. For its persistence owes much to a remarkable synergy with literary-critical scholarship, in which critics committed to a range of recent (mostly poststructuralist) the-ories of language and culture have taken the initial synthesis and run. The result has been impressive: studies of the language and ideas of the revolu-tionary moment with far greater nuance, precision, depth, and scope. Among the best illustrations of the megasynthesis has been Michael Warner's promi-nent *Letters of the Republic* (1990), which enthusiastically endorsed Bailyn's assessment of the "intellectual's revolution" while surprisingly characteriz-ing the synthesis as "now relatively uncontroversial."[20] Warner drew on Foucauldian narratives of the decentered subject, Habermas's account of the emerging public sphere, and Anderson's account of the imagined na-tional community, ultimately giving the original synthesis greater subjective specificity *and* social location: the workings of America's public sphere were

elucidated, the intricacies of citizen subjectivity carefully delineated, and
the synthesis extended to a wider range of cultural expression, from the novels
of the 1790s to the plebeian writings of William Manning.

Although some might snipe that literary critics were once again lagging
behind the historians, joining the movement as it was beginning to lose credibility, the critics were far from simple apprentices, and quickly moved from
junior partners to the very reinvigorators of the synthesis. Warner's work
was one among several works of the late 1980s and early 1990s that initiated
the remarkable critical explosion of the print–speech debate that, in ques-
tioning the formation of subjectivity and nationhood via the written or oral
construction of culture, has largely shaped the field for over a decade.[21] And,
as if to demonstrate the resurrection of the synthesis by this newer literary-
critical wing, there has been an increased complication of the synthesis in a
focus on competing or complementary discourses. Bruce Burgett, for instance,
has drawn on Pocock's work to stress tensions between republicanism and
liberalism; Christopher Looby has sketched a "revolutionary rhetorical hybrid-
ity" uniting "two powerful idioms, that of Protestant millennialism and that
of classical republicanism" (224); Thomas Gustafson has ambitiously outlined
an "archaeology of sovereign discourses" including "the language of republican ideology, the rhetoric of the jeremiad, the persuasions of Jefferson and
Jackson, and the lingua franca of parent-child relationships" (15)—the list
could go on. Philip Round's formulation of the megasynthesizers' project
gives a fine sense of its promising new developments:

> [the new] discourse analysis focuses on a broad range of cultural acts—textual,
> oral, and material—in order to describe how the *processes* of borrowing,
> arrangement, and emendation yield more insight into the formation of
> revolutionary ideology than more static concepts like 'idea' or 'origin.' For
> language, like commerce itself, is defined by relations, and the formation
> of a revolutionary interpretive community was a function of the formally
> established relations between different uses of the same English language
> in the colony and the metropolis. (235–36, emphasis in original)

We might call this literary-historical convergence the republican *megasynthesis*, and if cultural critics have a faint sense of déjà vu, it may be because the development of early American Studies has so closely paralleled
an earlier theoretical shift from a stark Lévi-Straussian structuralism to a
variety of poststructuralisms. The resulting critical hegemony has produced
a double-edged project. On the one hand, the historiographic focus on the
organizational ideas has been enhanced by the insights of cultural critics.
However, this union has simultaneously reinforced the marginality of the

sociological, the inarticulate, and specifically the backcountry. Inasmuch as the project of the megasynthesis has been discourse analysis, it implicitly privileges the most articulate (and, generally, written) forms of discourse, almost invariably found in the cities. Whatever accounts of backcountry life emerge from social history and ethnohistory, these will be a priori situated within a larger discursive network, for which seaport intellectuals serve as the best exemplars. Because the original synthesis pledged its methodological allegiance to the Founding Federalists and their project of ordering and organizing the masses, even the most finely nuanced extension of the synthesizing project will carry with it a commitment to the federalist view of the unruly back populations. Republicanism remains the purview of the urban intellectual, the theorist, and the writer, who give signification for those who messily live it.

Practical Ensembles

In moving toward an alternative framework for thinking about the early American backcountry, we might turn to a work seemingly distant from the field but inspirational nonetheless for this study: Barrington Moore's *The Social Origins of Democracy: Lord and Peasant in the Making of the Modern World* (1966), a work that appeared the same year as Foucault's *Les Mots et les choses*, the same year that Bernard Bailyn was seeing *The Ideological Origins of the American Revolution* to press. A pioneering work of comparative sociology, Moore's project coalesced around a number of Cold War interests—Sovietology, the debate on German fascism, and the burgeoning studies of the "Third World." What these fields had in common was a growing awareness of, and concern with, the relationship between rural classes and political revolutions. But unlike Eric Wolf's *Peasant Wars of the Twentieth Century* (1969), which examined revolutionary moments in Mexico, Russia, China, Viet Nam, Algeria, and Cuba to foreground the clash between the "industrialized" and the "underdeveloped" worlds, Moore's study disrupted such distinct world tracks by illuminating the hidden rural past of "capitalist democracy." He began with accounts of England, France, and the United States, all of which (with Japan) experienced "peasant revolutions that fail[ed]," in contrast to India, China, and Russia, which experienced "peasant revolutions that succeed[ed]."[22] To demonstrate the point, Moore reconstructed accounts of the English and French Revolutions and the American Civil War, challenging the retrospective narratives that focused on emergent classes and dismissed lords and peasants as anachronistic dregs. His account of the English Revolution, for instance, stressed the conflicts among the various rural classes (lords, gentry, yeomanry, poorer peasants), which allowed for the commercialization of the countryside as well as of the cities while also removing the threat of peasant-based violence or conservatism. So, in England, a rural modernity closely tied with urban development proved central to subsequent British political development. In France, by contrast, absolutism allowed for the persistence of lordly power and the corresponding weakness of the peasantry. When the revolution commenced, the more radical peasantry became a decisive motor for change in an alliance with urban classes, while later (in the Vendée, for instance) resisting urban-based transformations. "There were at least two peasant revolutions," wrote Moore, "that of the peasant aristocracy and that of the larger and more diffuse majority, each following its own course and also from time to time fusing or opposing revolutionary waves in the cities"; within such a context, "the peasantry was the arbiter of the Revolution, though not its chief propelling force" (73, 77). In Moore's account, then, "agrarian strata are the strategic actors in the political institutions from above or below which create the conditions for the development of various forms of political institutions in industrial societies."[23] Even in nation-states with seemingly weak agrarian classes, their relational position was necessary to understand the apparently urban order of things.

Moore's argument still has considerable influence on contemporary Latin American studies, with which current U.S. studies are increasingly seeking a dialogue, so why has this argument had such negligible impact on scholarship on the United States? Moore's assessment of the American Civil War stressed similar antagonisms and alliances between rural and urban forces— whether the alliance between western farmers and northern industrialists that consolidated the North–South split, or the subsequent one between northern and southern elites that left a postemancipation Black tenantry without remedy, largely determining U.S. racial politics for the next century. As for 1776, though, Moore viewed the War of Independence as a nonrevolution. "Since it did not result in any fundamental changes in the structure of society, there are grounds for asking whether it deserves to be called a revolution at all," he wrote. The "great, transforming debate" notwithstanding, the revolution was finally "a fight between commercial interests in England and America," and if the "claim that America has had an anticolonial revolution may be good propaganda . . . it is bad history and bad sociology" (112–13). (It's not clear if Moore was familiar with J. Franklin Jameson's argument sixty years earlier, that the Revolution radicalized rural America, ending royal

restrictions on land use, abolishing the quasi-feudal quit-rent system, confis-
cating Tory estates, and prompting the related reforms of entailment, primogeniture, and franchise requirement laws.[24] But the two assessments are less
distant than they may seem, for if Jameson insisted that legislative reforms
of the confederation period guaranteed the continued strength of the yeoman
farmer in the new democracy, Moore was similarly stressing the persistence
of the prerevolutionary status quo ante, denying any sharp break between
"colonial" and "national" eras until the Civil War.)

Surely a major disincentive for developing Moore's analysis was its consistent portrayal of agrarian culture in negative terms, as a cultural absence
or backwardness. British traditions of parliamentary democracy owed much
to the *absence* of peasant violence thanks to the gradual elimination (by
enclosure, migration, class mobility, etc.) of the poorer peasantry; meanwhile,
landlords and rich peasants had adopted a capitalism congruous with urban
developments. France "enter[ed] the modern world through the democratic
door" because aristocratic landlords were largely eliminated in the Terror,
thus achieving with a violent negation the long "development of commercial agriculture" accomplished in Britain (105–6); the French peasantry in
turn prevented political radicalism beyond the British model. The deficient
yet well-grounded democracy of the United States after Reconstruction was
likewise determined by the specific *weaknesses* of the Black peasantry (never
an organized class before or after the war), the Western farmers (secondary
partners before the war, marginalized after Reconstruction), and the plantation aristocracy (subordinate to Northern capital after defeat). In each case,
the elimination, weakness, or failures of Western rural classes ruled out the
messier developments of China, India, and Russia, a point driven home by
Moore's counterfactual of "what would have happened had the Southern
plantation system been able to establish itself in the West." The United States
"would have been in the position of some modernizing countries today, with
a latifundia economy, a dominant antidemocratic aristocracy, and a weak
and dependent commercial and industrial class, unable and unwilling to
push forward toward political democracy" (153). Here a hypothetical plantation culture is not quite Western; it is moderni*zing*, weak, antidemocratic,
dependent, unwilling, lagging. The particularity of Western political culture
stems from the weakness of the rural, while variants (mostly non-Western,
but including the deviations of European fascism and communism) must be
grasped through the strong presence of agrarian forces. The result is a paradoxical formula of Western development, at once insisting upon the crucial
relational position of rural classes while finally evacuating their positive

cultural significance: in cultural terms, the agrarian is form without content. Not surprisingly, then, Moore's argument would have influence in regional studies where the peasantry remained a powerful force (most notably in Latin America) and where historians, with a complementary tradition of peasant studies, could overlook Moore's dismissal of agrarian culture. In studies of the United States, though, Moore could only stymie cultural historians with his mixed message; his thesis could not be taken seriously unless fundamentally surpassed with an account of agrarian culture.

To consider whether and how agrarian classes may be fundamentally constitutive of the political and social culture of the United States, we need a clearer sense of what makes up backcountry *cultures*. Will we find it in the statistical data of social history, or the anthropological surveys of ethnohistory? In detailed narratives of discrete events, or in the occasional written text produced far from the city? My response to Moore's challenge has been to adjust the scale of his inquiry, to look for those larger class antagonisms in eighteenth-century *practical ensembles*. One of the remarkable features of colonial and early national life is the persistent, even obsessive, concern with collective forms. Constitutions, councils, tribes, confederacies, leagues, courts, parties, cabals, clubs, salons, juntos, corporations, schools, synods, meetings, missions, plans, societies, wards, regiments, markets, associations, guilds, crews, mobs, marches, parades, conventions, committees, companies, charters, lodges, expeditions, factions, compacts, revivals, sects, workhouses, assemblies, congresses, hospitals, plantations, parishes . . . the terms leap out at us from early documents, not to mention the tables of contents of today's scholarly journals. I've argued elsewhere that these practical ensembles took on special significance at this moment because of the relatively high opportunities for "interstitial emergence." The weakness of European collective forms, the adaptations and encounters of the New World, and the clash of conflicted imports with local developments together defamiliarized collective forms of life, prompting such phenomena as conspiracy theories.[25] It was within, through, around, and against the practical ensembles that early American cultural praxis occurred, took shape, and acquired meaning. Eighteenth-century actors understood themselves as living in a society of relatively fluid collective forms, and through these local building blocks they approached those matters we more loosely capture with generalities like "politics," "economy," or "culture."

Talking about this intermediate terrain of practical ensembles poses its own challenges. If today we have extremely well-developed critical vocabu-

laries, inherited from American social sciences and Continental structural-
isms, for talking about Self and System, the same conceptual tools are not
readily at hand for the social spaces in between. To give an obvious example,
we today use the term "institution" to refer to voting and marriage, legislative
government or the House of Representatives, the marketplace or the Bank of
North America: our impoverished vocabulary for collectives slides carelessly
from the precise acts and attitudes of the here and now to the general systems of history. Additionally, the reification of the long established ensembles
of our present-day government, workplaces, and homes does not defamiliarize
them as they once were in the colonial and early national periods. Relatedly, the segmentation of disciplines that made sociology a specialized area
of study has not been seriously challenged in the recent growth of interdisciplinary work, to which an empirical sociology remains a relative outsider
if not an outright embarrassment; long gone are the days when theory
anthologies included a section on "Sociological Approaches." Finally, the
language of ensembles often seems simultaneously static, anachronistic, para-
noid, and arcane, as if talking about practical groups conjures up management seminars, wacko conspiracy theories, obsessive military history, or an
embarrassing and schismatic Old Left enthusiasm for organizational minu-
tiae—evoking, in other words, Tom Peters, Agent Mulder, Jeb Stuart, or
Lenin. Perhaps the clearest marker of our blindness to practical ensembles is
found in the case of Gramsci's reception. Although Gramsci is well-known
as the theorist of "hegemony" and "advanced capitalism," his interest in the
culture of unions, syndicates, cells, councils, soviets, and *squadristi* is generally ignored. In a similar way, we are much more comfortable with Tom
Paine's broad-stroked "Common Sense" or *The Age of Reason* than with
"Agrarian Justice" and all the jabber of mints, banks, and pension plans.

Yet it was through the vernacular terminology of practical ensembles that
the backcountry–city axis and its numerous antagonisms—between seaport
merchants and rural producers, between Native American nations and
speculators and traders, between statehouse purses and the inhabitants of
the imperial buffer zones—were experienced. An Indian treaty was not a
merely local instantiation of dominant discourses, but marked the engagement between multiple practical ensembles, from various Native American
polities, to colonial executives and legislatures, to traders and speculators.
Likewise, yeoman petitions are not simply expressions of a dominant republicanism, though with bad grammar and misspelled words; they instead
mark a particular meeting of dispersed farmers trying to organize themselves

in relation to an administrative body and a perceived threat. Mapping these ensembles thus allows us to situate discourses within the colonial project, and in so doing understand that project as the attempt to organize, control, manage, and supervise agrarian settlement, production, mobility, warfare, and trade. Even during the earliest brutal moments of seizure of Native American wealth and lives, colonization was defined by an antagonism between the metropolitan extension and the hard-to-manage inhabitants of the interior. What developed into the struggle between seaport cities and back-country residents was largely an extension of this overarching imperial pattern, with an ever-expanding cast and repertoire of problems. Practical ensembles were the localities within which these battles were waged.

Such an analysis of collectives has its own obvious problems, not the least of which is the problem of terminology. Are we to catalogue the endless ensembles as so many unique particularities? If so, can we make any generalizations? In dialectical terms, how do we make the move from regressive to progressive analysis? Here I've taken as my guide Jean-Paul Sartre's study of practical ensembles (his term) in *Critique of Dialectical Reason,* a work written at the fruitful conjuncture of Annaliste history, French structuralism, phenomenology, and historical materialism. Making essentially a long polemic against Stalinism, Sartre sought to insert a new vocabulary into a "sclerosed" and reductive historical materialism. Against the orthodox formulations of Class and Society he unexpectedly drew on the "microsociology" promoted by American businesses for more effective management of the firm. Following their lead, he sought to take seriously the "structures and laws" of local collectives. He characterized his approach as starting with "a structural and historical anthropology" that would provide "the basis of the intelligibility of sociological Knowledge," in turn grounding "the intelligibility of historical Knowledge."[26] There is no history without, first, some basic claims about human social life (how we perceive and make the material world, how we communicate with Others, how we become individuated, how we interpret), which allows us then to understand basic collective structures in social life (the practical ensembles, from series to group to institution), before finally examining the clash of historical interpretations. "An anglers' club is neither a small stone nor a supraconsciousness nor a simple verbal rubric to indicate concrete, particular relations among its members," he wrote (126). Not a thing, not an idealization, and not simply a label; rather the anglers' club was a social form, a specific relationship to material surroundings, to other members of the ensemble, to others outside the ensemble, to the action undertaken in and by the ensemble, and so forth.

I have found the broad contours of Sartre's project particularly helpful for thinking about the local and the general in eighteenth-century America, and the remaining chapters of this book will gradually develop the details of his argument, with some reservations, in their early American contexts. Whether this engagement with Sartrean theory is useful is for readers to decide: the leap from Parisian existentialism to colonial Philadelphia will strike some as odd and no doubt inappropriate. So it may be worth noting that Sartre's historical touchstones are generally from the early modern period to the French Revolution. His introduction of the practico-inert is essentially a long gloss on Braudel's *The Mediterranean and the Mediterranean World in the Age of Philip II* and its account of New World gold (167–80); an analysis of serial inflation focuses on the French revolutionary government's attempts to regulate the market (288–93); a treatment of serial opinion draws on Georges Lefebvre's *The Great Fear of 1789* (293–307); the discussion of fused groups is an extended reflection on the storming of the Bastille (351–404); and a critical example of institutional dynamics focuses on the Reign of Terror (591–99). From the slow collapse of feudalism and the rise of the capitalist market, to the development of absolutism and the stages, divisions, and aftermaths of the French Revolution, the *Critique* often draws on the vernacular political terminology (the sovereign, fraternity–Terror, the constituent and constituted dialectic) of that development. My goal here is to give this analysis a bit more of a Gramscian twist, to bring the everyday theorists of early America into some engagement, however staged, with Sartre's later reckonings.

More important, I hope to suggest an engagement between these vernacular self-theorizations and the discourse analysis of the republican megasynthesis. The exchange is often like the one Gramsci described, between a French Catholic worker and an author awarded a prize from the Paris Academy of Moral and Political Sciences. When the author condescendingly reminded the worker of Christ's claim that there would always be rich and poor, the worker responded, "we will then leave at least two poor persons, so that Jesus Christ will not be proved wrong."[27] So we often find creative adjustments of discursive "imperatives." But an early American example of this methodological exchange may be more germane here, and as an illustration I take the following declaration made by James Wilson:

Is a toast asked? "The United States," instead of the "People of the United States," is the toast given. This is not politically correct. The toast is meant to present the first great object in the Union: it presents only the second: it presents only the artificial person, instead of the natural persons, who spoke it into existence.[28]

This passage might be read as a fine expression of republicanism, with the appropriately whiggish gesture of placing the people over the governmental form. A republican synthesizer might tell us that this is the synthesis in action, with Wilson himself speaking into existence the proper relationship between people and nation. We hear those eloquent phrases associated with the political theory of the time—"the first great object," the "artificial person," the "natural persons," and, elsewhere in the statement, the abstract "principles of general jurisprudence," the "laws and practice of particular states and kingdoms," and the nature of the Constitution itself. For the literary critic, meanwhile, there is the requisite appreciation of language, a confirmation of the linkage between nationalism and the discursive construction of republican citizenship: a nation "spoke[n] into existence by its citizens." One recent study, in fact, goes so far as to grant "the logic of Wilson's argument" a prime theoretical position from which to confirm "the origin of legitimate authority in the voice of the people."[29] We might finesse this argument any number of ways and further explore the tension between the nation and the people—there is the political correctness of a particular relationship of people to nation, or the self-reflexivity of the people asserting themselves through a rhetorical objectification of "the people," or the fascinating distinction between natural and artificial—but these analyses too will stick close to the discursive logic of the statement.

What of the context of Wilson's statement, though? It appeared in the U.S. Supreme Court's decision for *Chisholm vs. Georgia* in 1793, part of an appended opinion of then–Associate Justice Wilson. At issue in the case was the right of an individual to sue a state and, on a larger scale, the validity of the new federal constitution. Like all of Washington's appointees to the court, Wilson had been a strong advocate (in fact, a framer) of the Constitution, and he had played an active role in framing Article III, the article in question. A veteran of Pennsylvania's bitter battle for ratification, Wilson was well aware that, without some strategic maneuvering on the part of federalists, the "natural persons" of his state had almost sunk the whole project. His enemies had nicknamed him "James the Caledonian" for his scheming Scottish sophistries. And, like some other court members, he was actively engaged in land speculation in a number of states, including Georgia, and eventually earned the distinction of being the only justice of the high court to have served time (for debt) while also serving on the court.[30] In 1793 the battle between supporters and opponents of the Constitution was still on, if dissipating, and the *Chisolm vs. Georgia* decision prompted such a backlash from the states that the eleventh amendment was soon thereafter passed to overturn this decision. But although it is useful to pluck Wilson from the ethereal heavens of the nation and place him back in the scraps of Philadelphia politics, I don't sketch this context to crudely debunk Wilson's words. My point is not that Wilson was a conniving land speculator rather than a grand republican theorist; he was something of the latter, though the label seems so vague as to be of dubious use. Nor do I mean to suggest that Wilson's republicanism is explained by his land speculation and his commitment to elite federalism; any number of Founding Fathers combined such interests without drafting Wilson's fascinating passage, or expressed such sentiments without extensive land speculation. Rather, these contextual markers should remind us that Wilson's republican theorizing was an engaged and very particular praxis, here most clearly signaled by the reference to "the toast," which shifts us from the ether of pure utterance and places us in the banquets of early national Philadelphia.

After Louis Capet met the guillotine in January 1793, there was an increasing factional polarization in Philadelphia that found expression in such rituals as political toasts, and Wilson's reference ("Is a toast asked?") not only attempts to guide the interpretation of words uttered in the set forms of party heat, but also to evoke and recast the speech of the people within the organizational parameters of the party dinner. In the practice of the time, toasts were not offered spontaneously but rather "asked" in careful sequence by the presiding host. As one of the "most popular forms of the celebration," toasts embodied a "marriage of debate and declamation," writes David Waldstreicher.[31] But "debate" may be an inapt term here, for toastly suasion came less from a verbal argument presented for rational evaluation than from the dynamics of the practical ensemble in which the toast was presented and where participation was already regulated. The toast was answered by a second-order (seconding) response. But Wilson's opinion, of course, was a written text, and indeed most contact with toasts was surely mediated by print. Toasts were not only "the most important business of any partisan celebration," but also "the most widely published genre of popular political culture." Printed in local papers and reprinted "in other regions of the country, toasts served as informal platforms for whatever local community, party, or faction had organized the gathering, and they were carefully parsed for the subtle and not-so-subtle indications they gave as to the balance of forces and the state of public opinion in a given area."[32] Did this textualization reproduce the practical ensembles in which they were presented? Of course not, but neither did the print medium render toasts just another form of circulating discourse. Rather, a new relation was established between the ensemble of the factional party and the ensemble of serial readers who would "parse" the words for the "balance of forces." And this was no abstract exercise in political analysis, but an attempt to *shape* the balance of forces. With the printed toast, the toasting group extended its range, drew readers into (or away from) the dynamics of toasting, but always at the margins, away from the past rowdy praxis of the toast, unless the readers could reproduce the conditions of toasting, in their own festivity at some future time, to answer (with agreement or with challenge) the printed version. Thus we cannot really speak of a "debate," but rather of an exchange of some sort, either an uneven and imagined exchange between the single reader of the toast and the original toasting collective, or perhaps an enacted exchange between a new collective and the previous imprinted one.

With Wilson's court opinion, then, we must go a further step: from within a newly established institution, a judge issues an opinion correcting the content of partisan toasts. "The People of the United States," not "the United States," he writes, assuming that this mild rebuke will influence the praxis of toasting, and further that this corrected formula will enable the printed toast to have greater power among the serial reader. Wilson issues his corrective in print, but this is hardly print in the same sense as the newspaper story, for when Wilson's words make the gazette, they have already come from the Supreme Court (where an "original" opinion resides), not a partisan journal. So the implied reader might imagine this correction enacted in a toast in the future, and will hopefully sense the power of the improved, more "natural," and *politically correct* wording. Do the people of the United States speak "it into existence" then? Is this Wilson's observation about how language works—citizens speak society into existence? Not quite. What is at stake for Wilson is, rather, how the United States will be spoken by *partisan groupings*, who will then exert their influence on serial citizen readers. To say this is a theory of "the origins of legitimate authority in the voice of the people" is to miss the insights of Wilson's praxis, which rather concerns— and participates in—the assertion of legitimate authority in the expression of a practical ensemble. This is not to suggest that Wilson's speech doesn't mean what it says, or to appeal to some hidden motives or secret sociology that will unlock Wilson's discourse. For the language of toasts is there on the surface, and to pay attention to the practical ensembles through which cultural battles are waged is in fact to take Wilson's discourse more seriously, to track the social uses of language while resisting the leveling of federalist fantasy. In the terms I'll be developing in this and the following chapters, Wilson's words achieve their power from their engagement with overlapping feelings of structure, taking their position within a rhetorically conjured phenomenology of collective life. They posit a *fused* practice of toasting existing *serially* throughout the United States *(all around the country groups are making political toasts)*; they assume these words are undermined by a serial misunderstanding that accentuates the distance between citizenry and institutions *(all these people confuse 'the United States' with 'the People of the United States' because this is a common toast)*; they exercise a corrective, institutional oversight *(the toast must be made correctly, per Wilson's explication)*. Such is the sense in which Wilson understands "the origin of legitimate authority in the voice of the people": this authority has meaning thanks to the hermeneutic oversight of toastmasters and judges operating in established, institutionalized settings. Speak when and how you're directed; understand that toasts are happening around you; ignore the separation you feel between "the People" and "the United States": *then* the United States will be spoken into existence.

Beyond Philadelphia

Two approaches to reading a republican, then: on the one hand, that of the republican synthesizers, we seek the articulation of a discourse of structuring values; on the other, we seek a guide to a mapping of the practical ensembles through which discourse finds form and praxis. In the former mode, Wilson is a nodal point on the flat landscape of republicanism; in the latter, Wilson is an institutional figure publishing to groups, series, and institutions. To put this in Roland Barthes' still useful terms, the republican synthesis *mythologizes* Wilson through an act of "language-robbery"; it creates a "second-order" system of analysis that, however sophisticated in its tools, remains close to the more popular myth of the Founding Fathers. In the "inflexion" given to republican discourse, the metasynthesis fundamentally distorts by recasting the messiness of situations as a commanding "metalanguage."[33] The privileged terms of the republican lexicon become a bit like the Vaseline rubbed on the actors in *Julius Caesar* to prove enormous thinking. We would do better to follow Barthes' "ethic of signs," and demythologize this discourse, finding it "deeply rooted, invented, so to speak, on each occasion, revealing an internal, a hidden facet, and indicative of a moment in time, no longer of a concept."[34] This means venturing beyond the most formalized and abstracted language of what we consider "political theory" to seek a broader range of vernacular theorization. When John Adams wrote to Benjamin Rush about the lack of "human understanding" in matters of "government," he clarified his remarks with the observation that "A strange disposition prevails throughout all stages of civilization to live in hollow trees and log houses without chimneys or windows, without any division of the parlor from the kitchen or the garret from the cellar." Rush's reply offered a riff on Adams' imagery: "Ever since the Revolution, our state has been like a large inn. It has accommodated strangers at the expense of the landlord and his children, who have been driven by them from the bar and their bedrooms and compelled at times to seek a retreat in their garret and cellar." And Adams, in a further response to Rush, assessed the situation in Europe with this remark: "Commerce, manufactures, and science will languish under this gloomy tyranny and Europe grow up into a forest inhabited only by wild beasts and a few hunters who shall have fled into the wilderness from the tyranny of pen and ink."[35] Ignorance in the log cabin, understanding in the parlor, the American state as landlord of an inn, European revolutions as a return to frontier savagery: these are more than quaint metaphors to be confined to collections of correspondence, and though we have long privileged Adams' "Novanglus" essays, his *Thoughts on Government,* or the *Discourses on Davila,* a more comprehensive account of his cultural praxis might emerge from a better sense of its practical referents.

This is not to suggest that this book ventures a new reading of republicanism, now resituated within its varied institutional deployments in country and city. My focus, rather, is an explication of the practical ensembles of the backcountry–city divide within which republicanism, federalism, and nationalism (and their respective myths) might be more productively situated. And although I hope that such a change in focus might help us better understand New World colonization and better locate the United States in its hemispheric context, I should here address what I take to be this study's greatest strength and its greatest shortcoming: its focus on Pennsylvania. I've focused on this middle colony for two related reasons. First, although I do offer some speculative generalizations about North American backcountry–city relations, my emphasis upon the *colonial* foundations of these conflicts must eschew any retrospective characterizations of the "thirteen colonies" as a future United States. The varying regions, times, and participants of New World colonization rendered the particular provinces distinctive in crucial ways, and these differences should be foregrounded in any study of early American culture. As Franklin once put it, the colonies were "not only under different governors, but have different forms of government, different laws, different interests, and some of them different religious persuasions and different manners."[36] "[H]istorians of colonial British America," as Jack

Greene has noted, "have always been most impressed and given most emphasis to the extraordinarily visible differences among colonies, among regions, and among subregions."[37] The same has not always been true of cultural critics, but these provincial specificities deserve our attention.

In the Pennsylvanian case, the relevant particularities include its relatively late, compacted, and intensive colonization, beginning (for the English) in the 1680s and 1690s, roughly a half-century after the Chesapeake and New England ventures had consolidated the north–south split. The relatively late opening of the colonial enterprise contributed to extraordinary population increases: the non-Native population grew from 11,400 in 1690 to 18,000 in 1700, 31,000 in 1720, 85,600 in 1740, 183,700 in 1760, 327,300 in 1780; 434,000 in 1790, and 602,300 by 1800.[38] Much of this growth was concentrated in Philadelphia, where the population jumped from about 2,200 in 1700 to 5,000 in 1720, 9,000 in 1740, 14,000 in 1750, 18,000 in 1765, and over 25,000 in 1775; by 1800, the city's population was around 67,800.[39] Most of Pennsylvania's growth was in the countryside, however, with about 88 percent of the population rural through to 1820.[40] Within this context of simultaneously rapid ruralization and urbanization, there occurred an institutional improvisation informed by the strengths and weaknesses of earlier colonial enterprises. The proprietary family, the Penns, sought a strong executive embodying the administrative functions of a state landlord, but with a compliant and streamlined legislature. After some initial conflicts in the first decades, however, this quasi-feudal executive was set against a frequently antiproprietary, unicameral Assembly that seemingly simplified and polarized provincial politics. In addition, Pennsylvania would contain the most ethnically diverse white population among the thirteen colonies. By 1790, about one-third of the population was English or Welsh in origin, another third from German-speaking regions, a quarter or so Scottish, Irish, or Scots-Irish, with about a tenth from other backgrounds.[41] This diversity would prove significant, for it signaled a wide range of religious-cultural denominations (Quakers, Pietists, Baptists, Lutherans, Presbyterians, Anglicans, Roman Catholics), without the hegemonic consolidation of any one set. If the streamlining of the macropolitical sphere heightened the colony's political battles, this ethnic-religious diversity tended to foreground and exacerbate rural–urban conflicts, while calling attention to the organizational innovations of different sects. Finally, the geographic centrality of the colony, and more importantly its proximity to the Iroquois Confederacy to the north and the Ohio Valley to the west, would make it the center of British–Indian diplomacy in the middle decades of the eighteenth century, as well as a central location for pan-Nativist movements among the so-called "tributary" polities, including the Shawnees and the Delawares. Not surprisingly, then, we find recurrent and relatively concentrated rural-urban violence in the region, from the early border conflicts with Maryland and Delaware to the Paxton Riots of 1763–64, the Yankee-Pennamite conflict in the contested Wyoming Valley, and later, after the Revolution, the Whiskey and Fries Rebellions.

These particularities, discussed in more detail in chapters 2 through the Conclusion, contributed to Pennsylvania's cultural centrality by century's end. Here, rapid urban development is a decisive factor in explaining not only the concentration of publishing in Philadelphia but its eventual political symbolism as the frequent home of the Continental Congress, the site of the Constitutional Convention, and the United States capital from 1790 to 1800. Printing and publishing developed quickly in the colony, with two English-language newspapers operating in the 1750s, six in 1775, nine by 1789, and twelve in 1796. There was at least one German-language newspaper from 1740 on, and two or more after 1770. In the 1790s, over ninety newspapers appeared in Pennsylvania—about fifteen in German, many short-lived.[42] Publishing entrepreneur Benjamin Franklin's association with the region is well known, but Philadelphia would also become prominent as the publication site of Thomas Paine's "Crisis" series, John Fenno's *Gazette of the United States*, William Cobbett's *Porcupine's Gazette*, Philip Freneau's *National Gazette*, and Benjamin Franklin Bache's important opposition paper, the *Aurora General Advertiser*. Susanna Rowson's *Charlotte: A Tale of Truth*, later to be published as *Charlotte Temple*, was first published in the United States in Philadelphia in 1794, a sensible choice for a novel writer. It is similarly no coincidence that such prominent novelists as Charles Brockden Brown and Hugh Henry Brackenridge were Pennsylvanians and used the colony/state as an important setting, nor that non-Pennsylvanians like Crèvecoeur, Tabitha Gilman Tenney, and Gilbert Imlay chose the state as the setting for their works.

If these particularities warrant this provincial focus (and this is for readers to decide), the corresponding shortcomings should be evident. Neglected are several important seventeenth-century patterns of colonization: the corporate system of Virginia, the Dutch and feudal roots of New York, the battle between planters and small farmers of Barbados, the careful church settlement patterns of New England. Neglected as well is the impact of the English Revolution, so important for New England and the greater South of the Chesapeake and Caribbean. Neglected too is the decisive impact of large-scale slavery—relatively small in Pennsylvania, with only 2.3 percent of the population Black in 1760, as compared with Delaware's 20 percent or even New Jersey's 7 percent.[43] (It was to some extent the weakness of slavery in Pennsylvania that made Philadelphia such an important urban center for African Americans by 1800.) The extension and testing of this analysis in the American South will require study of the planter–farmer–slave triad and its impact on Bacon's Rebellion, the Carolina Regulations, and slave rebellions and maroonage. Finally, I have not attempted here any systematic comparative study of the connection between region and printing, which would at the least have to reckon with the particularities of New England publishing and certain generic divergences evident in early American literary history.[44]

But if Pennsylvania cannot be viewed as "representative" or "typical" of early America, we may say, with caution, that Pennsylvania ultimately achieved a *modular* cultural significance for other colonies and states. Attracting a range of writers, traders, diplomats, and politicos to its late eighteenth-century capital city, the Pennsylvania conflicts and their responses assumed a greater intracolonial and later national importance. By the 1790s, Pennsylvania had become profoundly associated with settler insurrections and, in the Ohio Valley region, with white–Indian contact, be that military conflict, captivity, diplomacy, swindling, or trade. Philadelphia's strong institutional foundations for literary culture meant that, in this environment, early American letters were profoundly concerned with, even haunted by, the backcountry. To some extent, the paradox of American literary development—a predominantly urban phenomenon within a profoundly urban society—is exaggeratedly true in Pennsylvania. For that reason, a cultural history of the backcountry–city divide there may serve as a useful starting point.

2
Seriality

Le Grand Dérangement

On 31 July 1755, early in the Seven Years' War, British administrators in Nova Scotia ordered the removal of Acadian settlers from the Bay of Fundy area; in August and September, as many as 800 Acadian men were summoned to British forts, where they were imprisoned; and as the first phase of Acadian deportation wound to a close, as many as 5,400 individuals were on their way to Britain or British possessions.[1] By late November, three British ships arrived in Pennsylvania, carrying 454 prisoners-of-war. For months they were detained outside Philadelphia, but in the face of high expenses, the Assembly in February of 1756 directed James Pemberton to frame legislation to deal with the Acadian problem (47–48). The resulting statute, passed in March, was entitled "An Act for Dispersing the Inhabitants of Nova Scotia Imported into this Province into the Several Counties of Philadelphia, Bucks, Chester and Lancaster and the Townships thereof, and Making Provisions for the Same." On the premise that "dispersing the several families and persons into different townships and parts of the province may give them an opportunity of exercising their own labor and industry, whereby they may procure a comfortable subsistence for themselves and ease the public of heavy expense," the law distributed one family per township throughout the easternmost counties of Pennsylvania, quietly denying access to western lands.[2]

We may concede the ostensible agenda of the law—to distribute the burden of public relief among the population of Pennsylvania—but the call for "dispersal" opens up a broader cultural map of colonial Pennsylvania. Dispersal is, here, as the Acadians well understood, a cultural and political program to scatter and disintegrate—to promote assimilation, to atomize and fragment—opposition. As such, the statute was one small moment in the broader imperial strategy to break up French pockets of culture; as Pemberton noted: "the danger of a frontier settlement heretofore occupied by the said inhabitants of Nova Scotia and others commonly known by the name of the French neutrals appears to have been the motive of their dispersion into other His Majesty's colonies in North America, and it may be for the service of the Crown to unite them with his loyal subjects in the said colonies" (218–19). Hence the refusal to allow the Acadians into the western counties where they might re-form into proper "settlements" and establish ties with French forces or Native Americans. What's most illuminating about the bill, though, is that it explicitly links a strategy of cultural warfare with an economic system, that of yeoman farming. For the Acadians were identified as "hav[ing] been bred up to the management of farms," and their establishment "on rented plantations" was deemed the most effective form of dispersal (217). Farmers were already and naturally dispersed; and the best way to treat potential enemies of the state was to make them farmers. Dispersal was disintegration, fragmentation, isolation, scattering. The French term for the Acadian relocation, le Grand Dérangement, aptly captures the project's various dimensions—military, political, economic, cultural—with its connotations of strategic placement, ordering, even (in the pun on insanity) cultural regulation. And, recognizing the stakes of this project, the Acadians refused to comply with the law before relocating to Louisiana in 1766–67; there they would maintain their cohesion with a different kind of ordering.[3]

The imperial concern with dispersal, far from being exceptional, was ubiquitous in the colonial period, an essential and recurring dimension of New World modernity. We might think back to different colonial contexts, like that in which the New England Confederation (1643) was established to remedy the unintended consequences of settlement dispersion: "whereas in our settling . . . we are further dispersed upon the seacoasts and rivers than was at first intended, so that we cannot according to our desire with convenience communicate in one government and jurisdiction."[4] In Virginia, John Smith explained the notorious 1622 "Massacre" in terms of colonists unable "to defend themselves against any enemy, being so dispersed as they were."

But he likewise noted practices of strategic dispersal among the Indians, who "disperse themselves in small companies" to "mend their dyet," or militarily "disperse themselves among the fresh men" of an enemy company.[5] Each instance illustrates a fundamental concern, central to settler colonization, with the political, economic, military, and—in all cases—*cultural* dimensions of population distribution and oversight. From some viewpoints, dispersal is desirable, necessary for maximized settlement, rent collection, or cultural control. In others, it is the essential peril of settlement, of isolation and separation, vulnerability and violence. In all, *dispersal* alludes to the fundamental practical ensemble of colonial life, *the series*.

The ubiquity of seriality make it difficult to discern, and in some theoretical formulations, it has become something of a degree zero for early American culture. Two influential examples may illustrate its significance. In Benedict Anderson's insightful but overgeneralizing account of "creole nationalism," the experience of simultaneous, serial newspaper reading plays a critical role in the formation of the "imagined community" of the nation. Although reading takes place "in silent privacy," every reader knows that the experience "is being replicated simultaneously by thousands (or millions) of others of whose existence he is confident, yet of whose identity he has not the slightest notion."[6] We see something similar in recent and related applications of public-sphere theory, which posit a serial community of citizen-locutors. Michael Warner's influential study, for instance, argues that the public sphere "incorporates *into the meaning of the printed object* an awareness of the potentially limitless others who may also be reading. For that reason, it becomes possible to imagine oneself, in the act of reading, becoming part of an arena of people that cannot be realized except through such mediating imaginings." This serial relationship, Warner concludes, "was to become the paradigmatic political relationship of republican America."[7] These intertwined frameworks of nation and public sphere certainly identify important forms of seriality that formed in eighteenth-century America, but in reifying and exaggerating the importance of these series, such frameworks distort our understanding of the period. Before we craft such grand totalizations that take the colonial and early national periods as synonymous with this or that series of "citizens" or "readers," we need a clearer sense of what seriality is. We need to think about a host of other series (of Black slaves, farmers, women, indentured servants, traders, soldiers, ...) and their relationships to other, nonserial ensembles, like the guild strike, the slave insurrection, the militia, the club, the tribe, and the farmer's march (to name just a few).

To gain greater conceptual purchase of the colonial series, this chapter surveys some vernacular theorizations of the feeling of seriality in the Pennsylvania backcountry. My focus will be on the seriality of backcountry populations in matters of agrarian settlement and Indian management, and I take as guides Michel-Guillaume Jean de Crèvecoeur's *Letters from an American Farmer* (1782), proprietary documents about judicial control of Indians and squatters, and wartime petitions from backcountry farmers. I have also taken as a critical foil the historiographic project commonly called "social history," for which a serial, statistical empiricism has become fundamental. Further, in this and subsequent chapters I shall argue that the vernacular sociology of practical ensembles is inseparable from early American understandings of race, class, and gender relations in early America, and here I will be suggesting that the common understanding of seriality was strongly gendered as a feminine condition. Ultimately, I want to insist that agrarian seriality was fundamental to a colonial modernity defined by the forbidding task of managing vast new spaces and resources in a context of institutional weakness. As the practical matrix of backcountry populations *and* the foundation of rural insurrections, agrarian seriality posed the basic problems taken up by group action and the institutional innovations of what came to be called federalism.

Reciprocal Isolation

If the series is ubiquitous in colonial life, it is equally so in contemporary liberal societies, with the result that much cultural theory, knowing little else, reifies, exaggerates, or altogether misses the phenomenon. Jean-Paul Sartre, who called the series "the basic type of sociality," was arguing against precisely such overinflated mistheorizations, specifically focusing on Kurt Lewin's then-popular extensions of Gestalt theory. The complexities of seriality were misperceived, such that the "*apparent* structure of the milieu makes sociologists like Lewin tend to take it for a *Gestalt* which performs a synthetic action on its structures as a *real totality* and determines the behaviour and processes of every part in so far as it communicates directly with all the others through the real presence of the whole in every one of them."[8] Sartre's critique of the bogus notion of the whole present in all parts could be applied equally to traditional notions of "the culture of the times" or contemporary poststructuralist assertions of discursive interpellation, whereby the messy forms of social life are collapsed and explained via a cultural system "instantiated" in all subjects, actions, and expressions. Clarification of the series, then, is crucial to countering our favored methodological shortcuts.

Sartre identifies the series as "the being of the most ordinary, everyday gatherings" (269), so, although his examples include the mass media, the free market, rumors, and the working class, he focuses first on the deliberately banal, small-scale phenomenon of the bus-stop line. The bus queue cannot be explained in terms of some gestalt or "culture of the time": we must start, instead, with the practico-inert realities of transportation systems (roads built, tracks or sidewalks laid, cars or trains manufactured), all the result of human praxis continuing to exist inertly, directing our movements (or, if abandoned, marking past movements). The bus stop marks the external determinants of a specific practico-inert field—where we board, where the buses run, their schedule, the number of seats, the payment system—within which passengers travel. People standing in line are thus not living some "communal fact" or group unification, but are rather a collective of individuals acting "separately as identical instances of the same act" (262). This will be particularly evident in a line of seven, when the bus arrives with room for four: the individuals will then realize their isolation from one another (*some of us board, some don't*), as well as their arbitrary interchangeability (*I happened to get here third*). So the line is an "*inactive human gathering*," its "visible unity. . . only an *appearance*" (264).

The real force of Sartre's analysis comes, however, in the extension of this example to large-scale phenomena like the radio broadcast, an example of "gathering at a distance" (272). Listeners are aware of, imagine, other listeners, and, though their reactions will be shaped by additional cultural influences, the experience is fundamentally serial: while one listener exults in hearing the Top Ten song, knowing that millions of others love it too, or while another listener feels frustration imagining millions being misled by a pundit's commentary, their relationship to other listeners is one of "*being-outside-themselves-in-the-other* of the members of the practico-inert grouping," the radio audience (268). The listeners, feeling their interchangeability in isolation or membership, "perceive in themselves and Others their common inability to eliminate their material differences"—here the mass media, as well as the practico-inert of household or car radios—keeping them separate (277). Such, too, is the lived experience of the free market, which is not, Sartre insists, the subjective internalization of economic logic by a process of interpellation. It is rather a case of an exterior relation to the practico-inert and an interior relation to other buyers and sellers: the farmer must sell grain as the price drops, or buy fertilizer as the price rises, not because she is committed to the free market (she may or may not be), but because she knows no one individual can influence a market driven by the seriality of Others buying, selling, hoarding, or overproducing.

An analogous diagnosis can be offered for class location or forms of identity politics. The "common-class-Being as an interiorized common object is *neither* a totality imposing itself on its parts but differing from them, *nor* a word connoting the indefinite repetition of particular class-being as a universal reproduction of the identical" (316): not a totality from without, not a classification from within, but instead a material phenomenon—the aggregation of working peoples—with a particular cultural relationship to one another of isolation, interchangeability, and inertia (313). The seriality of the working class, in its exteriorized (practico-inert) and interiorized (hermeneutic) dimensions, becomes *the* enormous obstacle for workers seeking transformation. Common forms of identity function in a similar, if less obviously "material," way: "*The* Jew (as the internal unity of Jewish multiplicities), or *the* colonialist, or *the* professional soldier, etc., are not ideas.... The theoretical error... was to conceive of these beings as concepts, whereas—as the fundamental basis of extremely complex relations—they are *primarily* serial unities" (267). The "being-Jewish" of *the* Jew is not simply ideology, for the practices of a persecuting anti-Semitism create lived relationships that make "being-Jewish" a practical question. "Being-Jewish" then becomes a "relation in so far as it is lived by every Jew in his direct or indirect relations with all other Jews" (268). The interiorized alterity is two-fold, "being-Jewish" as an imposed "statute *for non-Jews*" and the "common-being-outside-oneself-in-the-other" (268): non-Jews will view the Jew as one in a series of Jews, and the Jew will come to see other Jews as imposing Jewishness through this seriality. The important qualification that distinguishes this account of the series from the common view of identity politics is that Sartre is *not* speaking of identity "in a deep psychological sense" but in terms of a response to "a more practical-material mode of the social construction of individuals," here the materialized discourse and practices of anti-Semitism.[9]

The series has its particular forms of communication, which Sartre explores with the example of peasant rumors. Drawing on Lefebvre's *The Great Fear of 1789*, he counters the common account of public opinion "as a collective consciousness arising from the synthetic unification of the citizens into a nation, and imposing its representations on everyone as an integral part of the whole" (294). In the aftermath of the storming of the Bastille, the Great Fear of late summer, 1789, "did not break out everywhere at the same time" and did not develop throughout all of France; specific waves of rumor were "propagated *serially*" (295). The Fear's intelligibility must therefore be discovered in "a structure of alterity in relation to Paris" (295). Peasants spread rumors of an aristocratic conspiracy, of hired bandits set to attack the countryside, not with accurate information but because, in their serial weakness, the peasants felt their isolation in the antagonistic agency of the Other (actual aristocratic organization in Paris), and felt that what could happen to *those* peasants could happen *here*. The rumor developed not out of some organic "hysteria" or a common belief system that emerged spontaneously, nor because of organized and conscious praxis on the part of peasants; it depended instead on the sense of alterity (toward aristocrats and brigands) perceived by some, the felt interchangeability with other peasants, the passing on of information and fear, and the sensed need (because of other peasants, other aristocrats) to act against an immediate threat. Critical to this account of seriality is the way the material environment (including the practico-inert of discourse) directs this culture of seriality. So, in another example, centuries of appropriation of arable land through intense deforestation result in run-off, erosion, and intense flooding (161–62). The serial praxis of individual land-clearing becomes a collective setting in which the transformed practico-inert acts as what Sartre calls "counter-finality," not as matter apart from human beings but as a "passive force within a process of signifying unification" (180). The practico-inert of seriality is not, then, matter *apart from* human transformation or meaning, nor is it a tidy correlate of cultural signification. In this sense, anti-Semitism is like peasant deforestation insofar as the anti-Semitic discourse about Jews is as materially real: a counterfinality constructed by human praxis that becomes a force acting on the series of Jews and non-Jews. The broader point is that seriality exists as a cultural phenomenon in relation to a material environment that it somewhat creates but somewhat encounters.

Sartre had earlier toyed with the concept of the series in *Being and Nothingness*, arguing that any given phenomenon could be adequately perceived only through an infinite and therefore impossible series of perceptions.[10] In this account, seriality amounted to the infinite obstacle to knowledge, an endless, unavoidable fragmentation of perception. One can see here the origin of the series as practical ensemble—the endless dispersal of understanding and action across interchangeable and isolated actors. Seriality is always a liability or limitation in Sartre's view, as evident in his account of workers continuously separated and weakened, save for those rare moments of group unification. This assessment of the series, a reaction against the individualism of Sartre's early work, is decidedly undialectical, in ignoring the possibilities of strategic resistance through dispersal. Here one might contrast Lefebvre's account of the Great Fear, so influential for Sartre, with David Hardiman's account of the 1922 *adivasi* religious movement in Gujarat; Hardiman describes a traveling "purification" movement that eventually provided the foundations for political self-organization.[11] If Lefebvre's rumor emphasizes panic, confusion, misinformation, and vulnerability, Hardiman's traveling movement stresses creative modification and adaptation. We should be attuned, then, to the positive potential of seriality, resisting the purely negative valence given it by Sartre. As I shall discuss below, Crèvecoeur, in his multifaceted but qualified celebration of rural seriality, recognized in the agrarian series a powerful resistance to the institutional culture of the Old World, going so far as to define the paradigmatic American as the serial freeholder.

This sketch of the series may serve as our initial guide to the New World modernity of agrarian populations: not a unified mass, but an inactive gathering of reciprocal isolation; not a society mystically at one with the countryside, but a collective of individuals facing the counterfinality of their praxis; not a unified rural culture but a common-being-outside-oneself-in-the-other, a culture of traveling rumors. And if this brief summation highlights the challenges faced by backcountry populations, it also foregrounds the problems of their management by colonial and imperial elites, not to mention some potential resources of resistance to such management. What Sartre characterized as the weakness of those *in* the series was as much a problem for those seeking mastery *of* the series, shaping the stark colonial opposition between backcountry and city. In colonial modernity, the first problem of the backcountry would be its serial dispersal. How would scattered Indian populations be assimilated and mastered? How would orderly settlement be carried out, and rents collected? How would white settlers remain connected with the political and cultural institutions of the seaport cities? How could serial dispersal serve as a means to resist administration?

In such a context, the orderly liberal seriality of citizenship in print or nation was more a utopian fantasy than a practical reality of the backcountry's sullen seriality. Let us start, then, with Crèvecoeur's insights on the matter.

The Phenomenology of Plowing

Eighteenth-century America's theorist of seriality par excellence was Crèvecoeur, whose *Letters from an American Farmer* is largely an exploration of the material and cultural dimensions of seriality, in dialectical fashion. Here the

French ex-soldier, settled and farming in the colony of New York, constructs a naturalized persona—Farmer James, third generation Anglo-American— conjoined with an idyllic portrait of rural seriality in the Pennsylvania countryside. It's tempting to read Crèvecoeur as a regional theorist, sketching the Middle Atlantic, which is then contrasted with New England and the South. But the translation of colonial New York into colonial Pennsylvania—a reasonable shift, given the heavy rural immigration to Pennsylvania, and the comparative absence of the feudal structures that distinguished the Hudson Valley—suggests that Crèvecoeur was more interested in fashioning a *serial ideal* toward which Americans should strive, but which elsewhere was severely complicated or distorted by institutional developments (in New England by coastal clusters, in the South by plantation slavery). "Pennsylvania" is less a region, then, than a social mode and an historical stage (*after* frontier wilderness, *before* town development—much as Frederick Jackson Turner put it). The particularity of Crèvecoeur's vision should be stressed, in opposition to the tendency to see Crèvecoeur as a theorist of "the American character" and the like. He is more accurately a tendentious theorist of the American yeoman, of class and its concomitant political cultures. And if such epistolary titles as "What is an American?" seem to invite us to read him as a theorist of a national culture, we should temper this tendency with the realization that his is a class struggle, a project to make a certain kind of yeoman dominant, which Crèvecoeur must finally acknowledge a failure in the *Letters'* narrative denouement. The "most perfect society now existing in the world" is not *American* in some general or total sense, nor even the state of some particular region, but a specific, vulnerable situation linked to a particular practical ensemble.

"Industry, good living, selfishness, litigiousness, country politics, the pride of freemen, religious indifference"—so Crèvecoeur summarizes the various characteristics, economic, political, affective, and ideological, of the "race of cultivators."[12] It is easiest to begin, as do most readers, with the economic and political elements of this portrait. "James" stresses the "material difference" between European "husbandry, modes, and customs" and those of Pennsylvania, such that crucial economic and political distinctions exist between the "American farmer" and the "Russian boor" or "Hungarian peasant" (51). Land ownership provides an economic freedom grounded in "the bright ideas of property, of exclusive right, of independence" upon which "is founded our rank, our freedom, our power as citizens, our importance as inhabitants of such a district" (54). Small property owners, petty producers unbeholden to lords or employers, and thus freemen and citizens: what Crèvecoeur offers is a perfect portrait of what has come to be known as the Jeffersonian agrarian ideal.[13] This political-economic formulary, best contained in the widely anthologized second epistle, "On the Situation, Feelings, and Pleasures of an American Farmer," is certainly the easiest way to approach teaching Crèvecoeur, and a misleading one given the narrative conclusion of the *Letters:* the narrator is ultimately "driven from a situation the enjoyment of which the reader will find pathetically described in the early letters of this volume" (35). The danger of the Jeffersonian summation is that it seems like the prior material background for the "emotional" Crèvecoeur (D. H. Lawrence's label)—for the "farmer of feeling," as Crèvecoeur himself put it (53). That is, such readings encourage a crude economism (land ownership provides necessary preconditions to thought), before moving on to a misleading aesthetic and antisocial individualism (now that I own my land, I can watch the insects, ponder the egg, admire the bees). No wonder Leo Marx found the *Letters* "a delightful, evocative, though finally simple minded, book" that is ultimately about an individual using "the landscape, as an object that penetrates the mind, filling it with irresistible pictures of human possibilities."[14]

Actually, Crèvecoeur was theorizing seriality in a sophisticated fashion throughout the *Letters,* and the "emotional" and "aesthetic" observations are profoundly integrated in the politico-economic vision summarized above. The connection comes across most clearly in the celebration of religious indifference in the famous third letter, "What is an American?" This is no simple assertion of the gradual dissipation of religious dogmatism, but a prime illustration of serial dispersal's ideological consequences. The antagonists here are more cohesive collectives: sects, denominations, and congregations (74) that culturally echo the geopolitical opposition between "the chain of settlements which embellish these extended shores" and the "factions" afflicting Europe (66). The material distance provided by American farm ownership, the general scattering of ethno-religious groups, and the inability to achieve a critical mass of mutually reinforcing believers: these together prevent ideological development and force. Not caring very much becomes the theology of dispersal, and the implications of this doctrine extend far beyond religion, as the revolutionary context in which the *Letters* were written obviously suggests. The more profound adversary is *party,* political cohesion and resulting upheavals, as many of Crèvecoeur's metaphors suggest. "[Z]eal in Europe is confined," he writes in reference to religion, but "here it evaporates in the great distance it has to travel; there it is a grain of powder inclosed; here it burns away in the open air and consumes

without effect" (76): yeoman seriality as thousands of grains consuming themselves with no consequence.

This celebration of weak sociality would seem to shift us to an individualist account of culture, as seemingly reinforced by references to the yeoman
self as a "*tabula rasa*," a site of "instinct" and "spontaneous impressions"
(46, 47, 50). But the emphasis in Crèvecoeur's writing falls more profoundly
upon an elusive sense of collectivity—the feeling of structure of seriality—
that becomes the source for what is *experienced* as instinct or spontaneity.
This comes across in something as banal as James's celebration of plowing.
Although again he suggests that "the salubrious effluvia of the earth ani-
mate our spirits and serve to inspire us" and that "labour flows from instinct,"
Crèvecoeur more profoundly offers an odd vision (this time in the words of
James's neighbor, the minister) of the collective dimensions of plowing:
marching between his horses, "there is no kind of difference between us in
our different shares in that operation; one of them keeps the furrow, the
other avoids it; at the end of my field, they turn either to the right or left as
they are bid, whilst I thoughtlessly hold and guide the plough to which they
are harnessed" (47). James will repeat the image in telling of placing his
"little boy on a chair which screws to the beam of the plough" just as "my
father formerly did for me" (54–55), a familial practice that immediately
conjures first an Asiatic comparison with "the emperor of China ploughing
as an example to his kingdom," then the celebration of "the myriads of insects
which I perceive dancing in the beams of the setting sun" (55). This range
of images—repeated rows, horses and man trudging in parallel lines, generational continuity, the emperor plowing with millions of subjects, the myriad
of insects—suggests that the basis for the "salubrious effluvia" of plowing is
less nitrates, or some transcendentalism conjured out of the imagination, than
the felt interchangeability of the agricultural series evoked by the repetitions
of fieldwork. What we see in plowing are a range of sensations of being-
outside-oneself-in-the-other, materialized in a landscape of furrows, the mini-
series of the plow apparatus (horse/plower/horse), the generational continuity
of land ownership, even the patterns of surrounding insects.

This portrait of plowing seems particularly loaded, given another of James's
favorite analogies. "Men are like plants," he writes, "the goodness and flavour
of the fruit proceeds from the peculiar soil and exposition in which they
grow" (71). And again, "Every industrious European who transports himself
here may be compared to a sprout growing at the foot of a great tree; it enjoys
and draws but a little portion of sap; wrench it from the parent roots, trans-
plant it, and it will become a tree bearing fruit also" (80). The proper "expo-

sition" for plants provided by plowing has to do with even and predictable placement in regular and repeated rows. So too for humans. It's not that yeomen are *naturally* like vegetation *in general*, but that they're like evenly distributed *crops*, humanly arranged fields of serial citizen plants. This celebration of seriality holds for the various reflections upon animals, whether the hornets in their "curious republic" of "globular nests" and isolated "oblong cells" (63–64), or those "millions of insects" who "hide themselves and their offspring in so perfect a manner as to baffle the rigour of the season and preserve that precious embryo of life" (58), or those cattle that need to be bridled and fenced in the barnyard (57), an arrangement distinguishing them from European herds just as American yeoman are distinguished from "flocks" of peasants.

The American farmer's encounters with the landscape thus provide an important means of countering the "difficulty" of "viewing so extensive a scene" (67), a difficulty intrinsic to the serial condition of reciprocal isolations in yeoman farming. The result is a natural landscape of flora and fauna that one surveys to grasp the human sociality of the New World series. The *Letters'* narrator is not imprecisely perceiving a humanly modified landscape, nor is he naturalizing or mythologizing the Pennsylvania countryside: he is actively and socially transforming it as a human field. The well-known account of the bees illustrates this powerfully; James describes them as "like men"—a comparison that might be read to suggest that humans should become as "natural" as insects, living in healthy, thriving "republics" (60)— but his account in fact stresses a human modification of the apiarian order. The "profitable" hunting for bees involves the tracking and mapping of a series of vermilion-marked honey-yeomen, and the orderly, agrarian, serial placement and management of new hives and swarms, negotiated with those human yeomen who own the land on which "bee-trees" are found (59–60). James serves as something of an apiary land office, and the explicit parallels between human and bee (both seek honey, both work collectively to gather it) suggest not a transcendant modular order of nature but a hierarchy of social arrangements in which farmers must further socialize, Americanize, yeomanize, bees.

Perhaps the culmination of Crèvecoeur's celebration of seriality occurs at the conclusion of James's third letter, in the "History of Andrew, the Hebridean," the statistically exemplary settler and raw material for James's rural management. Andrew and his family are acculturated by dispersal—"I put them all with different families," says James (98)—before being given a lease and settled on the plans of James and his neighbors. James perceives the socialization succeeding at the moment when he "saw with pleasure . . . Andrew holding a two-horse plough and tracing his furrows quite straight," and tells Andrew "I see prosperity delineated in all your furrows and head-lands" (103), terms revealingly suggestive of the plowing of Andrew's soul as well. A turning point in the Hebridean's serialization occurs with a house-raising: "When the work was finished, the company made the woods resound with the noise of their three cheers and the honest wishes they formed for Andrew's prosperity. He could say nothing, but with thankful tears he shook hands with them all" (104). A fascinating account of sociality: Andrew receives his neighbors' labors, and without being able to communicate in any precise way with his peers nonetheless hears their cheers and wishes "resound," dispersed, in the surrounding landscape (104). The house becomes an architectural counterpoint to the cultural dispersal of the religious sec-tarianism. If, in the latter case, the collective is dispersed into insignificance, here the collectivity of house construction is linguistically and physically dissipated, the "square inclosure" (104) becoming a practico-inert residuum of Andrew's initiation into seriality. The farmhouse becomes the site of Andrew's nonexpressive isolation but also of his expressive link with other yeomen.

Quiet Possession

Let's return for a moment to contemporary public-sphere theory and its claims about print culture's importance. The public sphere, the argument goes, creates a relationship between readers "*not as a relation between them-selves as men, but rather as their own mediation by a potentially limitless dis-course.*" The citizen-reader, by this account, "incorporates *into the meaning of the printed object* an awareness of the potentially limitless others who may also be reading," such that it "becomes possible to imagine oneself, in the act of reading, becoming part of an arena of people that cannot be realized except through such mediating imaginings."[15] We could adjust these com-ments to consider the yeomen for whom farming creates a mediating rela-tionship *not as a relation between themselves as citizens, but rather as their own mediation by a potentially limitless system of smallholding.* The yeoman *incorpo-rates into the meaning of the land an awareness of the potentially limitless others who may be tilling. For that reason, it becomes possible to imagine oneself, in the act of farming, becoming part of an arena of people—the backcountry—that cannot be realized except through such mediating imaginings.* Could we venture to say that this agrarian seriality was itself "the paradigmatic political relation of republican America"? That would be premature: we still need to consider the additional dimensions, moments, and modes of rural seriality—how it was applied to Indian populations, for instance, or how it could also be perceived as a danger. We need to consider, as well, the practical ensembles that formed to counteract or regulate the series. Yet we first need to move beyond Crèvecoeur's idyllic portrait of seriality, through a more precise account of the material determinants of the yeoman series. The analysis offered here attempts a speculative survey of the basic coordinates of the Pennsylvania colony; again, other colonies must be examined in their own right.

Prior to November 1779, the land of Pennsylvania's white colonists was held in socage tenure from the proprietary family. Settlers were tenants of the Penn family, obliged to apply for land warrants from a regulatory land office and then owing the proprietors an annual quit-rent on land they occupied.[16] Like many of the mainland colonies, Pennsylvania was a transitional improvisation somewhere between feudalism and landed capitalism, and legally constituted "a seignory...divested of the heaviest burdens imposed by feudal law, and endowed with such powers of territorial control as distance from the realm of the lord paramount required."[17] This last qualifying clause is crucial: proprietary power depended upon proximity. William Penn initially approached the problem of long-distance management by planning settlement in the form of "a particular kind of supposedly communal 'English village,'" probably modeled on the New England settlements of the early seventeenth century.[18] One goal of such settlements was a cultural cohesion of the kind Crèvecoeur happily found wanting except among the Friends. "Despite the formal plans for township grid settlement," though, "Pennsylvanians soon adopted the isolated farm plan that would epitomize the American countryside for the next three centuries."[19] Also during the first decades of colonization (the 1690s to 1710s), conflicts arose over land settlement and rent. With the formation of the Commissioners of Estate and Revenue to manage rent, and the Commissioners of Propriety to manage land sales, an opposition developed between the Penn family proprietorship, allied with mercantile and land-speculating associates, and smaller settlers, allied with opposing merchants and speculators; the Lower Counties (which would become the Delaware colony) also rebelled against proprietary land policies of distribution and revenue.[20] So by the first immigration boom, following the 1713 Peace of Utrecht, provincial institutions and political practices had formed in which the land battle was essentially built into the antagonism between the proprietary executive and a loosely pro-yeoman Assembly. From the start of colonization, we discern two important tendencies: a widespread and largely passive resistance to land policies abetted by an ineffective administrative infrastructure, and an institutional political nexus in which an anti-proprietary bloc coalesced to hinder the proprietary's quasi-feudal ambitions.

The formative political period for rural seriality, however, occurred from the 1710s to the 1760s, during which time massive settlement, continued administrative failures, and aggressive efforts to reconsolidate proprietary powers all heightened land conflicts. William Penn, nearly incapacitated by ill health through the 1710s, died in 1718; his estate, and with it the proprietary charter, was contested until 1732, when his son Thomas disembarked in Pennsylvania to resolve the land problem with the reorganization of the Land Office.[21] The decade and a half of the estate dispute coincided with the aforementioned immigration wave, leaving James Logan, proprietary agent and Land Office secretary, to improvise land distribution and settlement.[22] On top of this was the long-simmering border dispute between the Baltimore and Penn families, the so-called "Conojacular War," which took the form of thefts, assaults, Indian insurrections, border raids, and attempted murders; these conflicts further encouraged settlers in the region to refuse quit-rent payments, given the uncertain status of their property. Within the political sphere, battles between the Quaker-dominated Assembly and the reconsolidated proprietorship weakened the latter's position vis-à-vis land disputes. The Assembly, for example, abolished the chancery court used by Penn to prosecute land disputes, while pro-Assembly political infrastructures were being developed in the new counties.[23] Meanwhile, the ad hoc formation of provincial institutions (an expanded court system, militias, a reformed Loan Office) made these become sites of polarized political conflict that further inflamed the land disputes. In the chaos of the colony's first decades, then, landlord-tenant relations were never meaningfully routinized by custom.

I have not offered this sociological overview to suggest that the land problem was a top-down relation located or initiated in macropolitical institutions. Nor am I speaking of debates over quit-rent rates or abstract principles of land distribution. It would be more accurate to say that a broad practical culture of seriality took shape in the settlement practices of the countryside, where antagonistic class relations were as much shaped by faltering attempts at administration as by the often nominal landlord-tenant relationship. If anything, the disorder of colonial politics necessitates the search for an emerging cultural politics beyond the institutional sphere. Mary Schweitzer carefully documents how, "[w]hen legal mechanisms interfered with the household goal of settling all adults on arable land, ... the community created its own land policy by using the court system and the rule of custom."[24] Rule of custom here essentially refers to widespread *refusals* of statutory requirements—quit-rents, warrants, surveys, deeds—and the emerging practice of "'quiet possession,' what later generations would call 'squatters' rights'" (99). As early as 1726, James Logan had estimated that one hundred thousand people had settled without consulting the land office, and it is in these mass refusals that we may piece together the seemingly inarticulate history of the moment. Of course this emerging culture of quiet possession had its Old World context for each major immigrant group. (Many of the Scotch-Irish arrived after 1717, when thousands of thiry-one-year leases, signed in the aftermath of the English Revolution, expired; in such a context, Thomas Penn's 1732 decision to retroactively raise land prices and quit-rents was a particularly volatile move. The slightly later migration of Palatinate Germans from the war-torn parishes of Northern Kraichgau brought a peasantry wary of, if accustomed to evading, the catastrophic politics of elites.)[25] But our task is to determine how a culture of "quiet possession" might have taken shape, what it might have felt like, and what its broader implications for colonial life might have been. This is challenging, given the paucity of records, but we may begin, following the lead of subaltern historians, to "seize on the evidence of elite consciousness and force it to show us the way to its Other."[26]

Expressions of this resistant dispersal are best found in the gaps of the Land Office's incomplete records, but there are refracted perceptions in the frustrated letters of the proprietary agents, as well. A 1719 letter from James Logan stated that "the lower Counties, since their Titles have been so openly disputed, have entirely declined paying any thing, and, 'till a full settlement, will never be compell'd to it without an armed force, unless all their arrears, which are very great, be wholly remitted to them." A decade later Logan uses similar language, speaking of "those vast numbers of poor but presumptuous People, who, without any License, have entered on your Lands, and neither have, nor are like to have, anything to purchase with." A passage from a 1727 letter is particularly evocative, Logan describing:

> Many thousands of foreigners, mostly Palatines, so called, already in the Countrey, of whom near 1500 came in this last summer; many of them are a surley people, divers Papists among them, & the men generally well arm'd. We have from the North of Ireland, great numbers yearly, 8 or 9 Ships this last ffall discharged at Newcastle. Both these sorts sitt frequently down on any spott of vacant Land they can find, without asking questions; the last Palatines say there will be twice the number next year, & the Irish say the same of their People; last week one of these latter (the Irish) applied to me,

in the name of 400, as he said, who depended all on me, for directions where they should settle. They say the Proprietor invited People to come & settle his Countrey, they are come for that end, & must live; both they and the Palatines pretend they would buy, but not one in twenty has anything to pay with.[27]

Striking here are the repeated references to number, which signal social *quality* as much as quantity. Number begets number, thousands signal thousands more, one person speaks for four hundred, the Palatines double, "People" suggests a flow growing exponentially. Number also defines the whole: that "many of them are a surley people" (what else could fifteen hundred poor and possibly armed people be?) is a sign of trouble for the whole lot, since "these sorts" define the entirety. Finally an inescapable sense of social inertia permeates these passages: in the use of the third person objective pronoun "them"; in the seemingly unavoidable use of the superlative (the numbers are *entirely* resistant, will *never* be paid unless granted *all* demands); in *their* surly sitting, settling, squatting, and surviving; and of course in their collective arrogance, destitution, and presumption. Even the attributions of settlers' agency seem inert: they ask for guidance, then "sitt . . . without asking questions"; they offer to buy, then don't; they appeal to the Proprietor, then ignore. It's as if *their* agency is about not acting in the conventional sense, but is rather the maddening surly sitting of serial dispersal. *Do with us what you can!*

When the Penns finally move to settle land claims, the "great numbers" respond with "great noise." Logan at one point assesses the practicality of working out a solution:

> Of those who have sate down on Lands divers neither are, nor are like to be, able to purchase them. They must, therefore, either be granted to others who can compound them with the People for their Improvements, or else to themselves on Rent, but then that will sound so high that it will be of ill consequence. In the lower Counties, where the richest Lands lie, they bellow out against a penny p. acre as the most grievous oppression. Nay, even the arrears of a bushel of wheat p. C. are to them become intolerable. . . . [Y]et if a settlement is kept in suspence on that account it may be doubted whether your Right & authority can be at all enforced without an army, for these Intruders will be all of one mind. That is, by some means or other to hold possession, and if they should unite, take head, & hold you at Bay, the remedy, where we have no executive Officer above a Sherif . . . will be exceeding difficult.[28]

Here "those who have sate down" are immediately conflated with the "divers" who are and will be perpetual squatters. So when the next sentence speaks of "others" who *can* pay for land and locally manage rent or improvements, these "others" are distinct from "the People." More interesting is the transformation of "They" from the "Lands" that can and must be dispersed (second sentence), to the bellowing resistant squatters (third sentence). Ultimately these two subjects, land and squatters, render the possibility of "settlement . . . kept in suspence." Most revealing, though, are the final references to the political challenge posed by the squatters, a challenge so significant that Logan, in a dramatic reversal of military imagery, envisions a corrective army *defensively* assaulting "these Intruders." It is here that Logan senses the paradoxical resistance posed by serial squatting in his account of yeoman collectivity. For, although he suggests that settlers "will be all of one mind," this is a conditional assessment: it is not that the yeomen *are* united but that "they should unite," that something in their occupation of the land makes them always *potentially* unified and resistant, particularly in the enforcement of "Right & authority." The decisive syntactic parallel here concerns *holding*; "to hold possession" also means to "hold you at Bay." Hence, too, the odd inversion of Logan's conditional in this letter: *if we tried to enforce rent laws, they should unite*, he initially suggests, but by the time he works out the scenario, he is saying *if they unite, we should never be able to enforce the laws.* Control of the conditional lies less with the proprietary initiative than with resistant possession; the rural series originally associated with brutish passive inertia becomes a potential source of dynamic resistance.

I will give some examples of rural self-theorization along similar lines, but Logan's reflections give us a fairly typical elite view of rural seriality, one that emerges not from the abstract and misleading platitudes of political theory but from the difficult and antagonistic praxis of managing the Land Office. We might even read these frustrated functionaries' fumings as the banal counterpoints to Crèvecoeur's exhilarations, *Letters About American Farmers* written from the remote urban offices. In any event, we find here a form of vernacular sociological mapping that, unable to take up the overwhelming colonial task of population management, turns by default to assess the feeling of structures, a feeling that proves the greatest obstacle. When proprietary secretary Richard Peters wrote Thomas Penn, "Your quit rents are shamefully in arrears . . . Your Manor Lands and Appropriated Tracts are settled as other parts of the Province promiscuously by good and bad people," he also was assessing the extensive and unregulated settlement of the backcountry. And, whatever the whiny moralizing of his remark, at some level he knows the problem defies moral, legal, and cultural notions of propriety. The settlers are "good *and* bad," and the shame is found in the blank spaces of the proprietary ledgers.

Numbers

In different ways, Crèvecoeur and Logan point to some of the historiographic challenges of depicting, let alone comprehending, the series. Crèvecoeur's series of American farmers, seeking to avoid faction, party, and sect, seems to vanish willingly in the dispersal of the backcountry, as if to elude the "hot" history of factions and institutions. Meanwhile, in the colony's executive offices, James Logan illustrates those same institutional cores processing reports, but is unable to get the series clearly in his sights. Nonetheless, Crèvecoeur and Logan do offer some of the information we today associate with "social history"—large and impersonal numbers, averages, patterns and tendencies, regional overviews—in ways that usefully situate or defamiliarize that historiographic project. The connection is not accidental: the social history of the twentieth-century necessarily processes elements of the serial social life it describes. If the present volume has relied heavily on social history, it also seeks to examine how the seemingly straightforward processing of data normalizes the phenomenon of seriality. Accordingly, a critical examination of social history has much to offer: a greater understanding of how seriality is naturalized in our historical imagination; a better grasp of the perils and advantages of serial life; and a sense of the social agency possible within the series.

A useful starting point is the influential work of J. Franklin Jameson, one of the turn-of-the-century academic elites who influenced and shaped American historiography for generations. A few biographical details may indicate his institutional significance: an 1898 Ph.D. in the pioneering program at Johns Hopkins; leadership of another preeminent program, at the University of Chicago, from 1901–5; presidency of the American Historical Association (1906–7); directorship of the Carnegie Institution's research division (1905–28); editorship of the *American Historical Review* and the annual bibliography *Writings on American History*; and oversight of the Library of Congress's manuscript division (1928–37).[29] At the pinnacle of his career, he produced one of the foundational texts of U.S. social history, *The American Revolution Considered as a Social Movement* (delivered as lectures in 1925, published as a monograph in 1926), which hailed the rise of "social history" in the new professional historiography.[30] Like his near contemporary Frederick Jackson Turner, Jameson sought to elaborate a "natural history of revolutions," one which, following the example of the "greatest of all revolutions" happening in Russia, would focus on social class (10–11). Social history's task was to track the "transforming hand of revolution" in the "economic desires" and "social aspirations...set free by the political struggle" (9). Central for Jameson were the yeomen, "the peasantry, substantial and energetic though poor,...the small farmers and frontiersmen" (18), and after preliminary observations about social classes, Jameson proceeded to focus on "The Revolution and the Land," insisting that "political democracy came to the United States as a result of economic democracy" in the countryside (27).

In the analysis that followed, Jameson offered a salutary assessment of the feudal elements of colonial agrarian life, shattering the myth of the eternal freehold, then documented a range of revolutionary-era legal reforms touching on settlement demarcation, quit-rent abolition, manor confiscation, primogeniture and entailment law, and franchise provisions. But in this account, as his chapter title suggested, the stress fell on "the land," not the farmers. A catalytic agency was transferred to the legislatures, passing reforms out of some vague response to the rural masses—in this way, they "set free" the "social aspirations" of the yeoman majority—and the "social movement" was less a form of yeoman agency than a revolutionized property structure for which small proprietors were largely place-holders guaranteeing their own persistence. In this early argument, we find characteristics of much contemporary social history, above all the shift to structural conditions, statistically verifiable tendencies, a naturalist theory of culture, and a metonymic depiction of social change in the description of material consequences. The "very conditions of life...tended to equalize men and to draw them together in the bonds of mutual sympathy," he noted, and the "process...which had marked the Atlantic settlements" was "to push forward still more the development of American democracy" (46). If Jameson downplayed the grand ideas of the Founding Fathers, we see him here implicitly identifying with the James Logans, trying to assess those squatters from a distance and resorting, finally, to generalizations about "conditions of life" and "process." But my point is not to dismiss Jameson's account as false in failing to register a clear yeoman voluntarism, for even with such obscurities, his treatment of the revolution as a materially grounded social movement seems more useful than the idealist accounts, a half-century later, of the republican synthesizers. We would do better to explore why and how his initial celebrations of "energetic" yeomen gave way to the social movement of "the land," and see what insights such conflations contain.

Helpful in this respect is a work closer to Crèvecoeur's vantage point and among the most influential social histories of the mid-Atlantic region, James T. Lemon's *The Best Poor Man's Country* (1972). Situating itself in a "general framework of social and economic history," Lemon's study opens with a "typical (if hypothetical) early Pennsylvanian," one Frederick Brown, "ordinary in the sense that he did the sorts of things that many rural Americans did in the eighteenth and nineteenth centuries."[31] Lemon outlines "the commonplace qualities of his life" in order "to understand their structure and rhythm, for they stood as a model for later Americans" (1). Yet, despite this initial presentation, Lemon's is a study that rarely if ever argues for uniformity. He repeatedly insists upon the diversity of yeoman life, stressing class distinctions and striations (10 ff), ethnic and religious differences (14 ff), diverse reasons for and patterns of settlement (chapter 2), different patterns of migration (chapter 3), and so forth. "Pennsylvanians," he notes, "thus were divided in varying degrees by nationality and language and denomination as well as somewhat by economic status." If these "divisions varied in importance," still "[a]ntagonisms among groups and also within groups" tended to arise during "such times of trouble as the debates over the Great Awakening, the controversy over defense against the French and Indians, and the Revolution" (23). Conversely, "these people with a common western European background and similar goals were able to cooperate with one another most of the time regardless of denominational and national differences." "Social unity," he concludes, "contributed to a prosperous society" (23).

These methodological and empirical claims are helpful for making sense of seriality. We may start by noting that Lemon's typical "American" functions differently from analogous idealizations of other historiographic modes. His is not, for instance, "the American" one finds in the history of ideas, who inevitably understands, believes, knows, and feels the ideas of the time. Rather, "Frederick Brown" is the proper name of a statistical mean, a norm toward which all variations trend. He is "ordinary," "typical," "hypothetical," and "commonplace" in the sense that he is *modular*. And this serial modularity will wax or wane depending on the interference of "events": it will have a centripetal pull evident in the "unity" of prosperous times, while giving way to "divisions" and "antagonisms" in the centrifugal "times of trouble." In this way, social history itself has an inverse relationship to the hot history of wars and revolutions, as is evident in Lemon's periodization of Pennsylvania settlement: in the fourth of these periods—"consolidation, disruption, and reestablishment" from 1760 to 1800—the American Revolution stands out as the disruption of numbers, averages, and means (219). It is not surprising that Lemon's analysis of the culture of seriality largely ignores the historiography of republicanism to insist upon "the 'liberal' middle-class orientation of many of the settlers who elected to leave their European communities. 'Liberal' I use in the classic sense, meaning placing individual freedom and material gain over that of public interest" (xv).

I will return to Lemon in a moment, but want to first stress the obvious similarities between his and Crèvecoeur's accounts of eighteenth-century Pennsylvania. For Crèvecoeur, too, is something of a social historian, and the *Letters* repeatedly mobilize statistics to describe American life. James tells of the 171 bees in the kingbird, 54 of which revive, and of the 14 dozen pigeons caught (56, 60–61). Later he gives the success statistics of the various immigrant groups, for which seven of twelve Scots will succeed, nine of twelve Germans, and four of twelve Irish (85). The use of twelve as the numerical base is revealing, highlighting the correlation between farm produce and people. Of a dozen Scots, seven will grow to farmers... and James will later observe that he has "caused upwards of a hundred and twenty families to remove hither" (212)—ten dozen. By the time Crèvecoeur has shifted to the story of Andrew the Hebridean, the numbers truly proliferate: Andrew will pay thirty-five shillings per acre, payable in seven years, for 150 acres (87); working for Mr. P. R., he will earn four dollars per month, his wife a half-dollar for spinning, his son a dollar for driving per time (96–97); Andrew will split three thousand rails for Mr. P. R. for a month before getting a contract from Mr. A. V. to lease 100 acres rent-free for seven years, after which he'll pay $12.50 a year for a total of thirty years (98, 101); his first year he sows 3 bushels of wheat, reaping 91.5 (104). The famous "What is an American?" letter itself concludes with the "account of the property [Andrew] acquired with his own hands and those of his son, in four years," totaling $640 (105). James tells us that he "has ordered [Andrew] to keep an exact account of all he should raise," and one assumes that in his fictional world he had done the same for the other dozens of families he had helped relocate to America; he finally tells us that he hopes to introduce book-keeping to the Indians when he relocates (223). Why all these numbers? There are not merely incidental, I think, but form an integral part of the acculturation to the yeoman world. When James writes about the wild inhabitants of the frontier, he explicitly assumes that "in proportion as the great body of population approaches them they will reform and become polished and subordinate" (79). In other words, they will become average, be averaged, as they learn the culture of statistical self-understanding, much as Andrew, who had accumulated 11.5 guineas in Barra seven years before, and then remained stagnant before moving to America, will become a member of the yeoman series once he can perceive, through an apprenticeship of contracts, saving, expenses, and quantified labor, the spectrum of his—and all—possibilities.

Crèvecoeur thus gives us an analysis of social history from within, where an agency integral to the series shows a lived feeling of structure that underlies Lemon's analysis. The sense of being-outside-themselves-in-the-other is the serial logic whereby one perceives an average and either works to achieve or surpass (and thereby change) it. This serial dynamic can indeed be called "liberalism" in the yeoman context, though the pursuit of "material gain" occurs individually in reciprocal isolation, not through an abstract adoption of values. That is, the liberal individual takes shape in the series-of-individuals that defines and directs the pursuit of wealth. Thus the history of the *longue durée*—the trends, patterns, and quantitative accumulations—do reflect an elusive agency within the series. If this agency sometimes appears a phenomenon of "the land," this is because the land does indeed mediate the serial relationship. The yeoman is literally a kind of placeholder; he holds his material place in part because others are holding theirs. Given the turnover of landowners, Jameson's focus on the land rightly locates the object, if not the subject, of serial agency. And if, as Lemon notes, this serial relationship sometimes breaks down, it does so because other series (of ethnic identity, for example) become more important, or because other practical ensembles and their modes of agency intrude. Social history thus gives us a still life, but one from which we can piece together a quiet if limited dynamic of the series. One buys or sells or squats or flees because others might or have, and in the long serial chain of transactions, what is left behind are the numbers of old accounting books.

The Wigwam Metamorphosis

Crèvecoeur's account of seriality is not simple celebration, however, and any account of *Letters from an American Farmer* must take into consideration his announcement of the collapse of rural yeomanry. Grantland Rice has provocatively argued that we should read the *Letters* as a novel structured around "gradual demystification" or "disabusement" of American myths; the twelfth letter thus becomes the moment when "James recognizes how his writing has, at best, veiled true socioeconomic reality, at worst, participated in the introduction of yet another degenerative historical paradigm."[32] This narrative map of a gradual "disabusement" is suggestive, but too quickly posits a pragmatist skepticism about master narratives, and I'd like to suggest a more focused reading of Crèvecoeur's vernacular sociology. If the seriality described by Crèvecoeur's early epistles explores the political and cultural *advantages* of a reciprocal rural isolation (secure distance from a central government, absence of religious disputes, relative economic autonomy, etc.), the narrative "disabusement" also takes up the dangers of serial dispersal. The third letter had already referenced the 1774 frontier violence in Virginia, in which "the crimes of a few" (anti-Indian violence by select settlers) triggered a wave of violence against "hundreds of innocent people" (79). James's account of the Acadian dispersal, the "greatest political error the crown ever committed in America" (69), is developed along similar lines. But in the twelfth letter, chronicling the violent disputes of "these calamitous times" of the Revolution (201), Crèvecoeur more aggressively takes up the limitations of yeoman seriality.

The serial countryside was never a unified collective in the sense of shared and coordinated group action, and this was the strength of a reciprocally isolated rural life into which ecclesiastic or state intrusions seemed next to impossible. Quiet possession was an effective form of rural economic and political security. But with the Revolution comes the formation of "parties" strong enough to transform the neutral, secure isolation into a distressing dispersal. "What can an insignificant man do," asks James, "in the midst of these jarring contradictory parties, equally hostile to persons situated as I am?" (205). The privacy that makes him feel like the emperor of China evaporates as he is now "no longer connected with society" and "finds himself surrounded by a convulsed and half-dissolved one" (201). It is the characteristics of this newly felt "insignificance" that the *Letters* go on to describe, in an amazing account of rural panic that parallels Lefebvre's study of the Great Fear. James feels he is always on the edge of "the most frightful precipices" (201), fearing incursions that never come to him but come all the time to others in the series:

> we never go to our fields but we are seized with an involuntary fear, which lessens our strength and weakens our labour. No other subject of conversation intervenes between the different accounts, which spread through the country, of successive acts of devastation, and these, told in chimney-corners, swell themselves in our affrighted imaginations into the most terrific ideas! We never sit down either to dinner or supper but the least noise immediately spreads a general alarm and prevents us from enjoying the comfort of our meals . . . our sleep is disturbed by the most frightful dreams; sometimes I start awake, as if the great hour of danger was come. . . . Fear industriously increases every sound; we all listen; each communicates to the other his ideas and conjectures. . . . what a dreadful situation, a thousand times worse than that of a soldier engaged in the midst of the most severe conflict! (202)

This is an "involuntary fear" for the individual, as affective agency has shifted to all the others in the series who relay reactions to actual violence; such is the swelling and spreading, for the contingency of one's place in the series means that the dashing of a child's brains, the scalping of a wife, the burning of one's own body, family, and house, are *potentially* taking place anywhere and everywhere. "If we stay we are sure to perish at one time or another; no vigilance on our part can save us"(208): the act upon the other announces our own fate from which we cannot save ourselves, since the other victims could not save themselves. The "successive acts of devastation" are thus both physical acts of violence repeating in time, and successive tellings and experiencings of these acts in serial communication, until the serial rumor of farmers telling horror stories is internalized in the household, until the domestic meal itself becomes the time of "general alarm," until the intimacy of the hearth becomes the countryside of galloping rumors. Now the grand and powerful scale of serial dispersal becomes oppressive, as James "hear[s] the groans of thousands of families now ruined and desolated by our aggressors," asking repeatedly, "What are *we* in the great scale of events, we poor defenceless frontier inhabitants" (205)? The cultural response to this dispersal-in-war is *flight*, which means not so much simple physical move-ment (although that is important) but the feeling of a structural need to move. This feeling of flight is signaled again in James's references to an uncertain movement just about to happen: "the certain destruction which awaits if I remain here much longer" (210), or "If we stay we are sure to per-ish." (208). Particularly powerful is the image of "every house . . . filled with refugees as wretched as ourselves" (208), with the designation of "ourselves" as *already* refugees and the bleak suggestion that the refugees have fled to a situation from which they will flee again.

But Crèvecoeur does offer a solution here—Indian society, surprisingly introduced through a discussion of captivity. Surprisingly, because the initial account of the Indians plays so heavily on the tropes of broken families (children wrenched from parents) consistent with James's frontier danger. "Many an anxious parent have I seen last war," he writes, "who at the return of the peace went to the Indian villages where they knew their children had been carried in captivity, when to their inexpressible sorrow they found them so perfectly Indianized that many knew them no longer" (213). But, in a sudden dialectical turn, Crèvecoeur moves to an appreciation of the alluring qualities of Indian life. That which serially plucks away pieces may reassemble them again. Captive children:

chose to remain, and the reasons they gave me would greatly surprise you: the most perfect freedom, the ease of living, the absence of those cares and corroding solicitudes which so often prevail with us, the peculiar goodness of the soil they cultivated, for they did not trust altogether to hunting—all these and many more motives which I have forgot made them prefer that life of which we entertain such dreadful opinions. (214)

Perhaps the greatest irony of Letter XII, then, is that the experience of *captivity* becomes the foundation for what James calls "this proposed metamorphosis" (225), whereby "we metamorphose ourselves from neat, decent, opulent planters, surrounded with every conveniency which our external labour and internal industry could give, into a still simpler people divested of everything beside hope, food, and the raiment of the woods" (222). As yeoman seriality disintegrates in war, *captivity* provides the cohesion necessary to recombine. This is not the total adoption of an Indian lifestyle, although it is often figured as similar to serial yeomanry: "the most perfect freedom" and "the ease of living" of Indian life echo the earlier epistles' accounts of American farming, and the accounts of Indian religion as free from sectarian disputes parallel James's celebration of yeoman religion. But now Indian life is subject to the modifications and innovations of yeoman life. Much as he serialized the bees, James plans on bringing the Gospel, inoculation practices, tilling techniques, and accounting to Indian life (220–23): these are large structures of seriality to be instilled and preserved. Speaking of his wife's inoculation techniques, he tells us "she inoculated all our children *one after another* and has successfully performed the operation on several scores of people, who, *scattered here and there through our woods,* were too far removed from all medical assistance" (220, emphasis added). Indian inoculation will be similarly serial: if they can "persuade but one family to submit to it" and then "carry one family through a disorder, which is the plague among these people, I trust to the force of example we shall then become truly necessary, valued, and beloved" (220–21). Implicit in this scenario is the contrast between a "plague" raging through the enclosed community like a raiding party, and an inoculation providing a safe, reciprocal distance. Inoculation offers serial epidemics of one, not the large-scale war of parties, and renders the virus as unable as the government to tyrannize the population.

Still, James's project is not purely to subsume Indian life under the clearly failed structures of the yeoman series in which "those cares and corroding solicitudes" ultimately collapsed. He realizes "there must be in their social bond something singularly *captivating* and far superior to anything to be boasted of among us" (214, emphasis added). In chapter 3, I'll discuss some of the ways in which mid-Atlantic captivity narratives became central to colonial cultures' rethinking of collective life, but we already see these tendencies in Letter XII, in which Indians serve as a foil through which to sort out the limitations of seriality. Crèvecoeur never clearly arrives at a solution to his problem, and he later proposes to "carefully study a species of society of which I have at present but very imperfect ideas" (226). But some clues to his tentative study may be found in James's account of the frontier offered in *Letters*. "As a member of a large society which extends to many parts of the world," he observes, "my connexion with it is too distant to be as strong as that which binds me to the inferior division in the midst of which I live. I am told," he continues, "that the great nation of which we are a part is just, wise, and free beyond any other on earth, within its own insular boundaries, but not always so to its distant conquests" (203). The frontier, then, is understood as the series *in relation to* conflicting ensembles, including the "large society" of the British empire that extends, in other series of colonial settlement, to the ends of the world. There are three problems here: factional groups can arise and, in their "incursions," assault the series; the yeoman series cannot remain secure under such pressure; and the "great nation" is too extensive to preserve a meaningful connection with its serial components.

"Indian" societies, however, remedy all of these problems. For one thing, Indians:

> know nothing of the nature of our disputes; they have no ideas of such revolutions as this; a civil division of a village or tribe are events which have never been recorded in their traditions; many of them know very well that they have too long been the dupes and the victims of both parties, foolishly arming for our sakes, sometimes against each other, sometimes against our white enemies.... [T]hey have no reasons to love us, yet they seem carefully to avoid entering into this quarrel, from whatever motives. (217)

There are two conflicting accounts of Indian cohesion here, the first the idealization—absurd in eighteenth-century Pennsylvania, as Crèvecoeur must have known—of a harmony so basic and primitive that the very idea of political disputes is alien to "their traditions." More interesting is the explanation later in the passage, which posits Indians as rebellious former victims: having been duped into ultimately self-destructive contests, they have carefully fostered an antipolitical culture. Although they formerly consisted of the very factions James decries, Indians now form isolationist factions defined by the avoidance of political, military, or ideological conflict.

Such a characterization may help us get at the slippery nature of the term "nation," used in the *Letters* to denote both global empires ("the great nation of which we are a part") and Native American tribes ("those nations with which I am best acquainted" [217–18]). In this yeoman variant of Montesquieu, the former use designates an extensive scale prone to faction and disintegration, as when James speaks of "a few hundreds of the worst kind [of Indians] mixed with whites worse than themselves...now hired by Great Britain to perpetuate those dreadful incursions" (218). The latter, more tribal, usage denotes a smaller, unified, apolitical collective living apart; "when once secluded from the great society to which we now belong," James imagines, "we shall unite closer together, and there will be less room for jealousies or contentions" (225). Removal from the entanglements of an extensive imperial system will prevent systemic breakdowns, reducing the "probability of adverse incidents as in more complex schemes" (225).

But Indian societies also address the more local, immediate, even domestic disintegration that turns a serial yeomanry into "cowards" (224) huddling in chimney-corners. And here James turns his attention again and again to the wigwam, contrasted with the yeoman dwelling celebrated in the tale of the Hebridean. The contrast is anticipated in the anecdote of Andrew's encounter with Indians. While Andrew is watching the house of Mr. P. R., "nine Indians...suddenly made their appearance and unloaded their packs of furs on the floor of the piazza." Andrew "took them for a lawless band come to rob his master's house," and dashes for his European "broadsword" to expel them; meantime, "they forcibly lifted the door and suddenly took possession of the house" (99). The ironic conclusion of this story, in which Andrew defends the integrity of the yeoman house, then pulls Mr. P. R. from the meeting-house, is a sort of domestic treaty unifying the two social forms, symbolized by the parallel fire of the calumet and the hearth. Already, a synthesis of yeoman isolation and Native American fusion has been imagined.

By the end of the *Letters*, James and his family will similarly achieve security by "abandoning the large framed house to dwell under the wigwam, and the featherbed to lie on the mat or bear's skin" (222). At first mention, the wigwam is a collective dwelling—"their honest chief will spare us half of his wigwam until we have time to erect one" (218)—a stronger collectivity implied, too, in the transmutation of featherbed, made from the feathers of those serial yeoman roosters and hens, to the bearskin won by hunting parties. Even in James's plan "to build myself a wigwam, after the same manner and size with the rest in order to avoid being thought singular or giving occasion for any railleries" (219), we see a departure from the seriality of

yeoman house-raisings, in the shift from a systemic and exteriorized con-
formity (in which naturally a house constructed by all neighboring farmers
will be like *their* houses) to an interiorized shame culture fitting for "a society of men who so readily offer to admit us into their social partnership and
to extend to my family the shelter of their village, the strength of their
adoption, and even the dignity of their names" (221). It is this cohesion
implicit in reproducing the wigwam that provides the security to "sleep
undisturbed by frightful dreams and apprehensions" (222). So yeoman seriality persists in the *Letters'* dystopic–utopic ending, but with two critical
modifications: the domestic space, the formerly privileged site of serial independence, will be more intimately linked with the community through collective cultural practices, while, on a more expansive scale, political links
beyond the tribal village will be avoided. Transdomesticity and isolation-
ism: dreaming of his children's future, James imagines that "[i]nstead of the
perpetual discordant noise of disputes so common among us, instead of those
scolding scenes, frequent in every house, they will observe nothing but
silence at home and abroad" (223).

Crèvecoeur's writing gives us one of the most sustained attempts to explore
the cultural dimensions of a seriality common to eighteenth-century America, a seriality of agrarian life so appealing that it has become one of the
myths of American self-understanding. But with a commitment to self-
disabusement, Crèvecoeur's greater cognitive achievement was in situating
the yeoman series in relation to broader social totalities and more immediate domestic forms. This places him in the company of many of his contemporaries, who also came to understand that one could not think about
farmers, or Native Americans, or the British Empire, or cities, in isolation
from one another; who came to see in the *relational links between these ensembles* the basic elements of New World modernity; and who finally came to
realize the potential for modification and metamorphosis of such elements.
Before exploring further these connections and modifications, we must briefly
survey the seriality operative in colonial Indian policy.

Treating the Series

To say that the backcountry's predominant collectivity or self-perception
was serial, using the isolation of settlement to resist proprietary management,
is only a partial assessment, inasmuch as the backcountry was also significantly
populated by Native Americans. Most Indians had not lived a serial existence after the yeoman fashion, though, with white incursions, Christian-

ization programs, and forced migration, a serial dispersal was gradually taking shape.[33] During the revivalist period of the 1750s and 1760s, as we will
see in the next chapter, some Native Americans of Pennsylvania came to
view themselves as critically dispersed and thus enormously vulnerable economically, politically, and culturally. Consequently, white colonials were
not inclined to view Indians as serial populations (with the Delawares the
notable exception), and instead understood "local" Indian life in terms of
group fusion or confederal administration. Nonetheless, some specific dimensions of Anglo–Native contact *were* understood in terms of seriality, and
more often than not in the double-edged terms outlined above—dispersal
posing a persistent threat to the established patterns of coexistence yet also
comprising, in other forms, the solution.

  We can begin with the phenomenon of rumor, that serial form of communication jumping like a panic from listener to listener, spreading out of control *because* of the reciprocal isolation of the population and the temporal
modification of the rumor itself. Colonial administrators repeatedly expressed
alarm at this form of communication, whether among whites or Indians. In
a 1743 exchange between the proprietary Provincial Council and representatives of the Six Nations, the chief Iroquois agent, Shekellamy, repri-
manded Delawares and Shawnees for spreading false information.[34] "This
String of Wampum serves to tie your Tongues and to forewarn You from
Lies," he told the Delawares, while warning the Shawnees, "You believe
too many Lies, and are too forward in action.... We are the Chief of all the
Indians."[35] Shekellamy then turned to admonish colonial administrators for
not controlling white backcountry rumors: "Your Back Inhabitants are People
given to Lies and raising false Stories. Stop up their Mouths; you can do it
with one word. Let no false Stories be told; it is dangerous to the Chain of
Friendship" (*Minutes of the Provincial Council* 4: 649). Less than two months
later, Governor George Thomas followed this advice upon receiving a frontier delegation's deposition from one James Hendricks. The document insin-
uated that Indians had murdered some white traders, and Provincial Council
minutes scornfully report that when the delegation was examined for first-
hand knowledge, they "related to no other Particulars than what were contained in the said Depositions, except some groundless insinuations of one
Peter Chartier, an Indian Trader." Thomas insisted that the settlers "might
be assured there was no Disposition in the Indians to begin a War, and that
the Informations given by Hendrick's and the rest were the Effect of fear &
Chartier's Villainous Reports, and advised them to return immediately to
their own Homes and to prevail on their Neighbours to disperse and remain

quiet" (4: 656). The obvious irony is that such dispersal created the conditions for the rumor, to begin with.

In these and other references to rumor we find a sense of intersubjective communication far removed from the simultaneity of Anderson's newspaper-reading imagined community or Habermas's deliberative public sphere: we find, rather, dispersed backcountry populations creating or distorting information in the process of serial relaying and out of fear of isolation, and without the centralized control of the sort of authorized account signified by Shekellamy's metaphorical wampum string. As a consequence of the rumor problem, treaties of the period consistently stressed the importance of sharing, regulating, testing, and overseeing information. Typical was a 1728 treaty among the Proprietary, the Conestogas, the Brandywine Delawares, the Conoys, and the Shawnees, which included as its fourth and fifth "links" the rejection of rumor and the orderly sharing of information:

> 4th. That the Christians should not believe any false Rumours or Reports of the Indians, nor the Indians believe any such Rumours or Reports of the Christians, but should first come as Brethren to enquire of each other; And that both Christians & Indians, when they hear any such false Reports of their Brethren, they should bury them as in a bottomless Pitt.
> 5th. That if the Christians hear any ill news that may be to the Hurt of the Indians, or the Indians hear any such ill news that may be to the Injury of the Christians, they should acquaint each other with it speedily as true Friends & Brethren. (3: 311)

What was agreed upon was a centralized counterresponse to serial communication, as when, in 1733, a Conoy delegation met proprietary agents to counter rumors of a Conoy murder of a white man, and to verify rumors of an anti-Conoy expedition from Virginia. In this case, the centralizing context of the treaty served as a court of communication at which Conoys countered the seriality of local settlers in the Donegal-Paxton area, while offering up as counterevidence two Tutelo scalps; in response, Thomas Penn assured the delegation that rumors of the Virginia expedition were false (3: 500–505).

There are important serial analogues to the uncontrolled flow of rumors that recur throughout the treaties. In a 1732 treaty with the Six Nations, Pennsylvania agents complained about "Warriors, who are often too unruly" and "come amongst or near the English Settlements" to "rob, hurt or molest, any English Subjects" (3: 448). Four years later the Iroquois were complaining about renegade traders, particularly those dealing rum and gunpowder, and about settlers who did not share provisions (4: 93). Unlike the Iroquois, who had earlier conceded "it is very hard for us to govern all our young men" while nonetheless promising to try (3: 451), the proprietary agents offered a rationale for this market seriality: "all the White People, tho' they live together as Brethren, have each, nevertheless, distinct Properties & Intrests, & none of us can demand from another Victuals or any thing of the kind without payment. One Man raises Corn & he sells it, Another raises Horses & he sells them, & thus every Man lives by his own Labour & Industry, & no one has a Right to take away from another what he thus earns for himself" (4: 94). The force of this brief tutorial on economic liberalism lies, I think, in its defamiliarizing gestures; the market is not a timeless, universal, or ubiquitous system, but a "White" seriality accepted and promoted in the domains of production and consumption. The white marketplace is distinct from the renegade serial actions of Indian men.

And yet, if market seriality was defended in terms of "Labour & Industry," colonial agents were more sympathetic toward Iroquois concerns about *land* settlement, which mirrored their own concerns about Indian population distribution. As early as 1728, Governor Patrick Gordon shared with a combined Indian delegation his concerns about recent settlement, admitting that "great Numbers now come in amongst us . . . not such good People as William Penn brought over with him, they are loose & idle" (3: 317). "[Y]ou are to consider this Country is full of People," he added, for "we have many weak & some wicked People amongst us" (3: 318). When the Onondaga diplomat Canasatego complained, in 1742, about white settlers intruding on Delawares in the Juniata valley, Governor Thomas agreed to work on removing them (4: 570–71). In support of regulated land distribution, the Iroquois also worked with the proprietary to abnegate improper land transactions. When settlers purchased land from some young hunting Indians near Conegocheege, the delinquent hunters were ceremonially chastised, the principle of central land transfer was reaffirmed, payment was returned, and the Provincial Council thanked the Iroquois for their response (4: 561–62). If unregulated serial exchange was defended in white commercial relations, the same was not true for the seriality of white squatting and settlement or decentralized Indian land sales, suggesting, in the colonial development of capitalism, a differentiated application of free market ideologies dependant on political circumstances.

If Native American and white elites resisted the seriality of unregulated land sales and white squatting, the same held true for Indian settlement. Again and again, we find Native American and white elites discussing and attempting to regulate the settlement of tributary Indian populations. During a 1731 Provincial Council meeting, Logan discussed the dangers of a

French–Shawnee alliance, and offered as a solution the controlled settlement of Indian populations: "a treaty should be sett on foot with the Five Nations, who have an absolute authority as well over the Shawanese as all our Indians," he argued, "that by their means the Shawanese may not only be kept firm to the English Interest, but likewise be induced to remove from Allegheny nearer to the English Settlements" (3: 403). Shawnee settlements alongside "English settlements," all part of "absolute authority" and the resultant hegemony of "the English Interest"—the same ideas are central to the treaty with the Iroquois the following year, when they were exhorted to "bring home all such of your People as live among the French; that so you may all be joyned & bound together as one very great Man, with one Heart and one Head, for so you will become much the stronger" (3: 448). Five years later, Lt. Gov. Clark of New York reported a Shawnee relocation away from the Susquehanna to "French territory," and stressed that he had informed the Six Nations "that they should use their utmost Endeavors to prevent the Removal of the Shawanese, since it would prove so considerable a Diminution to their own Strength; and those Nations had accordingly undertaken to do all in their Power to divert the Shawanese from settling amongst the French" (4: 234). And at a 1746 Albany treaty, a multicolonial statement was delivered to the Iroquois, requesting "That yourselves, who many of you live scattered and dispersed, should dwell in Bodies closer together, as you have heretofore promised to do" (5: 15). White–Indian relations, then, might be seen as the New World standard for the attempted control of backcountry settlement, insofar as a defining feature of "forest diplomacy" was the oversight of population location, always understood in cultural, military, and political terms. Iroquois oversight, particularly of the Shawnees, was often ineffectual, but one senses from Council documents that the Iroquois management of populations, imagined or real, served as an administrative ideal for colonial elites.

The overarching serial dimension of White-Native relations, however, concerned the imposition of a liberal legal culture upon Indian polities. Fundamental to the treaties were provisions for reciprocal criminal proceedings, of which this seventh link in the Chain of Friendship, as stated in a 1728 treaty, is typical: "But as there are wicked People in all Nations, if either Indians or Christians should do any harm to each other, Complaint should be made of it by the Persons Suffering that Right may be done, & when Satisfaction is made, the Injury or Wrong should be forgott & be buried as in a bottomless Pitt" (3: 311–12). A 1735 treaty described this as the "one Chief Article" initially "agreed on between Willm. Penn & the Indians":

"that if any Mischief or Hurt should befall either, they should assist one another. . . . That this Country, tho' it Might be filled with People of different Nations, yet Care should be taken that Justice should be done to every person" (3: 598). In many of these treaty declarations, specific cases of Indian-on-White violence were under discussion. In the 1728 treaty, for instance, recent violence against a "white man last year at Pextang" was addressed (3: 337). But it would be a mistake simply to view the justice provisions as cynical English arguments to punish crimes against whites, and not simply because whites were correspondingly punished. At issue was the serialization of members of multiple "Nations" as individuals under a central regulatory system. Here we return to the dangers of rumor, for legal serialization provided the Crèvecoeurian antidote to the potential formation of ethnic or racial parties, and the concomitant escalation of violence, in response to rumors of frontier violence. Crimes threatened to fuse populations, to cohere loose "nations" into oppositional camps, but a legal individuation guaranteeing reciprocity amounted to the juridical equivalent of orderly, dispersed settlement. During a 1738 conflict over White–Native violence in the Conestogoe area, James Logan insisted on this principle—"in all Cases of this Nature we consider the guilty Person only, if he be a Christian; no other Christian or white Man is putt to any trouble; & in the same manner if he be an Indian, we do not account any other Indian answerable for it but the guilty only, and he alone is to be punished" (4: 281). To control diverse collectives, there must be a moment of insisting that the collectives do not matter.

From White–Native relations, then, we can piece together the basic paradoxes and challenges of serial colonization and accommodation. An unregulated, serial market of commodity exchange was promoted by whites, though unregulated, serial land settlement was challenged; the serial proliferation of rumor was combated through a centralized distribution of information, while juridical treatment of crimes was undertaken through principles of seriality. We see here the essential contradictions of eighteenth-century (not to mention contemporary) seriality: serial distribution of culture and commodities is good, serial development of culture or capital is bad. More importantly, these applied theorizations and practices of seriality reveal a fundamental dimension of white–Native contact: the attempted imposition, by Euro-Americans, of certain forms of collectivity, of certain feelings of structures. This hegemony was by no means a unidirectional process, and, in chapters 3 and 4, I will discuss equally powerful Native American feelings of structure that profoundly influenced white colonial culture. Here, however, I want to stress the importance of vernacular theories of seriality reiterated by white elites in their contacts with indigenous elites, and the ways the contradictions in application provided insights to Native Americans. The explication of individuated market relations, the apologies for and polemics against unrestricted white settlement, the negotiated attempts to control the flow of information, the clarification of European legal principles: each provided Indians with a sense of basic colonial social structures, of their contradictions and tensions, and of the potential seriality of Indians in light of intensifying contact. If the structures and concepts of seriality were weapons in the colonial cultural arsenal, it is also true that a growing sense of seriality provided the foundations for the transition from tribal-national affiliations and accommodationism to pan-Nativist resistance revivals.

White Flight

If yeoman populations experienced a certain power through the seriality of quiet possession, they occasionally suffered dispersal as weakness too. And although Crèvecoeur's literary explication of flight is ultimately resolved in a utopia of yeomanized wigwams, the farmers' petitions from the wartime frontier suggest a very different practical outcome in which, mobilized by race hatred and terror of Native Americans, the farmers inch toward violence. What is more, we see in the petitionary flood an oddly far-reaching inspiration to economic and political analysis. A careful treatment of these petitions, then, will serve us well in thinking about the crises of seriality and the phenomenon of group fusion (the subject of the next chapter). Here the moment in question is the Seven Years' War, the region the wide English frontier subject to incursions by the French and their Native American allies. There were two waves of violence during this period, the first beginning in the summer of 1755, when about twenty white settlers were killed at Wills Creek, and stretching to 1758, when frontier attacks finally became uncommon; the violence would flare up briefly at war's end, culminating in the Paxton Riots of the winter of 1763–64. During the first crisis, that of the late 1750s, a flurry of petitions were delivered to governor or assembly declaiming the dilemmas of the yeomanry. The bulk of the petitions came from settlers in the interior counties, most frequently Northampton County, and reiterated two practical demands.

First, most of the petitions request a more strategic use and positioning of troops, whether allocated along a road, stationed in a settlement area, or clustered in local forts. Such demands consistently address immediate and short-term needs, and rarely speak of a general frontier strategy, although they show awareness of an overarching if ineffectual military policy coming from Philadelphia. A typical petition from the Mount Bethel area criticizes the past deployment of regional troops as "of Little or no Benefitt unto us," then "humbly" explains "That a Station for a Number of Men, somewhere near the Wind Gapp, under the Blew Mountain on the East side thereof, might have the best Tendency to Secure the Inhabitants of These parts."[36] But the petitions likewise suggest the first moments of self-organization, describing improvised paramilitary associations after the fact, then requesting financial support for such activity. Petitioners from Lehigh and Allenstown Townships announced formation of "a Party of Rangers," having "resolved to defend themselves wile they are able." To continue, however, they would need "immediate Relief" in the form of "a Company of Forces, or such other Relief as will assist the said Inhabitants to defend themselves."[37] Mostly Scots-Irish petitioners from Derry, Lancaster County, request money to continue maintaining "Guards in Hannover Township," having already spent £300.[38] A petition from East Pennsborough, Cumberland County, modestly states that "we have agreed with a gard of fourteen men in number, and if it were in our power to pay for a Geard we should be Satisfyed, but we are not able to pay them."[39] A petition from forty-one Lynn Township residents, mostly of German background, presents a variation on this theme, lamenting "the Natour and Mis Magegment of the Generaty Part of the Peopel" that prevented them from "associat[ing] oure Selves and others Immediately into Companies," but then describing in detail a more efficient arrangement of troops.[40]

We should not, however, reduce the petitions to practical demands; they are every bit as significant for what they tell us about the feeling of serial *flight* described again and again. A 1756 petition from Cumberland County explains the dangerous cycle feared by the settlers: frontier dispersal and governmental inattention invite greater attacks, further evacuations, and then greater weakness; the more flight, the more the dissolution of "this Frontier"; and now this dissolution has reached the petitioners who "(without a further Protection) . . . will shortly endeavour to save themselves and their Effects by flight."[41] A similar analysis arrives a year later from Hanover Township, alleged home later of the Paxton Boys. "We, in these parts, are at present in the utmost Confusion," write the yeomen, adding that "the greatest part of the Inhabitants nearest the mountain are fled long ago," as a result of which "the greater part of the remaining Inhabitants are now flying with wives & Children to places more remote from Danger." The consequence: "above

15 miles in length, & 6 or 8 Breadth, in a few days will be altogether waste, & we who continue must either fall a sacrifice to our Enemies Cruelty, or go with our wives and Children to beg our Bread."[42] A parallel petition from Derry encapsulates the point in describing the situation of neighboring Paxton and Hanover: "Hannover is upon the point of flying, and we cannot tarry if they fly, and our flight will open a way into the heart of the Province."[43]

This structural analysis from below offers two basic insights. Most conspicuous is the understanding of backcountry stability, which, to remain viable, must be able to maintain its potentially infinite and reciprocal, if isolated, seriality. The problem goes far beyond neatly quantitative factors; not solely the loss of so many people creates the crisis. Rather, *flight* triggers a social momentum that results in qualitative injury to the remaining settlers: they are unsure whether to follow, but are told, by the urgent and reasonable actions of their fleeing peers, that they should fly as well, that they are becoming more exposed, that flight is inevitable. Flight is thus temporally elusive, binding together the dangers and evacuations of the past with those of the future in a present disintegration. In this respect, the petitioners' predictions that their home area "in a few days will be altogether waste" *and* their desperate resolutions to stay cannot be simply ascribed to rhetorical excess. Rather, they express "the utmost Confusion" that reigns among those who have not yet fled, those who may or may not be on the verge of flight. Flight amounts, finally, to the negative, disintegrative correlate of quiet possession, a kind of quiet *dis*possession; serial disintegration proves the underside of serial stasis; the successful resistance of capitulation to contracts and quit-rents now collapses in flight from total loss and even death. Where an earlier serial opposition could be achieved partly through acts of avoidance, partly through dilatory political structures, partly through sheer physical distance—in other words, through the *social* distance of settlement practices—now, in a situation of violence, binding must be actively achieved through either of the petitioner demands mentioned earlier: either troops and forts could function as strategic obstacles to the raiding, or, with the proper financial assistance, settlement areas could bind themselves together in militia organizations. In the latter case, the resistance to flight is most obvious: settlers are practically fused into a group politically (in self-organizing and electing commanders), economically (by investing money and supplies), and militarily (through patrolling, guarding, or fighting). And petitioning in itself is a tentative pledge to follow through with this kind of cohesion, the series of signators reactively binding themselves into something stronger.

It's also worth noting that the stationing of troops was figured in terms of flight, albeit the flight of the native raider. Tactically, troops could not realistically prevent frontier incursions but could prevent the flight of the Indian in what were uncommon and disturbing conditions of warfare. Survivors, bound to victims through self-organization (and victims, living on through a binding with survivors), could sound the alarum and intercept the fleeing guerilla. This tactic is best described by the same Lynn petitioners who diagnosed their own "Mis Magegment":

> wee Do think that if the Garresens that is Now Lying over the Blue Mountaine in the Forests Was all Removed to This side of the Mountaine and Laid 4, 6, 8 or 10 men in a Good Houce at Not a grate Distance apart, and a Road Cut from one Plantation to the other, of About 3 or 4 Perches Broad, as the Plantations is Prete Neaire to Gether, one this Side of the Mountaine. We do think that it would Cause the Indians to be afraid to Com in Small Companies over the Road, as theaire yousel Way is to Goo for faire of Being taken agoing Back, for When Ever there is Murder Don Within the Road there must be A Good Watch Cept one that Rood to Take them as they Pas Back, and by Larem Guns there Can be many People Cald to Gether in Short Space of Time Besides the Soldiers . . . [44] (3: 152)

Compelling here is the orthographic unlocking of adverb into infinitive—"To Gether"—as well as the way in which the passage reveals the "Larem" of the situation—not in crude metaphorical fashion, as if an alarm gun fortuitously coincides with the social dynamic being described, but in practical and social terms. The alarum signals a past and present attack, which not only kills a member of the community, but also, for the present and future, encourages a spontaneous self-organization ("many People Cald to Gether" around a core group of soldiers) to interrupt, through annihilation, the flight of the Indian. The alarum thus reverses the social relationship with the Indian Other: white flight and Indian cohesion become Indian flight and white union. The practical and temporal dynamic envisioned here, then, reveals that soldiers are not simply a quantitative addition to frontier society (*more men with guns*) nor do they signify a differentiation of tasks (*they fight, we farm*), even for the disorganized people of Lynn. Instead the small series of soldiers plugs the gap in the yeoman series, providing skeletal support and a future: they cannot flee and will never succumb to flight, and, more importantly, they can serve as the future success, the wall of troops on the escape route, for yeoman organization.

At the same time, yeoman flight—and, we may assume, the self-theorizations offered in the petitions—led to some analogous theorizations by elites. In 1755, the chief proprietary diplomat to the Indian nations, Conrad

Weiser, wrote to the governor from war-panicked Reading, explaining that frontier flight threatened Pennsylvania's social fabric:

> Most of the Town are but day labourers, owing Money, are about to leave it, they have nothing at all wherewith to support their Familys. All Trade is stoped, and they can get no employment, and without the Govern^t takes about 30 or 40 of them into pay to guard this Town, they must go off and the rest will think themselves unsafe to stay, & the back Inhabitants will have no place of Security left for their Wives and Children when they are out either against their enemy, or taking care of their Plantations & Cattle, & when things should come to Extremity.[45]

By Weiser's account, flight occurs among three distinct social groups: the frontiersmen, the unemployed and indebted day laborers, and the refugee families. The day laborers are out of work because of the wartime situation, and now threaten to flee, taking with them so much accumulated credit— beyond redemption, wiped off the ledgers—that it could halt trade in the county's commercial township. Without military welfare, the town would become insecure, at which point the refugee "Wives and Children," the displaced domestic support of the frontier farmers, would also flee (again), prompting further flight among the frontier farmers. And so on, we assume. Weiser's is a fascinating extension of the petitioners' sociology, not simply because it acknowledges and incorporates the displaced domestic foundation of frontier economies—wives in towns become analogues to the troops and forts requested in petitions—nor because the crucial group holding the frontier together has become, ironically, the frontier lumpenproletariat, the debtor class bound together only through state intervention. What is most insightful here is the expansive view of the frontier dilemma—always figured in the petitions in terms of swathes of land, or counties and their township seats—to more variegated social clusters (families, laborer-consumers, and implicitly merchants). Here, the understanding of backcountry society as a series of radial social bands is clarified. In some respects, Weiser's is a de-familiarizing inversion of Turner's old frontier theory, which held the fringes of society to be areas of wild dispersion and freedom from social constraints, though "the interior" is entrenched within institutional relations. But for Weiser, who was surely tracking the frontier situation and the petitions pour-ing in, the terms are reversed. The frontier has become the anchor, its dis-persal the greatest threat to the interior. There is concerted effort to main-tain a cohered outer binding to the western counties, for fear that flight at the exterior will unravel the whole, will become flight all the way back to Philadelphia. In Weiser's account, with its social striations, the most vulnerable and volatile layer is in the interior, within the cash flow of the market economy.

This was not an uncommon construction in wartime Pennsylvania. We find a similar view in a 1755 letter from William Parsons, Esq., of the frontier town of Easton, to Assembly members James Hamilton and Benjamin Franklin, in which Parsons sounds the political alarm:

> Our poor people of this Town have quite expended their little substance & are quite wearied out with watching, and were all along in hopes the Government would have taken some measures for their Relief & for the security of the Town. But now seeing themselves as well as the Town neglected, they are moving away as fast as they can. So that if we have not help nor no orders from the Commissioners to use means to get help in a day or two, We shall every one of us be obliged to leave the Town & all we have in it to the fury of the Enemy... for all the Country is flying before them and no means are employed to stop them.[46]

Parsons' assessment of flight gives an added political inflection to Weiser's economic analysis, for here the consolidation and survival of institutional power, at least in the frontier towns, depends on the cohesion of a political public. Frontier flight collapses not only the fringes of the counties, but the political cores of the townships as well. This situation, too, is a matter of cash flight, for Parsons, having "expended what little stock of Cash I had, in Publick Services," wishes that "you had but given Encouragements to some Persons that you could have confided in, for their Employing people just for our present Defence, 'till you could have agreed on a general Plan."[47] In the hands of local placemen in the county seats, the savvy distribution of revenue could have masterfully unified the townships.

In noting such parallels, I do not mean to suggest that serial flight was the sole or the dominant metaphor for understanding society or conflict. But here we do see tentative theoretical *extensions* of the flight scenario in two important domains. First, Parsons, Weiser, and others extend the analysis of flight to the realm of economic tendencies, in contemplating the role of capital for social cohesion during moments of potential social disintegration. Here backcountry dispersal provides the cognitive key to a growing sense of the limitations of a proprietary mercantilism, through which political institutions are economically anchored. This analysis of flight also invites a further analysis of broader urban–rural relations, in which the flight of one population band might lead to subsequent series of flight elsewhere. In this view, urban cohesion hinges on the stability of surrounding protective layers of seriality. In both these dimensions, flight becomes something other than the imagined distress of the frontier; it is a sociocultural reality that must be understood, controlled, and countered in relation to other collective forms. For the petitioners of the late 1750s, flight was an element in the practical and theoretical constellation of seriality that revealed (as it did for Crève-coeur) the gaps in serial existence. In some ways the material sources of these vulnerabilities had been the source of yeoman strength during the first half-century of Pennsylvanian colonization, when institutional control was weak. But with the incursions of the Seven Years' War, the strengths of frontier individuation, passive resistance, and reciprocal uniformity became the terror of isolation and disintegration. This terror would become the basis for a unified collective resistance.

Serial Women

The selective survey of backcountry seriality offered here—in the fiction of Crèvecoeur, the methods of social history, the practice of quiet possession, the goals and principles of Indian diplomacy, the farmers' petitions, and the vernacular analysis of flight—is by no means comprehensive. It aims, rather, to highlight a feeling of structure that saturates the phenomenology of the backcountry, and that will appear as well in the discourses and practices surrounding group action and institutional administration. The expressions of the vernacular constellation of seriality figure more prominently than (and even subsume) the standard ideologies of republicanism or liberalism used to describe early American culture. In concluding this chapter, I want to highlight the important gendered inflections of eighteenth-century seriality, which, as we have seen again and again, is commonly linked with the position of the woman. If James Lemon gives us a man as the typical serial settler, we may again find a corrective in the writings of Crèvecoeur, for whom the American Farmer is unimaginable without his wife, now sitting beneath the tree watching him plow but, in moments of crisis, becoming the projected site of vulnerability.

It should not be surprising that the seriality of the colonial backcountry has strong if sometimes latent connotations of feminine domesticity, for "women" are themselves a series in this context. Iris Marion Young has sug-gested that predominant trends in recent feminist theory—gender essen-tialism, critiques of essentialism, identity politics—have made it difficult to imagine how "women" might be a meaningful, practical political category: there is a lapse into something discursively similar to biological essentialism, a fragmentation of the category of women to the point that it is meaningless, or finally a purely strategic and functionalist identification of women as a potential political grouping.[48] Young takes issue with these positions on methodological grounds, claiming that they overemphasize individual subjectivity as reality (following psychoanalytic assumptions based on childhood development) and problem; by contrast, "[t]hinking about gender as seriality" evokes a critical framework that "disconnects gender from identity" (223). Young seeks instead to stress the existence of "women" as a series, a "social collective whose members are unified passively by the objects around which their actions are oriented or by the objectified results of the material effects of the actions of the others" (213). "*Woman*," she writes, "is a serial collective defined neither by any common identity nor by a common set of attributes that all the individuals in the series share, but, rather, it names a set of structural constraints and relations to practico-inert objects that condition action and its meaning" (226). Young proceeds to sketch a range of material effects that render "women" a meaningful category— enforced heterosexuality, conditioning and coding of bodies, pronoun use, the sexual division of labor, habitual violence against women (217–20)— before insisting that these "forms of seriality...do not necessarily define the identity of individuals and do not necessarily name attributes they share with others" but "are material structures arising from people's historically congealed institutionalized actions and expectations that position and limit individuals in determinate ways that they must deal with" (221). A related analysis is found in eighteenth-century theorizations of seriality. In the yeoman petitions cited earlier, flight is symptomatically linked with the situation of women, as when the Hanover residents write of the possibility, in flight, of "go[ing] with our wives and Children to beg our Bread," or when Conrad Weiser writes of that dangerous moment when "the back Inhabitants will have no place of Security left for their Wives and Children." Such analyses suggest that rural seriality is anchored in the economic seriality of women—both the economic support of women and the domestic production by women—in ways that ultimately code rural seriality, at this moment of crisis, as feminine weakness. Frontier settlers are as strong as the condition of their women, and when women can no longer be protected by the men, the men have become as weak as the women, begging with them for subsistence.

I want to stay with Young in suggesting that this analysis is not *simply* an imaginary, patriarchal gendering of weakness as a feminine state. There is a material foundation for the analysis that has every bit to do with the household foundations of the colonial economy. As Schweitzer writes, "The economy of Pennsylvania centered on the household as the decision-making

unit of production as well as of consumption."[49] This is certainly the sense
of the independent farm one gets from Crèvecoeur, whose American Farmer
tells his wife, in the introductory epistle, "Hadst thee never employed thy-
self in thy father's house to learn and to practise the many branches of house-
keeping that thy parents were famous for, thee would'st have made but a
sorry wife for an American farmer" (45). In painting his utopic situation,
James also writes about his affective transformation once he marries and,
abandoning his desire to wander, discovers the pleasures of the isolated farm:
"I felt that I did not work for myself alone, and this encouraged me much.
My wife would often come with her knitting in her hand and sit under the
shady tree, praising the straightness of my furrows and the docility of my
horses; this swelled my heart and made everything light and pleasant, and I
regretted that I had not married before" (52). The clear implication is that
the reciprocal masculine isolation is affectively acceptable when joined to a
feminine seriality. James even speaks defensively of women as legitimate
foundations for land development:

> Some people are apt to regard the portions given to daughters as so much
> lost to the family, but this is selfish and not agreeable to my way of thinking;
> they cannot work as men do; they marry young: I have given an honest
> European a farm to till for himself, rent free, provided he clears an acre of
> swamp every year and that he quits it whenever my daughter shall marry. It
> will procure her a substantial husband, a good farmer—and that is all my
> ambition. (92)

Here the *daughter* becomes the mediation point between serial yeomen, the
link between James and a potential "honest European." Women become
the principle for settlement and clearance, the source of good neighbors,
the key to acculturation, and, in a reversal of European inheritance customs,
the ultimate destination for land. There is a similar implication in the subsequent anecdote of "friend B." After observing that B's wife renders the
home luxurious by sprinkling "her linen with rose-water before she puts it
under the press," James learns that her name is Philadelphia: "her grand-
mother was the first female child born after William Penn landed with the
rest of our brethren, and in compliment to the city he intended to build,
she was called after the name he intended to give it; and so there is always
one of the daughters of her family known by the name of Philadelphia"
(93–94). This is not a simple identification of woman with city, but rather
the initial association of the woman with the "intended" future development
of the city, and then with the perpetuation of this futurity in the country-

side, as if the same daughters who ground rural development provide the utopic potential for cultural cohesion, here the binding of *brotherly* love.

The foundational seriality of women is reinforced in the period of the wigwam metamorphosis, as James's nightmares repeatedly involve the situation of his wife. During an alarm, "my poor wife, with panting bosom and silent tears, takes leave of me, as if we were to see each other no more" (202). And dreaming of life among the Indians, the one obstacle James faces, at narrative's end, is how to tell his wife: "Nor can I with patience think that a beloved wife, my faithful helpmate, throughout all my rural schemes the principal hand which has assisted me in rearing the prosperous fabric of ease and independence I lately possessed, as well as my children, those tenants of my heart, should daily and nightly be exposed to such a cruel fate" (210). In these two observations we further see the seriality attributed to women, as their flight leads to the breakdown of the yeoman series, and as their imputed desire for solitude and isolation proves the greatest obstacle to Indian collectivity. One senses, in Crèvecoeur, that women's subjectivity (or, more accurately, the subjectivity serially imputed to women) provides the true *affective* anchor for the materialized seriality of the countryside. Thus "women" assume numerous practical and symbolic responsibilities in the serial collective: *othered* parallels reinforcing the masculine, mediators between serial men, promises of cultural cohesion. I would suggest that through the imposed domestic isolation of wives and daughters materialized in the farm economy, serial men not only perceive the seriality of women but comprehend their own seriality through these relationships, finding in women the secret threat of their condition, and the remedy.

Something akin to this idea finds expression in the Indian diplomacy of the time, particularly in the language employed by the Iroquois in reference to tributary nations. In a famous 1742 treaty, Canasatego chastised the Delaware representative Sassoonan, saying "You ought to be taken by the Hair of the Head and shak'd severely till you recover your Senses and become Sober; you don't know what Ground you stand on, nor what you are doing. . . . We conquer'd You, we made Women of you, you know you are Women, and can no more sell Land than Women."[50] Such references are not patriarchal European dismissals of the Delawares as effeminate subordinates, however the white Pennsylvanians may have interpreted them. Rather, the use of the term "women" in treaty language reflected a "sexual division of labor and responsibility in Iroquois culture," here specifying male privilege in diplomatic exchanges, including land transfers.[51] But here too we find an interesting intersection between rural and female seriality. In a 1728 treaty, Sassoonan confessed to Governor Gordon that the Iroquois "have often told them that they were as Women only, & desired them to plant Corn & mind their own private Business, for that they would take Care of what related to Peace & War, & that therefore they have ever had good & peaceable Thoughts towards us" (3: 334). Tellingly, the division of labor concerns more than who can treat with other nations; here it connotes the agricultural labor with which women plant and handle their own business. Clearly in the Iroquois context, then, "women" denoted not simply social function, but the serial collectivity that made the manageable, moveable populations of the Delawares and Shawnees analogous with farming, as opposed to hunting, trading, treating, or fighting.

The gendering of seriality, whether of the yeoman farmer or of the tributary Indian nations, is not simply a discursive construct that contingently ascribes an inferior gender to a weaker social position. In each case a sociological insight is generated out of an admittedly narrow analysis of women's positions, such that women serve as foils (and vice versa) for male rural populations. The deep association of seriality with women will be answered by the heavy masculinization of group fusion, most obvious in the moniker of the "Paxton Boys," and the tendency to celebrate the Native American warrior. It will also prove significant for early American fiction, where the blending of a vernacular sociology with the conventional family metaphor will allow authors to explore in greater complexity the links between women and farmers.

3

Fusion

Claims Clubs

In April of 1733, a party set out for the Paxton region to survey ten thousand acres. Seeking a guide to the area, the surveyors asked "one Sam. Smith a liver in Donegall," but Smith refused; "being apprehensive that we were going to Survey some Land," wrote William Webb in his journal of the trip, Smith "signified to us that we had better return home than go any farther on such an affair."[1] Another surveyor of the party, John Taylor, queried Smith "for what reason" he made his remark; "the answer was that the inhabitants met & was come to a generall resolution not to admitt of any Survey to be made, neither in Donegall Swataro Paxton Quetepehala nor any lands any where there or thereabouts." The surveyors "informed [Smith] the good purpose of the Proprietor towards the inhabitants of the places afforesaid, yet nott withstanding it was often repeated by him that a Survey would not be suffered—upon any pretentions whatsoever no not so much as to locate the Bounds of Donegall untill they knew the terms expecting the price would not exceed 5 £ per Hundred from a price they have seen & who was Proprietor threatening" (252). Insulted, the members of the survey party asked if the backcountry squatters "were got beyond Law," to which Smith answered "yes & Gospel too which caused some warm words to pass, threatening what they would do." When the surveyors asked "if they were resolvd to kill us, or to break our bones," Smith answered "no, but we should be blanketed if we offered any Survey" (252).

Hearing this, the party proceeded to the Paxton area cautiously, in smaller crews. Webb found one local magistrate unwilling to accompany him without a "Speciall order" from the proprietor, and, traveling on without him, found "people flocked in on all sides of the road to a very great number nere 40 or 60 in about one Hour[,] many of them having clubs with them in a very unbecoming manner & by their words & actions appeared fully determined to offer an abuse if we had proceeded to a Survey" (252). This threatening group traveled alongside Webb and his companions for some time. Then, meeting the rest of the original party, Webb learned that his fellow surveyor John Taylor—mistaken for Webb—had been thrashed by a squatter. Concluding "from the generall appearance of the people in all those parts we durst not proceed to the execution of our Business," he "so resolved to return" (253). Even leaving, the surveyors "were pursued by two men in an unbecoming manner giving us very unbecoming language"; fearing "a considerable number pursueing us," the party considered contacting another local magistrate, but one of two "unbecoming" antagonists rode along behind menacing them with a club, the other "hollowing as he rid to allarm the country which prevented our representing the case to a magistrate & obliged us to take a road for our safty" (253).

With Webb's account, we're at the moment of Thomas Penn's arrival in Pennsylvania, his attempts to modernize the Land Office, and the institutional offensive launched against backcountry squatters. But, in contrast to Logan's account of quiet possession, here is an account of the critical cultural moment when the dispersed series comes together around the alarm, to form a dangerous collective of a different sort: the "unbecoming" flock of clubs. The power of Webb's and similar accounts lies, I think, in their vernacular phenomenology of group fusion and its moments: how fusion emerges from the centralized serialization of a dispersed population; how the squatters already expect and fear the survey, much as Webb and his companions come to anticipate resistance after repeated threats; how the intrusion of the survey raises the alarm which then brings forth the ensemble of resisters; how the resisters travel alongside and thus shadow the surveyors; how moments or even gestures of violence become perceived as the immanent potential for mass violence; how official institutions evaporate into insignificance; and how the organized party journeying through the serial countryside is itself ultimately dispersed by the gradually cohering squatters. What Webb and others like him are attempting to explain is the problem Crèvecoeur found insoluble. How may the series become unified? How may rural isolation become the foundation for a coordinated group consciousness?

In exploring the eighteenth-century backcountry, we must consider not only the predominance of serial life, but the regularity of rebellious mobilizations, white and Native American. Continuing the analysis of the last chapter, I want to explore: how the fused group (variously called Mobility, crowd, rabble, trash, and riot) was formative for the development of American politics; how it posed a major *cultural* challenge, both practical (how to achieve/quell it) and theoretical (how to understand it), in the American colonies; and how the predominance of such fusion in the white and indigenous backcountry gave vernacular accounts of fusion, at least in the middle Atlantic region, a strongly agrarian inflection. Of course, the two other major forms of group fusion common in the eighteenth century were (urban and rural) slave rebellions and urban crowd actions (associated most frequently with the revolutionary crises, but including anti-impressment riots), and any comprehensive account of the broader culture of groups would have to take these into account as well, ideally in their triangulated relationship with backcountry rebellions. In focusing on backcountry fusion, I do not mean to downplay the significance of these other two groups, who clearly became more important in the late eighteenth and early nineteenth centuries, just as white backcountry actions diminished in relative significance. Yet backcountry rebellions were singularly troubling, if perplexed elite responses are any indication. One commonly finds urban elites avowing their ability to manage and manipulate urban crowds—if it is "impossible to stem" the stream, wrote New Yorker Robert Livingstone, just "direct its course"[2]—while, in light of the successful revolution in Haiti (which haunted American political leaders from Adams to Buchanan), slave owners aggressively developed methods for the better surveillance and management of Blacks. But from the Seven Years' War, Pontiac's Rebellion, and the Carolina Regulations through to the Whiskey Rebellion, Little Turtle's War, the Fries Rebellion, the Blount and Burr Conspiracies, and Tecumseh's Rebellion, backcountry agitations seemed to disturb colonial and national administration profoundly.

The most infamous illustration of rural fusion in this era is probably the Massachusetts Regulation, which became a motivating force behind the federal constitution as well as the best-known early American play, "The Contrast." That the insurrection is still primarily known as "Shays' Rebellion," after its imputed demagogic leader, offers some index of critical attitudes about group actions. Many remain content to attribute such actions to emblematic leaders; connections with other regulation movements are downplayed; and above all the rebellion itself seems a brutishly episodic symptom to which discursive culture responds. The insurrection thus exists in the register of an emotional, irrational outburst to be treated as an historical object, not as a recurring rationality of eighteenth-century subjectivity. Exploring the significance of group fusion, then, requires countering many of these tendencies: to think about patterns of connection between group actions, and how they may arise; to contemplate a temporality of the rhythm of mobilizations; to question the emphasis on individual instigators; to consider the *absence* of group actions where perhaps expected; to think about the vernacular discourse surrounding groups—in short, to consider the group as an essential element of early American culture. As an initial exploration, this chapter takes a literary guide of sorts, Colonel James Smith, whose late eighteenth-century captivity narrative illustrates many facets of that period's white American fixation on group culture, and whose writings on military maneuvers provide an interesting cultural map of fusion. Additionally, the chapter explores the Indian-modeled guerilla actions of the so-called Black-Boys and the broader movement of pan-Nativist fusion in Pennsylvania, and finally treats the large-scale farmers' insurrection of the Paxton Riots, as well as the accompanying and characteristic historiography about that event.

Third Party Passion

What makes the group so hard to understand? A first obstacle is formed by the sociological clichés, ranging from the "organicist idealism" that sees in the group a "hyper-organism" of contagious spontaneity, to a neopositivist rational-choice theory that understands the group as a simple aggregation of members for functional efficiency.[3] Organicism usually expresses a conservative "nostalgic yearning against liberal atomism" (345), though it is also integral to the bourgeois horror of the crowd (the organic monstrosity of the hydra so prevalent in eighteenth-century discourse).[4] Neopositivism simply finds the same liberal individualism of the series in all collective forms. It is the obvious inadequacy of these two accounts of the group, combined with inexperience of, and skepticism about, the phenomenon itself, that hampers analysis of groups in contemporary cultural theory. Additionally, many sociological concepts conflate different practical ensembles under a single umbrella term, making the fused group that much harder to discern. The best example of such confusion is the term "class," which in the narrowest sense is a serial gathering, although historians and sociologists will conflate groups emerging *from* classes with their broader serial basis: thus a bread riot or a sit-down strike will be attributed to, say, the working class in toto. In fact "class" normally describes a relationship among multiple collective forms (serial, fused, institutionalized). Accordingly, we must sort out the relevant practical ensembles to understand the rural–urban "class" conflicts of early America.

Sartre approaches the phenomenon of fusion by stressing the necessary material conditionings that allow groups to emerge: "any restructuration of a [serial] collective into a group," he writes, "is a complex event which takes place *simultaneously* at every level of materiality" (349). That is, the material field must provide the conditions for fusion, a point stressed in the discussion of the storming of the Bastille. Residents of the Quartier Saint-Antoine saw in the Bastille the boundary of a poor urban district with set entry points for soldiers that would trap the locals within street massacres. The residents also perceived the Bastille as a source of arms, the only source from which the quarter could be defended from the west (358, 361). Thus "particular practico-inert structures of the environment" became a template on which potential group fusion "was inscribed in things as an inert idea" (361). The group-to-be had to perceive both its necessity (its danger) and its possibility (its defense) in the material environment. But material possibility, in this brute form, is not the crux of Sartre's analysis. "It is not enough that unity is possible" materially, for "it is also necessary that the instruments for wresting [the series] from recurrence"—Sartre is speaking here of the *cultural* tools—"should be present in the collective itself" (365). Here we must speak of "the group as *passion*" (348) in several dimensions: the perception of other groups and group members, a sense of serial impossibility and group possibilities, and a self-understanding of past, present, and future moments critical to the group.

Building upon historian Marc Bloch's thesis that aristocratic consolidation led to the consolidation of the peasantry (346), Sartre speculates that most groups form in response to other perceived groupings. In the Quartier Saint-Antoine residents perceive "France as a totality" in the new revolutionary government (352), feel the unification of the city of Paris by the mobilization of governmental forces and the declarations of Mirabeau and Louis XVI (353), and sense the possibility of local militia formation within the assembly's creation of militia units to "prevent public assemblies and disarm the citizens" (356). These perceptions may be false, as with the bourgeois nationalist fiction of a unified France, or the citizens' overestimation of the army's unity. Nonetheless, the perception of the Other group provides a model for the dispersed series. The militia units "represented, though negatively, a synthetic determination of the gathering"; as threats to the local

citizenry, they contributed to the idea of counterorganizing; defining themselves by such perceived external forces, the residents understand their protection must come "by means of a unification produced internally by the
gathering itself" (356). Does a group simply conjure forth other groups? Not
really, though it is often true that "a collective derives its possibilities of
self-determination into a group from its *antagonistic* relations with an already
constituted group or with a person representing this group" (362). What
results is more than simple mimicry, for "*imitation* is also *self-discovery* through
doing one's own action over there in the Other, and through doing the action
of the Other here" (354). Through the encounter with the Other group,
then, "the unity of self-determination...comes to the collective through
the Other in alterity as an *other structure* of the gathering, and as needing to
be realised by self-determination" (362).

   When, in 1798, Philadelphia's Democratic-Republicans formed the paramilitary Republican Blues in response to the Macpherson's Blues and Jack
Fenno's Philadelphia Grenadiers,[5] they did so not simply because they found
a model for organization, but because the threat of the Federalist black cock-
ades made them perceive the action of others, and their own need to respond
with self-determination. The Donegal claims clubs similarly cohered around
the semiaccurate perception of the surveying parties: facing the group
mobilized against quiet possession, they found self-determination in a parallel antisurveying party. As these examples will suggest, there emerges from
the antagonistic encounter with other groups (real or perceived) a crisis, a
moment "when impossibility itself becomes impossible," when the other
group "reveals that the impossibility of change is an impossibility of life"
(350). We're speaking specifically of the felt dangers of seriality, for it is the
serial gathering that "furnishes the elementary conditions of the *possibility*
that its members should constitute a group" (345). This is not a matter of
some sense of biological survival but rather of the hermeneutics of need, an
interpretive experience of finding the present reciprocal isolation unbear-
able, of finding one's seriality a threat demanding a response, of discovering
that flight is no longer possible. As serial possibility becomes serial impossibility and then has to become group possibility, certain structured objectives
will take form, shaped by the surrounding material field (what is possible in
this place, with these resources) and the sense of the imminently threatening countergroups.

   The material field, the antagonistic Other group, the crisis of impossibility,
and the structured objectives—all are necessary dimensions of group fusion,
but still do not explain the dynamics that take shape within the group. Here

we might usefully turn to a favorite self-designation of colonial groups, "Regulators," a label adopted from a sense of regulating not only a political system run amok but, equally stressed, themselves: *self*-regulation, their own group formation and activities. What constitutes group regulation? Every "individual's being-in-the-group" is given meaning by a "bond of interiority" that comes through a "regulatory third party" (381). Every group member becomes a "third party," both "*epicentre*" and "end," subject and object, organizer and organized (367). Group membership is not a "binary relation" between the individual and the abstract group, nor is it primarily a relationship between one group member and another. Rather, a "ternary relation" predominates, in which the internal third mediates the reciprocity between group members (374). Yes, one person in the group will help another, but in the third party I see "my objectivity interiorised"; my actions, though still "*mine*," have meaning because she, "*over there*," gives them meaning (377). At the same time, I realize that I too am a third party, that I give the other group members' actions meaning in the same fashion, as a kind of standard of group membership: I give meaning to *those actions over there*. Thus the actions of the group members—each a third party—become regulatory: the actions of every third impose ethics-saturated practical demands upon me, and require "the common unity of a *praxis* which is everyone's" (386). This means that every group member, by virtue of being a third party, becomes both a "*constituent and constituted power*," giving a stronger bond to the group's internal reciprocal relations while becoming bonded through other third parties (374). The group "leader is always *me*, there are no others . . . and *I discover in my own praxis* the orders which come from the other third parties" (396). In this respect we should take the Carolina Regulators' moniker seriously: they were not simply overseeing political actions within the macropolitical sphere, but understood themselves, through their group existence, to be enacting certain practical-ethical standards demanded by themselves *as a group*, and imposed on themselves *throughout the group*. They discover their own regulation and the regulation of others in their own actions. The addition of group members thus becomes more than a quantitative increase: "instead of being a mere inert summation of the units," addition "becomes a synthetic act for everyone: everyone joins the group *in order to be more numerous* and hence the increase of the group becomes everyone's practice" (394).

A group of 50 is not just 1 + 1 + 1 and so on, but 50 feelings of the presence of 50. The action at the Bastille cannot, then, be understood via an abstract template of values finally being realized on the streets of the Quartier

Saint-Antoine—these values (assertion of local authority against elite militia units) may have been present serially—but as a particular feeling of structure of greater cultural force. So the historian's challenge is to figure out how "the individual discovery of common action as the sole means of reaching the common objective" emerges from the "urgency, the imperious clarity, and the totalising force of *the objective* (that is to say, of the danger which has to be avoided, of the common means which has to be found)" (387). If this sounds like an idealization, it is: Sartre admits that the groups he has theorized do not actually exist in history. What he is attempting is *an approximation of the fundamental tendencies within actually existing groups*. Given the messiness of history, the variations among group members, "the theoretical schema . . . does not apply in reality: there are procrastinators, oppositionists, orders and counterorders, conflicts, temporary leaders who are quickly re-absorbed and replaced by other leaders" (403). Nonetheless, "if the group is really to constitute itself by an effective *praxis,* it will liquidate alterities within it" and "the common freedom will create itself *against them* until in the end the orders which circulate really are the orders which everyone gives himself in himself and in all" (403–4). Historical groups will have to tend toward this ideal group of fusion, to succeed as groups. The practical impossibility of the group is one reason Sartre characterizes it as a *process,* moreover one that is "limited" (390); this is also the reason Sartre will move to a discussion of what he calls the *statutory* group, which tries to prolong its regulatory existence through the self-imposition of statutes of membership— both sign and cause of further disintegration of the group into either series or institution.

So Sartre's account of group fusion is an idealization, one replete with a "revolutionary nostalgia" that "risks misleading the reader into an overestimation of the moment of group formation, and into a mystique of apocalypse."[6] The fused group is for Sartre an unambiguous moral and political ideal, the primary locus of freedom and agency. The theoretical antecedent of this view is perhaps the account of author–reader fusion in *What is Literature?*, where "the writer's universe will only reveal itself in all its depth to the examination, the admiration, and the indignation of the reader; and the generous love is a promise to maintain, and the generous indignation is a promise to change, and the admiration a promise to imitate." In "the aesthetic imperative we discern the moral imperative," Sartre continued, before concluding that "nobody can suppose for a moment that it is possible to write a good novel in praise of anti-Semitism."[7] Similarly, he cannot imagine or admit a group fusion of negative political values—an absurdity, as the case of the Paxton Boys will show. Nevertheless, a value-neutral account of fusion offers a useful corrective to the neglect and facile criticisms of historical groups, most evident in the convention of pairing a demogogic proper name (Popé, Bacon, Pontiac, Shays, Cresap, Fries, Tecumseh) with a term of sinister chaos (riot, rebellion). Something approximating group fusion was crucial to vernacular theories of social structure in early America, not only in accounts of *regulation* but in that favored elite trope of the time, the many-headed hydra. In the myth of the hydra of Lerna (a syncretic creature of multiple heads finally slain by Hercules), we can find an approximation of a theory of groups, right down to the conflicted depiction of the hydra's heads: when one head is cut off, two more grow in its place, until a central head is found, removed, and its stump cauterized.[8] What is this if not a vernacular account of the multiheaded ensemble of third parties, linked with the fantasy of a hidden leader as the secret weak point? As I will try to demonstrate in the remainder of this chapter, early Americans complemented vernacular accounts of seriality with analyses of fusion, frequently in the racialized battlegrounds of conflicts between whites and Native Americans. Group fusion would thus become a central means of speaking about racial difference, a pivotal motivation for institutional innovations, and a vital dimension of a popular and practical nationalism. It would be an overstatement to suggest that the massacre, the revival meeting, or the bread riot, as opposed to the public sphere or the constitutional convention, become the foundational paradigms for early American culture, although such a thought experiment would be intriguing. But no account of the dominant collectives of the period should ignore the *group*.

Beaver Ontology

We can begin to survey the vernacular accounts of group fusion in the captivity narrative tradition. Nancy Armstrong and Leonard Tennenhouse have suggested that the American captivity narrative, exemplified by Mary Rowlandson's 1682 *The Sovereignty & Goodness of God*, carved out the cultural space in which the English novel developed. "The exemplary captive" (Rowlandson) "existed for the early eighteenth-century reader as a kind of epistolary heroine, whose ability to read and write, more than anything else, distinguished her from her Indian captors."[9] As the lone letter writer, the Captive becomes the "solitary body" who "speaks out in isolation" and becomes "self-reflexive and thus a whole world unto herself"; through her, "the English subject becomes poignantly aware that survival depends on her ties to a community that cannot be experienced directly" (206–7). In the uniquely colonial experience of captivity, the modern self of the modern novel is created; Rowlandson begets Pamela, for "[i]t takes the solitude of her captivity to turn the narrator into a separate individual" (211). This is a suggestive reading of Rowlandson and some of the gendered origins of Anglo-American sentimental fiction. But like much new historicist criticism committed to the Foucauldian episteme, it totalizes too quickly, here dismissing variants within the genre. "Among the Indian captivity narratives," Armstrong and Tennenhouse write, "one kind in particular begins to reshape and dominate the genre," and other captivity tales are "curiosities" or "anti-tale[s]" that reinforce the dominant type (203). Consequently, they naturalize the captivity narrative as a *serial* tale, a discourse of isolated individuality formed in flight, and ignore a range of competing social modes in other captivity tales.

For equally or more significant in the mid- to late eighteenth century is the captivity narrative of *fusion*, the story of the serial white learning about group existence among the Indians. Many of these narratives emerged from the military culture of the Seven Years' War and the series of "Indian expeditions" that followed (up to and including Harrison's attack on Tippecanoe), and were collected by Archibald Loudon.[10] Here I would specifically like to examine the 1799 captivity narrative *An Account of the Remarkable Occurrences in the Life and Travels of Col. James Smith, During His Captivity with the Indians in the Years 1755, '56, '57, '58, & '59, In which the Customs, Manners, Traditions, Theological Sentiments, Mode of Warfare, Military Tactics, Discipline and Encampments, Treatment of prisoners, &c. are better explained, and more minutely related, than has been heretofore done, by any author on that subject. Together with a Description of the Soil, Timber and Waters, where he travelled with the Indians, during his captivity. To which is Added, A Brief Account of some very Uncommon Occurrences, which transpired after his return from captivity; as well as the Different Campaigns carried on against the Indians to the westward of Fort Pitt, since the year 1755, to the present date.* Smith's narrative, published in Kentucky in 1799 and reprinted by Loudon in 1808, not only illustrates some late-eighteenth-century tendencies in white characterizations of Native Americans, but also illustrates a sociological diagnosis common in captivity narratives of the time. The title's shifts—from personal recollection to ethnography, then to military culture, agrarian reconnaissance, and early national political conflicts—are suggestive in this respect, bridging the colonial–national divide. Not only does the work bridge the gap between the colonial and early national eras, but central to this narrative is a characterization of Native Americans (here the Caughnawaga Mohawks)[11] as a fused group, with a missionary desire to correct an overly individuated and serialized white society along Indian lines.

Smith's account may be read as a combination of several overlapping character developments, the first a strategically *deindividuating* strand chronicling Smith's gradual fusion with the Indians and troubling the self–group binary.[12] This strand is introduced with an uncharacteristically formulaic reference to "being born between Venus and Mars," for while Smith has "fallen violently in love with a young lady," he is likewise drawn into the war effort against the French (263). By narrative's end, this dilemma will be revealed as an opposition between ill-fated, individualist romance and triumphal collectivist conflict. Not only does Smith emblematically return home "a few days" after his "sweet-heart was married" (316), thus marking the abandonment of the "Venus" of individual romance, but a corresponding tale about the break-up of an Indian community hinges on his Indian brother's departure from the collective with an angry wife. The wife's departure (tellingly described as an "elopement") is prompted by a dispute over child punishment, and with this episode Tontileaugo, an important figure in Smith's own Indianization, leaves the narrative for good. Further, Tontileaugo leaves behind an all-male community of "Mars," marking an ascendant collective existence ultimately linked with the war of independence and American expansionism generally.

A few episodes may illustrate Smith's transition from seriality to fusion. Upon capture, he notes that the Indian party "divided the last of their provisions" and "gave me an equal share"—an unexpected instance of parity across enemy lines (264). At the town of Tullihas, Smith undergoes an adoption ceremony, which he again misunderstands as a ritual execution, provoking "loud laughter by the multitude" (268). And, following an early hunting trip, Smith complains about the load of meat he must carry. "They made a halt, and only laughed at me, and took part of my load and added it to a young squaw's, who had as much before as I carried." "This kind of reproof," concludes Smith, "had a greater tendency to excite me to exert myself in carrying without complaining, than if they had whipped me for laziness" (277). Each of these moments provides a social defamiliarization, as Smith's suppositions about groups and individuals repeatedly prove faulty. Where military conflict might predict maltreatment, he instead finds material equality; where he expects individual punishment and death, he finds inclusion, initiation, or group shaming. And this reeducation is much more than simply a correction of ethnographic attitudes about Native Americans, for Smith's

own *habitus* is being transformed as well. At Fort Ligonier he experiences—
and predictably misunderstands—the Indian gauntlet, "wishing them to
strike the fatal blow, for I thought they intended to kill me" (265). A short
time later, he explains the initiation ritual to another captive (suggestively
named John Savage), after which "I fell into one of the ranks with the Indians, shouting and yelling like them; and as they were not very severe on
him, as he passed me, I hit him with a piece of pumpkin—which pleased the
Indians much, but hurt my feelings" (287). So Smith is not only *learning*
about groups, he is *becoming* of the group, and is here torn between his serial
identification with a fellow captive and his role as a third with his fellow
Indians . . . feeling one way, acting another, and knowing both.

Smith's systematic reorientation continues throughout the narrative. When
he finds some of his books missing and "inquired after them, and asked the
Indians if they knew where they were," he assumes "they were displeased at
my poring over my books" and, glancing at a rack for drying skins, sees "a
gallows" for individual punishment (275–76). But, the following spring, the
Indians gather together upon finding his books:

> I was a little way from the camp, and saw the collection, but did not know
> what it meant. They called me by my Indian name, which was Scoouwa,
> repeatedly. I ran to see what was the matter; they showed me my books, and
> said they were glad they had been found, for they knew I was grieved at the
> loss of them, and that they now rejoiced with me because they were found.
> As I could then speak some Indian . . . I told them that I thanked them for
> the kindness they had always shown to me, and also for finding my books. . . .
> This was the first time that I felt my heart warm toward the Indians. Though
> they had been exceedingly kind to me, I still before detested them, on ac-
> count of the barbarity I beheld after Braddock's defeat. Neither had I ever
> before pretended kindness, or expressed myself in a friendly manner; but I
> began now to excuse the Indians on account of their want of information.
> (281–82)

Smith's admission that he "saw the collection, but did not know what
it meant" offers a nice précis for such scenes in which he must repeatedly
rethink his assumptions about collective life. And his narration of this episode strategically highlights the reconstitution of the self that takes place with
such occurrences, for here he first gives his reader his Indian name, describes
his first significant appreciation of Indian culture (which is implicitly a renunciation of his own serial culture), and first offers a translation of a speech *he*
delivers in Mohawk to the assembled Indians, in which "they," if only
indirectly, becomes "you." This episode also challenges a common trope of
the earlier captivity narratives, which treat the book as a cultural separator

(or, more sharply in Armstrong and Tennenhouse's formulation, as a constitutive element of bourgeois subjectivity). Smith turns out to be wrong again in his assumptions about Indian society, and learns that the group not only can accommodate books, but ironically can even facilitate his reading, and apparently without any fetishization of the book. A few pages later the renunciation of serial narrowness becomes more explicit, as Smith tells of giving meat to a "Wiandot" passing through the camp. When recounting this gesture to his brother Tontileaugo, the latter asks if he also offered sugar and oil. "I told him I did not; as the sugar and bears oil was down in the canoe, I did not go for it. He replied, you have behaved just like a Dutchman. Do you not know that when strangers come to our camp, we ought always to give them the best that we have" (283). Smith's response to this chastisement, an admission "that I was wrong" (283), now announces the superiority of Indian over European attitudes toward the individual, who must be viewed not as the isolated traveler but as the third, as me-in-the-other.

Perhaps the dominant form of celebrating the group fusion of Indian culture comes in repeated references to the hunt. There is an anecdote about the Catawbas faking buffalo tracks to capture their enemies, an explicit linking of hunting with military conflict (272). Another anecdote describes Smith hunting bear with Tontileaugo—a two-person task requiring one person to drive the prey out of the tree while the second shoots (278). Smith takes care to chronicle a moment when Tontileaugo "took hold of an arrow, and shot the bear a little behind the shoulder; I was preparing also to shoot an arrow, but he called me to stop, there was no occasion; and with that the bear fell to the ground" (279). The insertion of this detail emphasizes Smith's growing self-reflexiveness when it comes to his serial behavior, as he makes the transition from serial reiteration (*he shoots, I also shoot*) to the group identification of one member's actions in the other (*he is shooting over there on my behalf*). In another illustration, Smith and the Indians "scattered ourselves from the river to the lake" and drove the deer to the water, killing about thirty (304–5). Here, Smith demonstrates a strategic "scattering" that must be distinguished from uncoordinated dispersal, for the *deliberate* scattering, as in forest warfare, is the precondition for a deadly convergence of hunters and prey. In another anecdote, Smith describes a captured Virginian who teaches the Indians how to fish (314). Richard White notes that this exchange was typical—whites taught fishing techniques, Indians taught techniques for hunting on land.[13] From our perspective, the difference is critical: whites teach technologically individuated practices, and Indians teach necessarily grouped practices.

An additional episode exemplifying this deindividuating strand highlights some differences with Rowlandson's narrative. On the first full day of
his captivity, Smith arrives at the French Fort Ligonier, his first encounter
with large numbers of Indians, and he describes a hellish Babel of "continued shouts and yells of the different savage tribes who were then collected
there" (265). Smith estimates "that there were thousands of Indians there"
(265). This moment might be suggestively juxtaposed with that of Mary
Rowlandson's "First Remove," where, in a similar moment of racial enclosure,
she describes the hellish multitude of Indians: "Oh, the roaring and singing
and dancing and yelling of those black creatures in the night, which made
the place a lively resemblance of hell."[14] In Rowlandson's case, this undifferentiated perception serves to reinforce serial isolation, as when, during
the thirteenth remove, she writes about "how many times sitting in their
wigwams and musing on things past I should suddenly leap up and run out
as if I had been at home, forgetting where I was and what my condition was.
But when I was without and saw nothing but wilderness and woods and a
company of barbarous heathens, my mind quickly returned to me" (52).
But Smith's narrative explicitly challenges this sense of the horde, and he
admits his subsequent realization that there were only about four hundred
Indians at Fort Ligonier (266). This revision signals the recurrent thematic
of *number* throughout the narrative. In describing Indian combat more generally at the end of his narrative, in a section titled "On Their Discipline
and Method of War," Smith repeatedly insists that Indian organization
makes serial, statistical counting irrelevant: the official 1764 British count
of Indian forces was thirty thousand when "there were not above one thousand in arms against us," white casualties outnumbered Indian casualties at
a rate of fifty to one from 1755–58, ten to one after that, seven to two during the Great Kanhawa battle, and so forth (342, 345). So Smith explicitly
challenges the serial statistics associated with imperial administration, seeking instead an exponential theory of groups that might explain and direct
the magnification of social power.

If the first narrative tendency foregrounds the individual–group distinction, defamiliarizing the seriality of white yeoman life while stressing that
Indian collectivity is a puzzle to be taken seriously and solved, the second
tendency is an ethnographic riff, a more detailed exploration of Native
American groups in their varied manifestations. Having established the superiority of group existence, Smith aims to spell out not only an ontology of
group life but almost a metaphysics encompassing problems of Nature and
of God. And because he is still ultimately committed to the superiority of

Anglo-American culture, he must offer, observing the military and cultural destruction of Indian life, a related explanation for the fatal flaws of Indian fusion that an appropriating white culture must overcome. Some of this analysis appears early in the narrative, when Smith witnesses three ceremonies prior to a war against the Catawbas. The first is a war dance in which the warriors act out the dance together. "[A]ll those who were going on this expedition collected together and formed," and then, accompanied by music and drumming, "the warriors began to advance, or move forward in concert, like well disciplined troops would march to the fife and drum" (270). The seeming redundancy of the phrase "collected together and formed" is telling, asserting that a group is not a gathering based on number but a *form*, and here the war party's formal particularity involves a coordination attributed not to deliberation or debate but to a more primal musical tradition. Smith next describes "the war song," in which "only one sung at a time, ... while the other warriors were engaged in calling aloud *he-uh, he-uh*"; warriors avowed past and future achievements while others responded "with loud shouts of applause." This ceremony was so powerful as to draw in nonmembers of the war party who, "so animated by this performance, ... were then initiated into the present marching company" (270). What Smith observes, in this second ceremony, is a complementary inversion of the war dance that perhaps unlocks its secret. For if the first ceremony performed the collective, the second performs the individual's internalization of the group, the acting out of the role of the third. Significantly, this second ritual, not the first, draws in additional members. It is not, in other words, a matter of "herd mentality" or bandwagon effect, in which isolated individuals join the undifferentiated group to hide (thus accentuate) their isolation; rather, the war song offers a case in which assertions of individuality take the forms of commitment to the others (*I will kill with you and for you*), such that the group seems the only true ensemble for the expression of individuality. In a social context that condemns the undifferentiated mob as the many-headed hydra, the radicality of Smith's observation cannot be underestimated. And it is interestingly reinforced in his third example, that of "a kind of wooing or courting dance." Here, young men and women stand in opposing ranks, advancing to and retreating from each other as music is played. "The exercise appeared to me at first, irrational and insipid," says Smith, but he notes that amidst the musical syllables "*ya ne no hoo wa ne, etc.*" lovers are able to "intermix sentences with their notes, and say what they please to each other, and carry on the tune in concert." This ability to "say what they pleased in each other's ear, without disconcerting their rough music, and the others, or those near, not hear[ing] what they said" (271) again challenges the seriality predominant in Anglo-American discourse, even as it transcends the Venus–Mars opposition with which the narrative began: here the intimate sexual relationship is both private and collective. That such individuality not only survives but actually thrives within a culture of fusion, that wooing can coexist with and conform to the clearly superior military dimensions of a culture, not only complicates the traditional anthropological view of Native Americans predominant in English writing since Thomas Harriot, but reinforces Smith's view that the culture of fusion can be appropriated without, say, undermining the Anglo sanctity of love or marriage.

Smith is at his most ontological, however, in his repeated references to *beavers*, starting with a dispute with Tecaughretanego, "who was a wise man," but who nonetheless believed that the beaver population of isolated ponds was replenished by geese flying to the ponds and becoming beavers. Smith counters this "whimsical notion" with the theory that beavers travel to new ponds through "underground spring-related routes," which Tecaughretanego "granted . . . might be so" (291). In this first reference to beavers, Smith's rational deductions trump a seemingly demeaned Native American cosmology. The emphasis of his rationalist correction is significantly upon hidden forms of "communication" that keep the beaver pond "always clear, and never stagnated" (291). But this episode is immediately answered by another in which Smith is challenged for his belief that beavers eat fish; when asked where such ideas come from, Smith asserts he "had read of the beaver making dams for the conveniency of fishing," which makes Tecaughretanego make "game of me and my book" (291). Smith undertakes several experiments and "acknowledged that the book that I had read was wrong" (292). This opposition sets book knowledge against traditional observation, the former already characterized (in the earlier anecdote of Smith as isolated reader) as a serial activity, the latter (through the association with hunting) clearly a group one. With this anecdote, Smith not only undermines a favorite colonial convention, the assertion of white superiority through literacy, but complicates the earlier reason-myth antithesis, by aligning book knowledge with mythological beliefs, on the one hand, and experimental observation with group praxis, on the other.

Smith proceeds to detail lessons learned about the beavers: they cannot breathe under water; they construct dams "both for their safety and food"; and they use their "stones, or glands" to communicate with each other (292). The first of these points establishes the vulnerability of the beavers (they can be trapped and drowned), the second the cooperative compensation for that vulnerability (their strategic removal from the realm occupied by wolves), and the third the mysterious secret of their group projects. Because "the beavers are the dumbest of all creatures, and scarcely ever make any noise" (an observation sure to invite comparisons with stereotypes about Indians), the beavers "made use of this smell in order to work in concert. If an old beaver was to come on the bank and rub his breech upon the ground, and raise a perfume, the others will collect from different places and go to work; this is also of use to them in travelling, that they may thereby search out and find their company" (292). What beaver glands offer are a natural foundation for quasi-instinctual communication and group action, a form of species-being that goes beyond language as traditionally understood. It is this group essence that makes possible the amazing structural projects of beaver dams and thus an entire way of life.

But in the logical progression of Smith's narrative, enacted on a micro-cosmic level in this treatment of beavers, the stones/glands also constitute a fatal flaw, for "[c]unning hunters finding this out, have made use of it against the beaver, in order to catch them" (292). In some respects, this observa-tion might be taken as a summary of Smith's narrative—learning the secret of the Indian group, and using it to hunt Indians—though the observation is also, more locally, an ontological assessment of the beaver's fatal flaw. For beavers, unable to reflect on their fused collectivity, cannot discern when and how their instinctual communication is being used against them, but hunters can appropriate and redirect this instinctual fusion.[15] Not *Indian* hunters, we should note, for Smith proceeds to describe Indians hunting beavers in simpler fashion (drowning them, trapping them) and often fail-ing. In fact, Smith's long excursus on the beaver ends with an unsuccessful beaver hunt, a shift to hunting raccoon, and another (apparently unrelated but important) episode in which Smith gets separated from the Indians dur-ing a bad snowstorm (293). He survives by finding a hollow tree within which he barricades himself against the storm, during which we're given the strik-ing image of Smith "danc[ing] in the centre of my bed for about half an hour, in order to warm myself" (294). Thus the initial separation of being lost in the woods is doubly compounded by the tree-as-single-dwelling and the single-person dance. But these images should not be read as a reversion to individuality or a tragic loss of the group, for the episode concludes with Smith's triumphal return to the community, where, welcomed with a formal speech, he is told "we are glad to see the prospect of your filling the place of a great man, in whose room you were adopted. . . . You have given us an evidence of your fortitude, skill and resolution; and we hope you will always go on to do great actions, as it is only great actions that can make a great man" (295). The episode thus builds on the earlier lesson of the three dances: separation implies not serial isolation but an extension of commitment to the group, here in the battle against the elements which functions as a test of both the internalization of group knowledge and an externalization of group practices even when alone. In light of the beaver passages, we might read this episode as evidence that Smith has developed, and can respond to, some sort of Indian gland, a conclusion reinforced by a final "beaver" scene that achieves a synthesis of sorts. Two weeks after the snowstorm, Smith gets lost, "benighted, by beaver ponds intercepting my way to camp." Caught alone in the cold, he "danced and halloo'd the whole night with all my might" to stay warm. Returning to the camp, "they did not blame me," but Smith is told "that old hunters were frequently involved in this place, as the beaver dams were one above another on every creek and run, so that it is hard to find a fording place" (296). Smith is again welcomed and praised, and is now promised a gun, sign that he has reattained adult male status within the group. But in Smith's narrative, which ultimately moves toward the *transcendence* of Indian group fusion, this is not the triumphal moment that it appears, for the achievement of full membership in the Indian group still implies a confusion, a disorientation, a lack of self-reflexivity amidst the natural group landscape of the beaver ponds, as if the highest accomplishment of the Indian man is the stoic acceptance of his beaverdom.

The Hollow Square

Although Smith comes close to describing Indian life as the achievement of the Christian utopic group community—one that even "appeared to be fulfilling the scriptures beyond those who profess to believe them, in that of taking no thought of tomorrow; and also living in love, peace, and friendship together, without disputes" (287)—the Indians' is also a *doomed* community. And further episodes in his narrative extend and develop the flaw exemplified in the beaver (the lack of self-reflexivity, which renders group-ness a merely intuitive affair subject to appropriation by enemies) by stressing Indian incomprehension of white seriality, above all as manifested in commerce.

At one point, the Indians encounter a French trader with whom they trade for general supplies and alcohol. The group holds "a council about who was to get drunk, and who was to keep sober...to take care of the drunken people" (300-1). Smith is among the latter, one of "those who were to throughout conceal the arms, and keep every dangerous weapon we could out of their way, and endeavor, if possible, to keep the drinking club from killing each other, which was a very hard task." When the drinking bout is over, many are left "dejected," "crippled," and "badly wounded." Meantime, the trader moves on to an Ottawa town, where, after heavy drinking, "five Ottawas were killed, and a great many wounded" (301). This account is valuable in moving beyond the demonization of alcohol to some account of its interference with group dynamics; it makes the "drinking club" attack itself, and only having a designated alternative group prevents self-destruction on the scale of the Ottawas. Alcohol is thus a profoundly antisocial drug, one creating serialized drinkers. Critical in this account is the role of the trader, the epitome of mercantile seriality throughout Smith's narrative. The drinking episode is in fact introduced by Smith for contrasting the Indians' retrieval of furs left drying in "a public place," with white trading culture's propensity "to lie, cheat, and steal" (299). For the traders have not only broken ties with their own society so as to trade alone on the frontiers, but, in Tecaughretanego's words, have broken their ties with "Owaneeyo, or the Great Spirit," and their trade in alcohol is an attempt to play with their "glands," imposing a destructive white seriality upon Indian culture. Thus Indians fail not only to reflect upon their group-ness (like beavers): they similarly cannot grasp seriality and can be, through their contact with white culture, devastatingly serialized. Trade literally becomes intoxicating, instilling serial, individuated sins (covetousness, greed, lust, wrath) into Indian cultures.

With this analysis we can more clearly locate the third strand of Smith's narrative, its reconstructive program. For white culture, he is suggesting, suffers from related, if inverted, shortcomings—an inability to reflect upon its own devastating seriality, and a susceptibility (during warfare with the Indians) to groups. In an emblematic anecdote about the Seven Years' War, Smith describes the near-suicidal actions of one Colonel Grant, who "with his Highlanders, stole a march upon [the French-allied Indians], and in the night took possession of a hill about eighty rood from Fort DuQuesne"—a clever move admired by Grant's Indian adversaries. But Grant throws away his advantage when his men "beat the drum and played upon the bag-pipes, just at daylight," and the result is his defeat: "as he had his Highlanders in ranks, and in very close order, and the Indians scattered, and concealed behind trees, they defeated him with the loss only of a few warriors—most of the Highlanders were killed or taken prisoner" (314–15). When Tecaughretanego hears about the engagement, he naturally assumes that Grant must have "made too freely with spirituous liquors during the night, and became intoxicated about day-light" (315). This is no simple slur, but a rare and partial recognition of the seriality of intoxication.

A reconstructed postcaptivity Anglo-American culture, then, entails a self-reflexive adaptation of group culture and a war on commercial seriality. And the necessity for such a reconstruction comes soon after Smith's 1760 return to white yeoman Pennsylvania. In May 1763, "the Indians again commenced hostilities, and were busily engaged in killing and scalping the frontier inhabitants in various parts of Pennsylvania" (316). Having been driven from their homes in the late 1750s, many "thought it hard to be drove away a second time, and were determined, if possible, to make a stand" (316). With the help of "collections and subscriptions," Smith himself puts together a "company of rangers," choosing as assistants "two of the most active young men that I could find, who had also been long in captivity with the Indians" (316–17). The assembled rangers dress "uniformly in the Indian manner" and "painted our faces red and black"; Smith and his fellow ex-captives "taught them the Indian discipline" and the "Pennsylvania line" is formed (317). The company participates in the Susquehannah campaign (a precursor to Sullivan's deadly march through Iroquois country) and in Bouquet's campaign, where they win the release of about three hundred captives (317).

These events are narrated fairly quickly, for the thrust of Smith's account falls not on battles with Indians, as one might expect in what is partially a treatise on Indian combat, but *on battles with white traders and imperial troops!* When Indians break the 1764 ceasefire, the king's October 1763 prohibition on trade with Indians is still in effect, and some merchants violate the ban with illegal sales of supplies, including weapons. In the spring of 1765, "the firm of Baynton, Wharton and Morgan of Philadelphia shipped £30,000 worth of goods (which the settlers believed to include guns, ammunition, scalping knives and liquor) westward."[16] In response, Smith writes, one William Duffield assembled fifty armed men to stop the packhorses, confronting the traders with rational arguments, e.g., that the Indians "were almost naked, to supply them now, would be a kind of murder, and would be illegally trading at the expence of the blood and treasure of the frontiers" (318). The traders respond with a "ludicrous burlesque," but Duffield "would not compel them to store up their goods." In response, Smith "collected ten of my old warriors" and they descend upon the traders, surrounding them in the woods and firing steadily. "We then heard nothing of these traders' merriment or burlesque," he notes, and the traders are sent running while their goods are destroyed (318).

The first round, then, contrasts the ineffectual organizing of Duffield, who, for all his assembled force (fifty men), can resort only to argumentation, with the more concentrated (ten men, a ratio of one to five) force of Smith's "Black-Boys," who enact a demonstration of *group* reason along the roadside. The second round witnesses the return of the notorious Colonel Grant's Highlanders, who "without applying to a magistrate, or obtaining any civil authority," arrest mostly innocent suspects from the local population and "confined them in the guard-house in Fort Loudon" (318). Smith raises three hundred riflemen and marches to Fort Loudon, not to assault the fort in European fashion, but to systematically capture British troops coming and going. Grant sends a "flag of truce" and a prisoner exchange (at a ratio of two to one) is negotiated (319). When Grant continues to hold weapons "taken from the country people," he himself is taken prisoner until the weapons are returned; gunpowder that might be traded with the Indians is destroyed as well (319).

As Benjamin Franklin wrote to John Ross in 1765, after the first Black-Boy action, "The Outrages committed by the Frontier People are really amazing! . . . Rising in Arms to destroy Property publick and private, and insulting the King's Troops and Forts, is going to great Lengths indeed!"[17] And we too should pause to reflect on this remarkable situation: backcountry yeomen, led by "Indianized" ex-captives and themselves adopting "the Indian manner," stage Indian raids on Philadelphia traders and then British troops. Such "great Lengths" are repeated in 1769, when, as Smith tells us, "the Indians again made incursions on the frontiers," and traders again "continued carrying goods and warlike stores to them" (324). This time, at least as Smith tells it, a separate group of frontiersmen—"this new club of black-boys"—confronts the traders and destroys their goods, only to find themselves captured and "laid in irons in the guardhouse in Fort Bedford" (324). Now Smith "resolved . . . if possible, to release them" and "collected eighteen of my old black-boys, that I had seen tried in the Indian war, etc."—"etc." possibly designating subsequent conflicts with the white powers. This small party puts out word "that we were going to take Fort Bedford," then conspicuously camps near the fort before staging a surprise dawn raid, freeing the prisoners and departing. Smith writes proudly, "This, I believe, was the first British fort in America, that was taken by what they called American rebels" (325). Shortly after the raid on Fort Bedford, Smith is confronted on the road near Bedford; in the encounter, another traveler, allegedly unconnected with the Black-Boys, is killed. Smith is charged, arrested, convicted in an initial trial, and jailed in Carlisle (325–26). It is then that "we heard

that a number of my old black-boys were coming to tear down the jail."
Seeking legal exoneration, Smith turns away a group of three hundred Black-
Boys seeking to break him out of jail (326), and in the subsequent trial, the
judge's threats to the jury notwithstanding, Smith is found "NOT GUILTY"
(330).

With this vindication, the remainder of Smith's career, as summarized in
his narrative, concerns political and military positions—captain of the
"Pennsylvania line" during Dunmore's War, major in the Pennsylvania
association in 1776, one of Westmoreland County's convention delegates,
guerilla ranger (with "some of my old boys") in New Jersey in 1777, and, from
1778, militia colonel in Westmoreland county (330–33)—in which his
Indian skills allow him to achieve great successes (in Jersey, he routs over two
hundred British soldiers with only thirty-six men). In fact, so great are the
successes of Smith and other Indianized whites that they seem profoundly
constitutive of American independence. "May we not conclude," he asks,

> that the progress we [white Americans] had made in their [Indian] art of
> war, contributed considerably towards our success, in various respects, when
> contending with Great Britain for liberty? Had the British king attempted to
> enslave us before Braddock's war, in all probability he might readily have
> done it, because, except the New Englanders, who had formerly been engaged
> in war with the Indians, we were unacquainted with any kind of war: but
> after fighting such a subtile and barbarous enemy as the Indians, we were
> not terrified at the approach of British red-coats. Was not Burgoyne's defeat
> accomplished, in some measure, by the Indian mode of fighting? (343–44)

Although he tries to generalize his Indianization—"we" Americans all
adapted Indian techniques—Smith also calls attention to its exceptionality,
as when he daringly notes that "General Washington did not fall in with
the scheme of white men turning Indians" (332) or, more strikingly, when
observing that Indian antagonists could not "take the advantage" of Smith's
rangers, "as they commonly had done when they fought the whites" (333).
The whites? This strange differentiation demonstrates how, even as Smith
must describe the Indians as "subtile and barbarous," he views himself as in
some way ontologically reconstructed, and more profoundly views the Black-
Boys as models for politicized agency in the new society.

What Smith means by this is clarified when we return to his assessment
of the Black-Boys' seeming vigilantism, for Smith cautiously distances himself from charges that the Black-Boys became a law unto themselves. In
writing about the 1765 engagement with Captain Grant, he notes, "The
king's troops, and our party, had now got entirely out of the channel of the

civil law, and many unjustifiable things were done by both parties. This convinced me more than ever I had been before, of the absolute necessity of the civil law, in order to govern mankind" (319). This would seem an acknowledgment that the Black-Boys are a deviation from "the civil law" to the same extent that the Highlanders, agents of imperial prerogative, were. But there is a strong implication that the Black-Boys were *corrective* violators of the civil law, as Smith suggests in approvingly citing a song "composed by Irish immigrant George Campbell." The song begins with a celebration of established order, "What serves your country and your king," and an identification of the illegal merchant trade as "party interest" destined to meet "its merited fate." "Frontier inhabitants combin'd" in "joint league" to burn the goods; the Fort Loudon soldiers, who "scarcely knew which way to choose, / For blind rage and discontent," were sent out to arrest local citizens; and the farmers again "join'd a warlike band" to rescue their fellows (319–20). The final stanza assesses the political morality of the conflict:

> Let mankind censure or commend,
> This rash performance in the end,
> Then both sides will find their account.
> 'Tis true no law can justify,
> To burn our neighbor's property,
> But when this property is design'd,
> To serve the enemies of mankind,
> It's high treason in the amount. (320)

A quick deconstructive reading of this stanza would of course identify a fundamental ambivalence toward the Black-Boys (just but also dangerous), combined with the fleeting admission that the origins of law and justice (even when linked with principles of natural law) are to be found in rash acts of violence. Campbell, in seeing the "rash" actions of the Black-Boys as simultaneously illegal *and* righteous, gives an excess of meaning to the concept of treason: the Black-Boys are treasonous in violating the prohibition against property destruction, while also providing the necessary and just punishment for party treason (selling supplies to the enemy). But I think a better reading would maintain that Smith and Campbell, obviously aware of this apparent paradox, are attempting a sociological clarification of this recurring situation, in which five ensembles predominate. First is the vaguest of umbrella terms, "the civil law," designating an orderly social formation in which country, king, and property are duly respected. Threats to this civil law then come in three forms: from the tribal Indian enemy; from the "party interest" of the "Indian traders" who look out for themselves with no thought for their fellow citizens; and from the British soldiers who act out of "blind rage and discontent." How might we contrast these three ensembles with the fifth, *corrective* term, the "joint league" and "warlike band" of the Black-Boys? Smith and Campbell clearly cast the Black-Boys as the transcendent and narrative synthesis of the three second-tier groups. The Black-Boys bring the communal ethic of Indian tribal society to bear upon the class narrowness of the merchant "party," acting instead on behalf of the universal interests of society-at-large; they bring the emancipatory and strategic clarity of Indian combat to bear upon the blind and confining tyranny of the Highlanders; and to the primitive tribalism of the Indians they bring the prosperity, systemic sophistication, and established law and order of the merchants and military. And these syntheses make even more sense in narrative form, with the Indians constituting the positive primitive foundations of society as well as the primal threat of violence, the merchants signaling the civilizing but also divisive development of property and commerce, the military embodying the regulatory but tyrannical force of government, and the Black-Boys providing a synchronic combination of (Indian) origins with (white European) development while achieving a diachronic purging of the shortcomings of each. Put another way, the historical narrative offered here—which we might also read as an alternative myth of the American Revolution—is a whiggish tale of the fall and rise of the fused group, from its tribal American origins to its restoration by the frontier yeomanry, through whom fusion itself reestablishes social order. The vague and generalized "civil law" is thus achieved by the very material and episodic actions of a tightly fused ensemble, the guarantee of society itself.

If this is the temporal dimension of the political myth crafted by Smith, there is an equally important and fascinating *spatial* depiction offered here, spelled out most explicitly in the account of the 1778 organization of the Pennsylvania line. Smith was at the time "called upon to command four hundred riflemen," but without adequate provisions. To survive under this dangerous scarcity, Smith ordered his men to march "in three columns, forty rod from each other," "flankers" to march "on the outside" and in the front of each column, while within each column men marched one rod (about 16 1/2 feet) apart. "If attacked," then, "the centre column was to reinforce whatever part appeared to require it most," while during encampment the men "formed a hollow square, including about thirty or forty acres":

> on the outside of the square, there were centinels placed, whose business it was to watch for the enemy, and see that neither horses nor bullocks went out. And when encamped, if any attacks were made by an enemy, each

officer was immediately to order the men to face out and take trees, as before mentioned; and in this form they could not take the advantage by surrounding us, as they commonly had done when they fought the whites. (333)

The "hollow square," which would be visually diagrammed in Smith's *Treatise of the Mode and Manner of Indian War* (1812),[18] depicts not a cluster but a fortified periphery, which might be contrasted with his earlier account of a "ring hunt" orchestrated by Ottawa hunters. The Ottawa use fire to surround and concentrate hidden deer and successfully drive them into an ever-shrinking center, though when the anticipated quenching rains do not come the extended prairie is burned, "put[ting] an end to our ring hunting this season . . . so that upon the whole, we received more harm than benefit by our rapid hunting frolic" (306). Here we have a distinct variation on this model, in which the anticipated "prey," under-armed white yeomen, protect themselves in a broad and adjustable square ring that can maneuver to prevent encirclement. The "hollow" interior suggestively contains the livestock and supplies, as if the square marching through the woods has become a microcosm of the frontier, a mobile farmstead surrounded by a fused and circulating yeomanry. Spatially, Smith's map of yeoman fusion takes the weaknesses of the serial frontier population and turns them into strengths.

Little Gods

Far from enacting a construction or celebration of serial individuality, Smith's narrative actively promotes an explicitly revolutionary culture of groups. His endorsement is by no means unambivalent, as the narrative's temporal and spatial depictions should reveal: the Black-Boys exist episodically to restore an institutional order, and to complement defensively a serial yeoman existence, while, on a grander scale, fusion allows whites to reestablish colonial control in a commercially liberalized society. We should appreciate the irony that, at the end of his life, Smith would find himself battling what he saw as a diabolical and conspiratorial fused group—the Shakers. His 1811 denunciatory pamphlet almost reads as an inversion of his own captivity narrative, documenting the captivity of his son James while providing an ethnography of Shaker society (including dance and courtship practices, and an account of proselytizing methods). It is difficult to read passages like the following without sensing that Smith has finally lapsed into a Rowlandson-style captivity tale, complete with feminized accents: "They have a large party on Turtle creek, another on Eagle creek, both in the state of Ohio. Also a considerable number in Kentucky, and on the Wabash river. But admitting there is no general danger as to our government shall not the innocent be protected? Shall the children be torn from the mother's breast and subjected to servile bondage, and she be left without redress?"[19] Further, Smith's conceptualization of fusion depends upon a tendentious representation of Native American culture overdetermined by various racialized beliefs, including a Christian mythology of Old Testament "tribes," the naturalization of Indians, overemphasis upon "primitive" communism and unadulterated military prowess, and a blinkered gendering of the Native American group as masculine. (A more complete accounting of Smith's racial thought would have to triangulate his account of Native Americans with his account of the Kentucky expedition of the late 1760s. The episode is critical in depicting Smith's return to whiteness: departing from three white companions, he journeys back to the Carolina coast with an eighteen-year-old slave named Jamie. He injures his foot and must rely on Jamie for his survival, but it is at this moment that he stresses, even celebrates, his "solitude" (321–23). It is almost as if Smith must make a circuit back to seriality via southern slavery in order to prove his racial purification.) There is a danger of reproducing this kind of racialized thought in assuming Indian cohesion: although the tendency demonstrated by Smith was critical for the cultural development of frontier groups (as the case of the Paxton Boys will further demonstrate), the hierarchical differentiation of Indian peoples was just as widely perceived and, as I will argue in chapter 4, provided an important model for imperial control of backcountry peoples, white as well as indigenous. Nonetheless, wariness about Native American cohesion should not blind us to an important indigenous movement toward fusion developing in the mid- to late eighteenth century and extending, in different forms, into the nineteenth and twentieth.

I am speaking of the pan-nativist revival movements, what Gregory Evans Dowd has termed "the Indians' Great Awakening."[20] More a tendency than a unified movement, the pan-nativist revivals signal a shift toward a monotheistic cosmology and what Eric Hinderaker has called a "syncretic, nativist gospel" consisting of a constellation of recurring principles: a polygenetic theory of two (or sometimes three) races; return to ostensibly traditional ritual; the rejection of white commerce and commodities, including alcohol; an insistence upon pan-Indian unity across ethnic, linguistic, and geographical lines; stress upon monogamy; the rejection of firearms; and the use of emetics. Pan-nativism might thus be seen as a cultural nationalism informed by, appropriating, and overturning white racial thought about Native Americans. Local movements appear as early as 1737 (when Conrad Weiser wrote of a "seer" among a Shawnee-Onondaga community) and arguably culminate, in the long eighteenth century, in the Shawnee-centered movement surrounding Tecumseh and Tenskwatawa. Dowd chronicles the regular appearance of prophet figures in the interim: the Delaware "reformer" observed by missionary David Brainerd in 1744; the Unami Delaware woman active in the Wyoming Valley in 1751; Wangomend (the Munsee Delaware Prophet of Assinsink), active in the early 1750s; the Delaware Scattameck mentioned by Zeisberger in 1771; and most prominently, the Delaware Neolin, whose movement was adapted by Pontiac for his political mobilization of the 1760s.[21]

Rather than focus on the various ideological tenets of pan-nativism, however, I shall examine the movements' attempts to create fused groups in response to the encroachments of settler colonialism and European imperialism. A useful way of approaching this may be to ask why so many of the first prophet figures were Delaware Indians. The geographical and political situation of the Delawares, discussed further in the next chapter, has been nicely summarized in Anthony F. C. Wallace's *The Death and Rebirth of the Seneca*. From 1670 to 1740, traditional religious forms had been maintained, but with gradually declining morale; at the same time, a period of rising white racism, the Delawares had been almost entirely displaced from their traditional territories east of the Alleghenies, to become tributaries to the Iroquois. Then, between 1740 and 1760, various missionaries achieved mass conversions, sometimes of whole Delaware communities, in camp-meeting settings, but with imperial wars breaking out in the region, the Delawares were simultaneously forced to migrate and take sides in European political conflicts. Finally, between 1760 and 1800, relations with whites continued to deteriorate, while displacement continued, with catastrophic consequences, and the convert communities gave way to at least four revival movements (Wallace, 14–16). Without endorsing Wallace's tendency to psychopathologize the Delawares—he speaks of an "epidemiology of religious movements" (2)— we may find here the basic contours for pan-nativist movements: economic catastrophe in the form of displacement and the intrusion of white commerce into native economies; a field of shifting political alliances and hostilities in which Indians are repeatedly separated and whites emerge victorious; and a complicated encounter with Christianity, characterized by the rise of racist thinking, a celebration of community cohesion, a tendency toward abstraction, and the aggravation of economic and political difficulties. In the

Susquehanna Valley, the Delawares, more than perhaps any other Native American group of the eighteenth century, found themselves facing, in concentrated and truly critical forms, conditions that had plagued and would plague mid-Atlantic Native Americans throughout their contact with whites: displaced early in the century, with settlers and missionaries encroaching from the south and east, the English, French, and the western Indian nations vying for power to the west, and the Iroquois ruling from the north. (Analogous conditions would lead to the rising prominence of the Shawnees in the pan-nativist movement of the early nineteenth century, and to the Handsome Lake movement among the Senecas at about the same time.[22]) The Delawares, in this geopolitical context, were subject to conditions of extreme serialization.

In such conditions, an ideological counterresponse was necessary, but equally important (and inseparable from this ideological response) was an *organizational counterculture*. It was this that most whites found fascinating, in part because of a pictographic image of the revival that circulated in the 1760s. One account of the Delaware "Indian bible" comes from John Heckewelder, a Moravian missionary in the Pennsylvania-Ohio backcountry, who described a "map ... about fifteen inches square" with an "inside square ... of about eight inches." Two lines of this inside square, "however, were not closed by about half an inch at the corners," while barring these small gaps were other lines "of about an inch in length ... drawn to represent a strong inaccessible barrier, to prevent those without from entering the space within, otherwise than at the place appointed for that purpose." The inner square was called "'the Heavenly Regions,' or the place destined by the great Spirit for the habitation of the Indians in future life"; the two gaps were called "avenues," one originally "intended for the Indians" but now "in the possession of the white people," the other a newer avenue "made on the opposite side, at which, however, it was both difficult and dangerous for them to enter, there being many impediments in their way." At this spot an "evil spirit" kept "continual watch for Indians, and whoever he laid hold of, never could get away from him again."[23] The revival's cosmological map here designates a utopic space—the "Heavenly Regions"—at the center of the world: we might see this as a site of concentration, of drawing together, against the chaotic world of the Susquehanna Valley. Yet this cohesion is not depicted as a mass or aggregation, but as four walls— in other words, something remarkably similar to Smith's "hollow square" military formation. Since the space between the two squares is depicted as the space of movement and blockage, we might view the inner square as at once besieged *and* on the attack. The blockage of the traditional "avenue" of access suggests the identification of whites as a countergroup to be symmetrically matched by a cultural-racial nationalism, while the more difficult, alternative "avenue" metonymically signifies both a cultural renewal and a physical migration that can only be survived if the group sticks together. Thus there are impediments in "their" way, including a gulf "they" have to cross, but the evil spirit preys on the individual and may capture the serial "him."

Slightly different maps are described in the journal of James Kenny, a Quaker teacher serving the Pennsylvania Assembly's Commission for Indian Affairs at Fort Pitt.[24] Kenny wrote of an "Imposter [prophet] which is raised amongst the Delawares," describing this prophet's "plan" depicting the "right way to Heaven." Between "Earth" at the bottom and "heaven" at the top was a "straight Line from One to the Other, by which their forefathers use'd to assend to Happiness." Now, however, "a Long Square" separates "thire way to Hapiness, at right Angles, & stoping them representing the White people." On the "left Hand Issuing from the White peoples place is cut many Strokes parralel to thire Squair or Situation," these strokes representing "all the Sins & Vices which the Indians have learned from the White people, through which now they must go, the Good Road being Stopt." Specifically, the Indians must "learn to live without any Trade or Connections with the White people" (171). Days later, Kenny described how the local Delawares prayed "to a little God who carries the petitions & presents them to the Great Being, which is too High & mighty to be Spoke to by them; this little God lives in some place near them" (172). And some related practices were confirmed several weeks later when a Delaware acquaintance "shewed me his Book containing their new Religion," in which "he seemed to Adore the Image of the Son or Little God at the top of it, it shewes no Image of the Great being, but he says he is higher" (173). About a fortnight after this, Kenny records a dream told to him by an elderly visiting Delaware:

> As Dreams often come from the Idies or thoughts that are prevalent in the mind, I shall take notice here of a Dream the above Old Indian informs me he dreamed several years ago & informed me of it without our having any discourse about dreams. Says that in his dream he was conveyed as it seemed, in the Air to a Spacious Building, which seemed to be upheld there without any foundation or Stay to hang by & a door opened where he went in, being conveyed into an inner apartment he seen the Great Creator of all things,

sitting an a Glorious Seat & appeared like a Man (as he Immagined like the King of the White People); he discoursed with him & told him the Indians did not do right in giving such particular Names to Creatures as they had done, & told him that he had Created all things & that he had given Names to all Species which was enough & took him where another Door Opened, & the Almighty being Called all Species of Creatures One after another with a mighty Sound, & each kind of Creatures appeared & took notice of their name when called, so after shewing him this said, the General Name was Enough for Each Species; so conveyed the Indian to the inner Door as he was going away took leave & awaked. The Indians give themselves the Names of many Beasts & Wild Creatures, Vermin, fish & fowls of the Air, which may be Abomination. (176–77)

One further narrative, this one recorded in 1745 by the Presbyterian missionary David Brainerd upon meeting a Delaware prophet, may provide a point of entry to these various visions: "He likewise told me, that departed souls all went southward, and that the difference between the good and the bad, was this: that the former were admitted into a beautiful town with spiritual walls; and that the latter would forever hover around these walls, in vain attempts to get in."[25]

What emerge from this sequence are cosmological antipodes aimed at correcting the growing serialization of the Delawares. White culture is cast as a countergroup (the "Long Square" obstructing access to utopia) sponsoring a destructive serial culture, here the emergent parallel strokes slicing Indian polities into a series of sins and vices linked with trade and commerce. Native fragmentation is depicted as well in the chastisement by the great Creator, who blames Indians for "giving such particular Names to Creatures." This is a likely reference to kinship differentiation or tutelary practices, nominally associated with animals.[26] What is called for is a greater level of generalization and abstraction—"the General Name was Enough," a message obviously applicable to native peoples. Matching this analysis of serialization are structures of fusion: the "beautiful town" surrounded by hovering idiots (and again echoing the hollow square); the Christ-like god who petitions the Great Being; the Great Creator's "Spacious Building." What is striking about these images is less the physical cohesion implicit in town, building, or the place "near them" occupied by the "little God" than the explicit abstraction of the material—the "spiritual walls," the building "without any foundation or Stay to hang by," and the petitions delivered by a god. These abstractions, I would suggest, signal approximations of feelings of structure experienced by the Delawares in their revival movement: a cultural

unification solid enough to feel like spiritual walls against the Whites, yet
so immaterial as to give the sense of an abode without supports above or below.
The construction of the god figures is most revealing. Neolin and other
Delaware prophets had repudiated spiritual guidance by *manitous*, personal-
ized and differentiated manifestations of spirit, in favor of a single supreme
being.[27] But this new supreme being was often inaccessible—in one Delaware
map, not even depicted—and necessitated a mediating figure similarly abstract but also localized. That the Great Creator, in a contemporaneous tradition, reclassifies animals in larger groups according to species (*liquidating
alterity*, Sartre would say) suggests a similar gesture for the "little God" who
apparently exists as a small or local version of everything—God, but "little"
and "near." We might see in the little God, then, the ternary relationship
Sartre found in the third party; the little God mediates the reciprocity between the Indians and the Great Spirit, and as deity *and* petitioner is at
once a constituent and constituted power, asking and asked, over there and
nearby. The little God becomes the group itself, the godly concentration of
power granting success in an arena of antagonism.

The maps of Neolin attest to the fusion some Native Americans attempted or were able to achieve. For, although Neolin's preachings were initially concerned with fusion among the Delaware alone, extensions of pan-
nativist thought by Pontiac, Tecumseh, and others sought cross-tribal alliances
that might overcome the differences of local communities in the practical
organization of armed resistance. Did white colonials take note of this movement? Apart from scattered missionaries, diplomats, and frontier functionaries like Kenny, few seemed to attribute much significance to the prophetic
movements—until, that is, such movements became associated with large-
scale political insurrection. But there is another site of influence, one I would
suggest is more important. It can be argued that the pan-nativism of the
Delawares, Shawnees, and other Indians of the Pennsylvania-Ohio backcountry became a significant source of white American "nationalism," at
least in the mid-Atlantic region. To reconstruct the path of this influence,
we must turn to the history of the Paxton Riots.

The Hourglass

The logical approach to the Paxton Riots would seem to be through the
historiography of the crowd. Pioneered by the British marxist historians,
above all George Rudé, E. P. Thompson, and Eric Hobsbawm, this body of

work aimed to translate an older pejorative discourse of "mobs" and "riots" into more nuanced accounts of "crowds" and "actions," with a corresponding new vocabulary of history from below.[28] These works were not without their American correlates in the history of the "inarticulate" pursued by Jesse Lemisch, Pauline Maier, Edward Countryman, and others.[29] Yet what emerged in the American context was a debate largely contrasting the consensus-oriented crowds of revolutionary action, and the conflict-oriented crowds mobilized around impressment, debt relief, and other class-related issues.[30] The consensual crowds of the revolutionary period were "symptomatic of a profound change taking place in the Americans' comprehension of the people's proper role in the affairs of government," whereas the conflictual crowd fighting impressment demonstrates a particular "concern for liberty and right," a deep "sense of injustice."[31] Consequently the American version of crowd historiography reiterates the value emphasis of the republican synthesis while reproducing an older opposition between mobs and crowds. The latter distinction depends on a focus on the social values manifest in the crowd, from their origins to their results, with minimal account of the dynamics of fusion or the lasting impact of the feeling of group structure. The feeling of being-in-the-group, far from a value in itself, becomes a passing means to an end, an arbitrary vessel of discursive content. Neglected is the relationship of the group to seriality or institutionalization, the importance of groups to the fabric of political theory and practices, and the related absence of groups where they might be expected.

This negation of the group quality of collective action has been usefully explored by the Indian subaltern studies historian Ranajit Guha, who finds the dismissal of group actions an essential formula of imperial administration later unwittingly adopted by historians.[32] Writing about peasant insurrections in India, he begins with an examination of a series of hegemonic fallacies dominant within historiography: peasant action is instinctual, spontaneous, mindless; peasant action is merely reactive and functional; insurrections are sporadic and episodic. Although he undertakes the clarifying work of debunking, Guha's greatest insights are to be found in his cognitive mapping of these dominant accounts. A narratological scripting of imperial reports yields the following basic sequence:

Alarm → Intervention

The former term signifies both cognitive machinery and informational programs, the latter the administrative responses and counterresponses.[33] Such secondary materials of reportage and response are then typically reformulated in the tertiary accounts of conventional histories in a way that "distributes the paradigmatic relata along an axis of historical continuity between a 'before' and an 'after,' forelengthening it with a context and extending it into a perspective." The result is a "representation of insurgency. . . intercalated between its past and future so that the particular values of one and the other are rubbed into the event to give it the meaning specific to it."[34] This military-administrative distortion lives on in an hourglass narrative in which the insurrection is reduced to a tiny outburst dwarfed by a context and perspective traceable to an earlier sense of alarm and intervention:

$$\text{Context} \rightarrow [\text{event}] \rightarrow \text{Perspective}$$

This elite historiographic pattern prevails in accounts of colonial group actions, for which the Paxton Uprising may serve as an illustration. Historians of the event typically identify three constitutive moments emerging from three general causes and leading to three general consequences.[35] The "event" itself begins on 14 December 1763, when a group of fifty to sixty men, allegedly led by Matthew Smith of Paxton Township and Lazarus Steward of Hanover Township, massacred six Indians, formerly of the Six Nations but subsequently resettled on the Penn manorial lands in Conestoga. Fourteen surviving Conestoga Indians were relocated to the Lancaster workhouse for protection, but on December 27 they too were massacred, again by a group of about fifty men led by Smith and Stewart. Following this pair of massacres, the Pennsylvania executive issued proclamations calling for the swift punishment of the vigilantes, but to no avail; it also tried unsuccessfully to relocate a large group of "Moravian" Indians from the Philadelphia area to Sir William Johnson's estates in New York, but, in the face of opposition from the governors of New York and New Jersey, these Indians were returned to Philadelphia, where they were put under guard. In Philadelphia there followed a period of panic and fear as rumors began to circulate that Paxtoneers were marching on the city to kill the Indians and wage civil war. In response, Ben Franklin wrote an anti–Paxton Boys pamphlet (discussed below), the Assembly passed a riot act, and militia units (which included some erstwhile pacifist Quakers) were organized by an alliance of urban forces. The panic culminated in the anticlimactic march of the Paxton Boys to Germantown, just outside Philadelphia, in early February 1764. The frontiersmen were met at Germantown by representatives from the government (including Franklin), and after discussion the march was disbanded. Two

designated representatives, Matthew Smith and James Gibson, were allowed
to enter Philadelphia, where they inspected the local Indians and crafted a
petition to the Assembly. There was no further violence, no civil war.

Such was the thing called the "Paxton Uprising," conventionally attributed, with only slight dissent, to three factors. Historians first refer to the
Seven Years' War and the resulting dislocation of numerous white settlers.
Backsettlers, blindly fearful of and hatefilled toward all Indians, targeted them
with violence. Before this degeneration, however, settlers had appealed to
the government in Philadelphia to assist them with troops or funds with
which to organize themselves, but support had been minimal, sporadic, and
slow in coming—to some extent because the western frontier counties were
drastically underrepresented in the Quaker-dominated Assembly. Finally,
some historians have found ethnic-religious hostility a motivating factor,
although always on the side of the settlers: the Presbyterian farmers felt ani-
mosity toward the Quaker merchants and politicians. As to the significant
consequences of the Paxton Uprising, three are most frequently invoked.
First is the absence of any meaningful political response in Philadelphia,
although, coming at the end of the Indian crisis, this stonewalling did not
further provoke the Paxton Boys. Second, within Pennsylvania politics the
uprising marks the beginning of a power realignment, a descending Proprietary Party being displaced by an ascending Presbyterian Party taking shape
around backsettlers and the urban poor, the latter having been hostile to
the Indians and reluctant to mobilize militarily against the farmers. And
finally, in the big picture, historians have seen early signs, among the masses
at least, of a shift to a revolutionary consciousness, a "prelude to the revolution," above all in emergent complaints about underrepresentation and the
need for a responsive government. The hourglass narrative, then, gives us
racism, war and related policies, and ethnic communalism resulting in a
gradual political realignment and growing prerevolutionary whiggishness.
In the passage from ideological systems to ideological systems, the violence
itself becomes an irrational blip, a one-dimensional outburst of spontaneous
hatred, dwarfed by the Before and After of broader societal shifts and values.

i. Racism		a. Continuity
ii. Wartime Anger	→ [riots] →	b. Political Realignment
iii. Ethnic Conflict		c. Revolutionary Consciousness

With the Paxton case in mind, we can see more clearly what is at stake in
expanding our understanding of group action. What we risk losing is an
understanding of the group dimensions of the Paxtoneers' racism and their

changing political sensibilities; we miss the cognitive dimensions of the remarkable political fusion the Paxton Boys achieved, including the connections with, say, the concurrent pan-Nativist fusion or the subsequent formation of the Black-Boys. What we need, in other words, is a different account of the Paxton Riots that allows for the play of the feeling of structures, so we may understand the transition from a serial racism to a group massacre to an institutional realignment. Such an account need not reject or dismiss the ideological coordinates of the conventional narratives: rather, it will make them more intelligible, explaining for instance the contextual link between racism and a revolutionary consciousness.

Guha's solution to this challenge was to "seize on the evidence of elite consciousness" to "force it to show us the way to its Other"—that is, to piece together, from records of numerous insurgencies, the patterns of a "rival cognition" of peasants.[36] His analysis postulated the following progression:

Negation → Ambiguity → Modality → Solidarity →
Transmission → Territoriality[37]

Briefly, *negation* (in the sense of the Gramscian category) involves a growing, if still episodic, oppositional self-awareness that will gradually extend into more and more spheres of social life. *Ambiguity* denotes the continuation of competing ethical codes (elite and subaltern) during this period of extension, and *modality* describes the social dimensions of that gradual expansion: action will be public (not secret), collective (not private), destructive (not appropriative), total (not partial). This collective, public, total action must then face the problems of *solidarity, transmission,* and *territoriality.* The first term designates the problem of internal cohesion and organization, solved to some extent by allegiances of class, ethnicity, tribe, and caste, as well as the related problem of betrayal; the second designates the consequent problem of the extension of solidarity through what is often called "contagion" by the enemy; the final term signals the spatial limits of such transmission. Guha's is a suggestive mapping of collective action, though it strikes me as methodologically divided in a fairly conventional way. The initial terms of the sequence stress consciousness; the latter denote the nuts and bolts of organization: class consciousness naturally preceding class struggle. But the initial moments of negation, ambiguity, and modality are not preorganizational any more than the subsequent moments of solidarity, transmission, and territoriality are simply practical; it seems more useful to think about a progression through different forms of organization *and* consciousness. Thus, although my own analysis of the Paxton Riots will be appreciatively informed by Guha's work, I want to propose an alternative sequence for thinking about yeoman insurgency:

Dispersal → Alarm → Flight → Parade → Massacre → March

In the previous chapter, I outlined the moments of dispersal, alarm, and flight: *dispersal* as a consciousness of one's serial arrangement in the form of reciprocal isolation; *alarm* as the serial communication of a mortal threat and a crisis of response requiring a drastic reorganization; and *flight* as the creeping, apocalyptic, and seemingly fatal disintegration of the dispersed series. Each of these stages—evocatively sketched by Crèvecoeur, the back-country petitioners, and the Delawares—must be understood as both a moment of theory *and* of practical organization. And the stages need not be taken narrowly: we should resist the suggestion that what we most literally call flight is some obvious empirical reality (packing up one's homestead, urgently migrating), as if all other kinds of flight were metaphorical conceits, when it would be more useful to see in the various forms of flight (even, say, white suburban flight or the flight of capital) similar existential realities. And thinking back to the hourglass narrative of conventional group history, we find in these moments of dispersal, alarm, and flight a more precise sense of "context," which is not a static cultural state as much as the feeling of structure of a shaky cultural equilibrium, moving less toward a momentary or accidental interruption than to a resolution, of sorts. In the same way, we need to rethink "perspective"—how we view the After of the insurrection, or the insurrection itself. This question, we may approach through the sequence of parade, massacre, and march.

Massacre of the Nation

It is with the parade that we begin to witness the transition from seriality to group fusion. Some of the Caughnawaga ceremonies described by Smith, the Black-Boys' ritualized uniforms and forest mobilizations, the Delawares' emetic rituals accompanying prophetic explications—all can be classified as demonstrations of solidarity (practical and symbolic) preparatory to group action. In the case of the Paxton Riots, the initial anticipatory parades arguably occurred in 1755, after the summer killing of twenty or so white settlers at Wills Creek. Casualties continued into the fall, and the lists of fatalities in the farmers' petitions give an orthographic sense of the seriality of frontier isolation:

                    In Paxton
        Oct 25, 1755   at Machania
            James Armstrong
            Richard Cabit
            Michael Paxton
            John Stevenson
            John Murrey   Killed and Scalped
            Thos Woods
            Thos Colliar
            James Mc. Creery[38]

Finally, in November 1755, between three hundred and seven hundred settlers, mostly German, descended upon Philadelphia to demand action from
the government. In response they received a relief bill and a militia law.[39]
But reports of yeomen descending on Philadelphia persisted: in late November, the Governor received reports from a military officer stationed in Chester
County of "2,000 Inhabitants preparing to come to Philadelphia from Chester
County, to compel the Governor and Assembly to agree to pass Laws to
defend the Country and oppose the Enemy"; this notice coincided with a
similar report from Berks County.[40] In a letter to Thomas Penn at about the
same time, Governor Morris also anticipated "Mob" actions from York and
Cumberland Counties, adding that "This manner of applying is extremely
dangerous, and I am satisfied will be productive of mischief of some sort or
another."[41] These potential parades were defused by Pennsylvania's declaration of war against the Delawares. But several months later, in April 1756,
the Provincial Council "received Letters from Lancaster, containing Intelligence of a great Body of the Inhabitants of the Back Counties being to
meet there and proceed to this City, with design to force the Governor and
Assembly to pass some Laws that they have prepared for that Purpose."
Morris responded with a note to the Assembly, and immediately informed
the Council that he had sent officials "to the People that might be assembled at Lancaster to persuade them to desist . . . and that he had wrote to the
Justices of Chester and Lancaster Counties, recommending it to them to be
careful that the King's Peace might not be disturbed by so uncommon a
Meeting."[42] Why this concern? Between the November and April threats,
an action more aggressive than the November petitioning had taken place.
On 14 December 1755, a group of backcountry yeomen marched to the
Assembly House in Philadelphia to exhibit the frozen cadavers of several fel-
low settlers.[43] William Smith, an adversary of the demonstrators, reported

that bodies were flung "at the Stadt House Door" with threats that, if the settlers "should come down on a like Errand again, and find nothing done for their Protection, the Consequences should be fatal."[44]

We might read this parade, this careful and symbolically charged demonstration, as a tutorial in frontier dialectics—as it was surely intended to be. For this action sought to educate government elites about the state of the backcountry and possible future actions. The parade of anxious demonstrators with the corpses of their fellows is, first, a staging of frontier flight—the flight to the city—that explains, through enactment, their gradual decimation and disintegration. But it is also the symbolic and practical performance of their cohesion into a potentially dangerous political force: it is the constitutive declaration of intent for a future action, a moment when the elements of flight (people fleeing their homes, frozen corpses) will combine as a violent force, using live and dead bodies as weapons. David Waldstreicher, in his study of early American nationalism, has rightly insisted that we need to rethink the importance of parades and other political rituals, so that we may appreciate the political conflict enacted in the early rituals of nationalism. He rightly stresses the frequent origins of these actions in the "older customs like ritualized crowd actions."[45] But in focusing on primarily urban rituals of periodic and ceremonial regularity like Fourth of July parades, we risk ignoring the broader practical and threatening dimensions of parading—the parade as the rehearsal for more serious actions and interventions, the parade as demonstration of things to come.[46]

Further action did not materialize immediately after the German parades on Philadelphia: the militia provisions and the gradual waning of frontier actions forestalled any action until the next large wave of violence at the end of the Seven Years' War, which violence prompted not only the Black-Boys' mobilizations but the notorious Paxton Riots. Perhaps the most significant link between the two moments of parade and murder, however, can be found in the intelligence reports communicated during the war. Many were in the form of micro–captivity narratives, sometimes as depositions sworn for the Provincial Council. One September 1756 account, by "John Cox, a Son of the Widow Cox, who had made his Escape from Kittannin," recounted the pan-native actions of the region around Paxton and an Indian plan "to fall upon the Inhabitants of Paxton" and "to kill all the white Folks except a few, with whom they would afterwards make a Peace."[47] Numerous such reports continued throughout the war, as with the October 1756 account of Thomas Moffit and Daniel M'Mullen, who told of seeing "One hundred Delawares and Shawonese with their Families, mixt with a few Mohocks," and we can assume some similar accounts, formal and informal, proliferated following the large prisoner exchanges of the 1760s, as hundreds of frontier captives escaped or were exchanged and ransomed.[48] Such narratives differ from what we consider conventional captivity narratives in downplaying the subjective experiences of the captive, but they accentuate another important feature of the genre: the sociological reconnaissance of the Other against which the self is defined. Here the concern is with a covert racial community of Indians transcending tribal or community boundaries— with, that is, a military and political pan-nativism; the mode of communication is *rumor*, the serial proliferation and magnification of information received. Although acknowledging the likely exaggerations of these reports, I want to recall the pan-nativist religious movements outlined above, and to suggest that the captives were also probably perceiving a growing racial fusion transcending traditional political boundaries and emerging in response to white racism. However accurate, the growing Native American fusion was a crucial rationale for the Paxton Boys' two massacres.

It is here, in the parade of captives, in the revived memories of the horrors of the late 1750s, that we can begin to see what might be called *nationalism*. By nationalism, I mean a growing feeling of the necessity for fusion— for a cultural, political, and military fusion of an ethnos—against the threat of seriality and against the divisions imposed by institutional management. The indigenous revival movements, repeatedly linked with political and military movements (of Pontiac, of Tecumseh), were themselves *nationalist* movements reacting against crucial elements of colonial modernity: the discourses and practices of white racism, including missionary work; imperial administrative diplomacy; and the dispersal of peoples caused by trade, law, and the system of landed property. As nationalist movements, the religious and political revivals attempted a lateral *mobilization* of the scattered around an urgent fear of annihilation. Only when fused and resisting as a group might the Indian tribes find strength and survival. Only when fused would they become the "nations" that they are imagined to be in the parlance of colonial ethnography and diplomacy.

In the Paxton movement, similarly, farmers mobilizing in the backcountry learned about, and appropriated, this native nationalism. Nationalism first appears not as some imagined sense of serial identification of fellow readers, as Benedict Anderson would have it,[49] nor even as the serial identification of fellow squatters (described in the previous chapter): farmers in that context still conceive of themselves as defensively carving out a niche in a feudal-imperial framework. But as Indians begin to map their situation more clearly, and adopt fusion as their response, farmers, already inclined by racism to perceive Indians as an undifferentiated collective, come to see Indians as *fused* in a life-or-death struggle to eliminate white settlers. And so *they* fuse as a counternation, as killers of Indians, in response to this perceived and actual fusion, *and in response to their own seriality.* They fuse, too, as antagonists of the Philadelphia elites, because they see, with some accuracy, that their situation is similar to that of the dispersed Indians: they are second-class resources administered by a centralized imperial system, and they are threatened with extermination. (The sequence of fusion by response continues, too, with the White Oaks, a group of ship carpenters, subject of James Hutson's important 1971 article on the history of the inarticulate; many of the White Oaks were instrumental in forming urban military associations to counter the impending march of the Paxton Riots on Philadelphia.[50]) It is not that white settlers sympathized or "identified with" the surrounding Indians, but that they nonetheless modeled their response on their enemies'. And it is in this light that we must understand the outrageous massacres of Indian families as the next step after the parade.

Following the parade, the farmers must act to materialize their symbolic unification, and they do this with spectacular violence, violence as a practical but also symbolic act. When the farmers kill Indian children, women, and old men rather than "just" the young men, it is no accident: they are out to eliminate the Indian nation. As a fused group, the Indians *all* represent a threat, past, present, or future, and must be destroyed as a *group*. And in this act, the Paxtoneers come to understand themselves as unified by the violence of slaughter. Just as their children or wives might be killed, they must kill children and women: this is the rationality of fusion implicit in their murdering.

Massacre thus becomes a crucial moment in rural mobilization, and not *despite* the breaking of the law, but *because* of it. For the killings and the subsequent proclamations condemning the "lawless" Paxton Boys now unite them. If they do not remain fused, they will become serial victims of the law, tried and executed for their crimes. But if they remain fused, they will come to embody a counter law and living proof that the existing laws do not apply and are beginning to wane. Thus it is in the group reaction against serial isolation, and in response to a perceived fusion, that a nationalism takes shape. In the case of 1763–64, the white farmers find a prior model in the nationalism of their deadly enemy—in the Native Americans' fusion to overcome serial isolation. The massacre (the breaking of the law in an act of outrageous violence) becomes the pledge whereby the farmers redefine their politics. Never mind the imperial and institutional niceties of the Quakers and the Indian tributaries: the massacre provides new spiritual walls akin to those of Neolin's map. Or, to think ahead to the Paxtoneers' fellow traveler James Smith, the massacring yeomen see the superiority of the Indians even as they see Indian inferiority, and their solution is to become their enemy even as they annihilate them. They will become "white Indians" by fusing. National violence, the nation symbolically and literally massacring the other nation, is the new order of things, at least for a significant portion of Pennsylvanians.

No, we cannot reduce the complex origins of American nationalism to these massacres by a few frontier farmers in Pennsylvania. We should rather consider a nationalism taking shape in phases, as for instance when slave holders, at a later date, fuse in their fear of slaves about to be freed by the imperial government. Both rebelling Indians and insurrectionary slaves, we may remember, figure in Jefferson's draft of the Declaration of Independence, while "Americans" figured themselves, in popular revolutionary culture, as independent and rebellious Indians *and* as oppressed slaves. But the moment discussed here—the flurry of white–Native American violence concluding the Seven Years' War—is a locally significant one with parallels in other parts of the colonies (with, e.g., the Cherokee War to the south), and its links with the immediately succeeding Stamp Act mobilization of 1765 have yet to be adequately discussed. The so-called Pontiac's Rebellion, as the most potentially serious Indian conflict during the war, also had significance beyond the British frontier forts.[51] Further, the conflict produced a host of widely read captivity narratives that, like Smith's, initiated a subtle cultural realignment attuned to competing feelings of structure, and we might again recall that Crèvecoeur, like so many others (including Mary Jemison), would later understand the American Revolution as an Indian war. Likewise, the Tory Pennsylvanian historian Robert Proud would later identify the Paxton violence against Indians as the beginning of political factionalism culminating in the American Revolution. This is not the place to develop this argument: here, I only mean to outline the importance of the feeling of fusion for an alternative account of American nationalism. But we may explore the relevant conceptual vocabulary that emerges in the aftermath of the Paxton Boys' march to Germantown.

Christian White Savages

The Paxton Boys' march to Philadelphia, halted at Germantown, has been deemed an anticlimactic failure, presumably because the powerful demonstration and violence feared by many Philadelphians never came to pass, and because the avowed intentions of the Paxton Boys were never fulfilled. True, the Indians and Quakers of Philadelphia were not attacked, but the march was not a failure insofar as the message of the massacre was clear. For the farmers were no longer parading to demonstrate *possible* actions; rather, they marched to affirm, defiantly, *past* actions. They were technically criminals—the Proprietor called for their arrest and punishment—but when they met with representatives of the Pennsylvania government, they made a treaty of sorts and returned to their homes, as if the conflict was a draw, a crime without consequences. Further, the farmers appointed two representatives, Matthew Smith and James Gibson, to continue to Philadelphia to draft a defense with a double-edged title, "A Declaration and Remonstrance of the distressed and bleeding Frontier Inhabitants." The ensuing pamphlet war, "unprecedented in quantity and variety," produced sixty-three publications, making the rural insurrection central to the urban public sphere and making Philadelphia the leading city of American publishing.[52] This barrage of pamphlets was largely an urban phenomenon, but its central concern was a debate about the feelings of structure appropriate to a growing colonial society, feelings of structure central in the recent clash between backcountry and city. It was this pamphlet war that demonstrated the victory of the march, as the problem of the *group* became more critical than ever to Pennsylvania politics.

Central to virtually all of the writings of the aftermath is the opposition between group thinking—associated with nations, ethnic communities, and denominations—and "the law" that links the individual with the imperial framework under the legal concept of the "subject." Relatedly, the pamphlets repeatedly attempt the vernacular analysis of frontier fusion. That these terms became central suggests how the debate became less and less about the Paxton Boys' actions (already accomplished) or defense policy (increasingly a moot point as the conflict came to an end), than about the very experience of government. *Experience,* not structure or philosophy: for rather than treat governmental policy, institutional reforms, or abstract political principles (what one might expect in a pamphlet war anticipating the "revolutionary consciousness"), the writers emphasize the *experiences* of civility, of fear of violence or recrimination, of inflammatory violence, of the tensions leading to rational or irrational understandings of social relationships. This emphasis upon the feeling of structures explains the remarkable stylistic and generic range of the pamphlets, the "countless formats, songs and plays, essays, mock epitaphs, parodied speeches and prayers, caricatures and satirical drawings" described by Alison Olson.[53]

One of several dialogues, for instance, features "Positive" and "Zealot" discussing the reception of the "Declaration and Remonstrance," with Zealot imagining cooler second readings even as Positive boasts of slaughter during "the next Visit."[54] They are interrupted by "an honest plain Man, one Lovell," who develops Zealot's perceptions; he concedes that "the common People of the town, and those many Readers, who judge of Books and Things like old Wives, for the sake of pretty Glosses, and fabulous Stories," will find the Paxtoneers' declaration compelling, having been swept up into the feeling of the "Herd" (115). Others, however, will accurately perceive the threats of "an angry, giddy, violent and revengeful People" (118) and the potential dangers of the fused group growing out of control. To drive this point home, Lovell offers a brief history of the Presbyterians as a practical ensemble: they began as mild nonconformists "comparatively few in Number," but "when they became more numerous . . . their Godly Zeal abated, and in its Stead grew up bigotry, Superstition and Party-Zeal; and by Degrees, the same bitter persecuting Spirit by which their Fore-fathers were persecuted took Place in them." Consequently today's Pennsylvania Presbyterians "are divided and sub-divided into so many Sects and Parties, every one thinking themselves most Orthodox, and condemning and charging their Dissenting Brethren with Error, Heresy and Schism, who don't jump into each of their Opinions" (122). The dialogue is fascinating not only for its explicit account of group dynamics, which figure much more prominently than the details of the massacres and march, but also for its fictive enactment of the breakdown of that dynamic. The fusion of Positive and Zealot is already beginning to break down in the aftermath of the riots, and the intervention of the lone, righteous-speaking Lovell rhetorically obliterates the group dynamic by describing it. The dialogue is thus a metafantasy of seriality undermining fusion: as the serial Christian, who "Loves-all," forces his way into the group, so the pamphlet about the Paxtoneers will undermine the group action. In this respect, the dialogue offers a nice complication to contemporary theories of the public sphere that emphasize the serial abstraction of positionally neutral readers. Lovell concedes that the public sphere contains competing ensembles—those common, stupid readers who will affirm and thereby reproduce the group, and those discerning individuals who will privately assess the facts, upholding institutional norms against group barbarity. By this account, the public sphere is *not* a serial venue, but a site in which the dynamics of different ensembles are reproduced rhetorically, prompting the appropriate, correlative styles. Here, the ideal style of seriality is the dialogue of reciprocal opinions.

A similarly complex account of the Paxton Riots is offered in "The Paxton Boys, A Farce." The first half of the farce depicts the citizens of Philadelphia unifying in the crisis as the rioters near Philadelphia:

> The Cause invites[;] in Crouds we fly,
> To join the Noisy routfull cry;
> What Joys from Cares and Plagues all Day;
> To hye to the Court-House, hark away:
> The brisk, the Bold, the Young, the Gay,
> All hye to the Court-House, hark away.
> The brisk, the bold &c. (156)

In their own counterfusion, the citizen companies stand "waiting impatiently for their coming," only to find it a false alarm—it is a bunch of German butchers coming to town, about whom the author parenthetically notes: "Happy Butchers, you were not butcher'd" (158). The second half of the farce shifts to the dialogue format, with *1st Presbyterian* declaring to *2nd Presbyterian* that group force will not be enough but will be supplemented with "Policy, and Cunning" after the fashion of "my Forefathers *Oliverian* Spirit" (158–59). *1st Presbyterian* then encounters *Quaker* in a dialogue that concludes with a cleverly Shakespearean apostrophe: "Oh! Lancaster, Lancaster, the blood of murder'd Innocents cry out for Vengeance? Oh! Presbyterians, Presbyterians, who shall deliver thee from the Wrath to come" (162). The final scene adds one more character, *Churchman*, who concurs with the Quaker's assessment of Presbyterian treason and the need to offer armed resistance. The play concludes with a poem and a postscript:

> Stir then good People[;] be no still nor quiet,
> Rouze up yourselves take Arms and quell the Riot;
> Such Wild-fire Chaps may, dangerous Mischiefs raise.
> And set unthinking People in a blaze.

P. S. Should they attempt, or be mad enough to come down again, it's probable I may change the FARCE into a TRAGEY-COMEDY. (164)

What is most revealing about this work is its ambivalence about groups, as it moves from mockery of the near-slaughter of innocent Germans by the frenzied urban countergroup, to the "Presbyterian" insistence that groups are

not enough, to the final rousing call for a group response to the next episode. The play's final words highlight the ambiguity, in calling on the "good
People" to "Rouze" while, in the next lines, dreading "unthinking People in
a blaze." The generic references of the postscript diverge in similar fashion:
fusion leads to farcical counterfusion, but *next time* yeoman fusion will meet
a tragic end in the comic counterfusion of none other than Quakers. The
structuring of the farce also extends the analysis of dialogue between Zealot
and Positive. Again, the dissipation of tensions in the public sphere is envisioned if only the conflict can be recast as a serial exchange between a Presbyterian, a Quaker, and an Anglican—that is, fictional agents defined by
spiritual temperament. By contrast, the mock fusion of the first half occurs
with agents defined by socio-institutional position: *Citizen, Express, Governor,
Watchman, Servant, Captain, 1st Artillery Man, Soldiers, One of the Crowd*,
and so on. In Amélie Rorty's terms, this is an opposition between "characters," actors defined by defined and delineated social positions, and "persons,"
defined by intentionality, responsibility, and moral judgment.[55] "Characters"
succumb to group fusion; proper "persons" resist: both exist in society, and
the political crisis of the Paxton Riots is the proper formation of "persons"
more resolutely serial.

The Paxton Riot pamphlets deserve more attention than I can give
them here, but the above two examples will help us better read two of the
most prominent and more generically conventional essays in the series. The
first is Franklin's famously polemical "Narrative of the Late Massacres," long
read as an enlightened counterposition to the irrational racism of the Paxtoneers.[56] But it would be more useful to read the pamphlet as an insightful,
if oblique, account of the backcountry nationalism, white and Native, taking shape. The dichotomy dominant throughout the essay is that between
Law—moral *and* civil, and mediating between just government and individual particularity—and ethnic, nationalist thinking. Where the George
Campbell song included in James Smith's captivity narrative found the
ethno-fused group to be the foundation of Law, Franklin argues the reverse:
that the fused group not only undermines specific ensembles like the Indians, known to be "of different Tribes, Nations, and Languages, as well as the
White People," but in so doing upsets "Government" and "all Laws human
and divine" (61, 63). He famously proceeds to give numerous examples of
law trumping such ethnic-racial thinking, for instance that of the Moor
who protects the hunted Spaniard or the African who protects the hunted
white. But most of these examples dangerously undermine Franklin's argument. The Moor, for instance, learns that the Spaniard has killed his son,

and is clearly torn by his self-imposed obligation to protect the man (68). There is a similar tension in the anecdote of the Good African, who protects a white sailor left in Africa by a New England sloop. Angry Africans come to kill the sailor, complaining that "[t]he White Men...have carried away our Brothers and Sons, and we will kill all White Men" (69), but the Good African insists that not all Whites are bad. Diegetically, the story affirms the decision of the Good African, but readers making connections with practical politics might perceive the problems with the allegedly true story: the sailor must also have been involved in the slave trade, and the angry Africans are therefore correct in systemically viewing him as a dangerous enemy. In his anecdotes, then, Franklin does *not* assert the fundamental priority of moral law over national-ethnic rivalry so much as he acknowledges racial or national identification as primary and overcome only in situations of exceptional moral and serial behavior. Further, despite his insistences upon Indian differentiation, Franklin repeatedly assumes that Indians will adopt a fused racial nationalism in response to the massacres. He warns settlers: "Think on the Destruction of your captivated Country-folks (now among the wild *Indians*) which probably may follow, in Resentment of your Barbarity!...but now provoked by your murdering one of their Tribes, in Danger of becoming our bitter Enemies" (73). Earlier Franklin had insisted that even the Indian "*Barbarians*" did not practice such violence against "their Friends" and could distinguish between criminals and ethnic groups; here, however, as in most of the essay, he suggests that Indians are clearly susceptible to racial thinking, with "tribes" becoming a subset of an unmentioned racial Nation. Thus there is a revealing irony in Franklin's famous characterization of the Paxton Boys as the "CHRISTIAN WHITE SAVAGES of Peckstang and Donegall" (72). What is intended as an ironic reversal—*whites are savages, not Indians*—in fact links the two groups, insisting that Christian whites can develop a pan-nativism of their own. In fact, in many of the passages about the Indians and the farmers, the argumentation and rhetorical flourishes become so entangled as to become interchangeable.

Most interesting, however, are Franklin's suppositions about the cultural dimensions of the fusion taking place among the backcountry farmers. Franklin first notes that, given the massacres, "the whole County seems to be in Terror, and no one durst speak what he knows"—an apt characterization of the terror intrinsic to fusion. Then, in a rhetorical move that would become common to polemics about the Paxton Boys, he compares them with the Old Testament acts of Joshua:

With the Scriptures in their Hands and Mouths, they can set at nought that expressed Command, *Thou shalt do no Murder;* and justify their Wickedness, by the Command given *Joshua* to destroy the Heathen. Horrid Perversion of Scripture and Religion! to father the worst of Crimes on the God of Peace and Love!———Even the *Jews,* to whom that particular Commission was directed, spared the *Gibeonites,* on Account of their Faith once given. (63)

Again, the account of the sparing of the Gibeonites undercuts Franklin's argument. The Gibeonites had tricked Joshua into forming "a league" when, had Joshua properly consulted the Lord, he would have learned that the people of Gibeon were "their neighbours, and that they dwelt among them"— and thus destroyed them (Joshua 9:16). (At episode's end, Joshua angrily asks, "Wherefore have ye beguiled us, saying, We are very far from you; when ye dwell among us?" He curses the Gibeonites, that "there shall none of you be freed from being bondmen"—so they are enslaved.) But a more fundamental issue is at stake in the scriptural reference. Norman Gottwald has argued that the Joshua narrative captures the transition between the "cultic-ideological" premonarchical period (unified only in retrospect) and the centralized and constitutional moment of Israel.[57] "Joshua," then, scripturally signifies not only the divinely sanctioned genocide of neighboring landholders but, concomitantly, the achievement of national unification among a pastoral people divided into tribes.

Finally, in what might be read as the conjunction of his sociological account of backcountry terror and his cultural analysis of religiosity, Franklin offers a psychological prediction for the Paxton Boys. "You have imbrued your Hands in innocent Blood; how will you make them clean?—The dying Shrieks and Groans of the Murdered, will often sound in your Ears," he writes. "Their Spectres will sometimes attend you, and affright even your innocent Children!—Fly where you will, your Consciences will go with you:—Talking in your Sleep shall betray you, in the Delirium of a Fever you yourselves shall make your own Wickedness known" (73). That this evocation of the "guilty conscience" echoes Crèvecoeur's account of frontier panic is no coincidence. But here the panic has been arrested, inverted even, by the counter-killing. The "Delirium of a Fever" and the attending "Spectres" are not, I think, mere rhetorical flourishes, but attempts to understand the fusion that has taken place on the frontier, and then to wish that the elements of that fusion might be accentuated in such a way as to halt it, to turn it back into flight and the seriality of haunting. The "Narrative," then, offers an insightful awareness of group fusion without easy solutions. Rather than simply insisting upon individual, serial morality, Franklin poses difficult test cases that challenge the naïve opposition between group and series; while evoking a New Testament morality of the spirit, he attempts to rewrite an Old Testament history of tribal violence; while insisting upon the individuality of the massacred Indians, he envisions Indian fusion as the natural response; and in fantasizing about the haunting spirits of the slain, he suggests that only spectral groups and the isolation of bad sleep can restore serial individuality.

If the anti-Paxton publications show the profound practical and theoretical impact of the group, the Paxton Boys' "Declaration and Remonstrance" demonstrates how the fused farmers sought to maintain their fusion. The "Declaration" gives a fairly detailed analysis of why and how they fused, stressing (in the racist-nationalist terms outlined above) the fusion of the Indians and, more oddly, the disruptive activities of the merchants and land speculators in driving the victimized Indians to this fusion. The proprietary had "cheated them out of a great deal of Land," whereas the merchants had "defrauded the *Indians* by selling Goods to them at too dear a Rate" (104). Elites, then, were to blame, forcing the Native Americans to unite while leaving the isolated farmers to be their prey. Ultimately, the farmers had to counterunite in the resultant extreme conditions: "nothing but Necessity itself could induce us to, or justify us in" such violent conduct, they wrote, "as it bears an Appearance of flying in the Face of Authority, and is attended with much Labour, Fatigue and Expence" (101). More suggestive, however, is the "Remonstrance" portion of the pamphlet, at first glance a mundane list of nine requested reforms. The first item, more equal representation in the Assembly for the backcountry counties, seems the most spectacular, the demand most anticipatory of "revolutionary consciousness." But it is in the other eight demands that the Paxton Boys may be seen thinking about the practical extension of fusion: strict maintenance of juries—because these local community groups will be comprised of "their Equals in the Neighbourhood where their own, their Accusers, and the Witnesses Character and Credit, with the Circumstances of the Fact are best known" (106); removal of the so-called friendly Indians from Philadelphia, for "Who ever proclaimed War with a part of a Nation, and not with the Whole?" (107); an end to all the "fatal Intercourse" between white merchants and Indians while conflicts exist; public support for the "Frontier Inhabitants as have been wounded in defence of the Province"; a scalp bounty to further motivate the fusion of anti-Indian groups; a halt to trade until "our nearest and dearest Relatives ... still in Captivity" are released; an end to private communications with the Indians, as "[b]y this Means the *Indians* have been taught to despise us as a weak and disunited People" (109); and better use of frontier garrisons as sites of frontier gatherings. It is in these seemingly picayune demands that we find the most creative innovations, the most insightful analysis, on the part of the rioters. From scalp bounties and juries to trade embargoes, these rioters demand an end to the forces that would serialize not only backcountry farmers but also *Indians*.

These cursory comments on Pennsylvania's first big pamphlet war should foreground the relation of these publications to the so-called public sphere. Rather than expressing a serial exchange of communicative, rational debate (as Jürgen Habermas would have it), this pamphlet exchange illustrates the clash between an urban-based seriality of opinions and values and a rural fusion of violent counteraction. The pamphlets thus express less a "public sphere" of Pennsylvanians than a clash between two models of communicative action, with urban essayists fighting a rearguard action to transform a politics of marching into the rational exchange of ideas. In this context, too, we should note that the "Declaration and Remonstrance" is less a minor publication after the failed march than the successful continuation of the march itself. It is difficult to read it as such today, but it was, at the time, a clear insistence that backcountry fusion would persist, as the march would go on and on in juries, captive communities, released hostages, defiant silence toward the Indians, provisioned garrisons, and the like. The march as demonstration of continued fusion takes many forms. Further, this reading of the "Declaration and Remonstrance" should suggest a rethinking of the insurrectionary hourglass. The rebellion is not the fleeting moment of spontaneity lost in the ensuing perspective of macrosocial changes: the reforms demanded by the Paxton Boys were directly related to the moment of violence. Understood as an experiential challenge to the political status quo, the riot lives on long after the killing. Finally, the insistence on a continued racialized fusion provides a further basis for locating the origins of nationalism in group violence. *Who ever proclaimed War with a part of a Nation, and not with the Whole?* The implicit corollary to this argument can perhaps be found in the question, *Who ever proclaimed War as part of a Nation, and not as the Whole?*

4

Institution

The Moravian Oconomy

In 1754, Thomas Pownall visited Pennsylvania's Moravian settlements, some ten thousand acres worth, along the Delaware River north of Philadelphia. In an account published two decades later, he described in detail the utopian project, "the Temporal & Spiritual Oeconomy," of the *Unitas Fratrum*.[1] "They are a Society of Christians," he wrote, self-organized according to "an Episcopalian Hierarchy both as to their Temporal as well as Spiritual Interests"; though adhering to "the same principles as the reformed Churches," they were not properly Protestants, "hold[ing] however pretty much in a catholick spirit" suiting the "Church & Legislature of England" (104). Pownall was critical of the Moravians' communistic spirit—they were closer to "Plato's Republick" than to the "Gospel of Christ of the Doctrine of his Apostles," he noted (104)—but nonetheless showed a fascination with the intense organization of the "United Community." Its 910 individuals were assigned a number of specific positions, including "the Bishops, Deacons, Ministers, Spiritual Labourers, & Superintendants," while larger groupings of "separate classes, which were called *Choirs*," differentiated infants, children, boys, girls, single men, single women, and married people, who were sometimes housed separately (105–6). Property, produce, and labor were similarly organized within this "Oconomy" uniting the six settlements of Bethlehem, Nazareth, Gnadenhütten, Christian Sprung, Gnadenthal, and Friedensthal (104).

Pownall admitted he found "Oconomy" a "peculiar term" for the experiment, but reflected that "as the animal Oconomy of Man consists of an Union of Soul & Body each having their respective powers form & operation; so here The Oconomy of this *Unitas* had a Spiritual & Temporal Form" (105). Perhaps the idea of a cultural economy made sense.

This could be a fairly normal episode in an eighteenth-century travel narrative, but it stands apart in its first published format, the 1776 *Topographical Description of Such Parts of North America as are Contained in the (Annexed) Map of the Middle British Colonies, &c. in North America.* Most of this publication consists of the empirical description one expects in eighteenth-century scientific writing. But amidst the roads, rock and soil types, vegetation and hills, rivers and waterfalls "Of the Western Division," we suddenly find this detailed portrait of the Moravians. Why? Pownall explains that "[a]s this Curious Settlement was an instance existing in fact & actuating the plan of Plato's Utopeia, I could not in the description of this New World, which is rising intirely on an experimental System, avoid describing it." Further, "apart the singularity of its System of Community, The Fineness of its Settlements & Farms did of themselves deserve a special notice" (108). An awe of New World experimentation, a fascination with the extension of a material economy to a spiritual or cultural one, an interest in backcountry settlements and farms, an overall concern with the "System of Community"—all can be further situated when we consider Pownall's exceptional career of service for the empire: unofficial representative at the Albany Congress of 1754, lieutenant governor of New Jersey, secretary extraordinary to commander-in-chief Lord Loudoun, governor of Massachusetts, appointee to the governorship of South Carolina. Pownall capitalized on this service (all during the wartime turmoil of the late 1750s) to prepare in the 1760s and 1770s a number of writings aimed at an administrative rapprochement of the colonies and the metropole. His masterpiece, *The Administration of the Colonies,* appeared in 1764, as the Paxton pamphlets were circulating through Philadelphia and environs, and *A Topographical Description* appeared in 1776, a last-ditch attempt to achieve reconciliation.[2] Pownall's career was one of innovation and reform, of a creative engagement with colonial institutions, and it's in this framework that we may best appreciate his account of the Moravian Oconomy as a special case of rural organization emblematic of the broader administrative potential of the empire. Bethlehem and its counterparts signified a revived colonial order that might be contrasted with the disintegration of the settlements during the Seven Years' War and with the cultural dissent of the years following the Stamp Act controversy.

Lest we think of Pownall's text as simply a revolutionary era work, we should consider one further dimension of his situation, namely the incorporation of Lewis Evans' 1755 *General Map of the Middle British Colonies, in America*. Pownall and Evans had worked on the mapping project at the outset of the war, and Evans had prepared a detailed map that located the "first Meridien of America" at the longitude of Philadelphia, "a fine City, situate near the Center of the British Dominions on this Continent," and a city that "far excels in the Progress of Letters, mechanic Arts, and the public Spirit of its Inhabitants" (13). Pownall reprinted Evans' "Preface" in the 1776 compilation, presumably endorsing the snipe at the "inattentive Observer" who "would imagine there was nothing but Confusion" in the landscape, "and at the same Time explain the Climates, the Healthiness, the Produce, and Conveniences for Habitations, Commerce, and Military Expeditions, to a judicious Reader in a few Pages" (2). The administrative eye, by contrast, needed more detail, particularly (in 1755) in accounts of Native Americans. Evans complained that many authors "have taken every little Society for a separate Nation," although he himself had more carefully distinguished between dispersed settlements and nations confederated around the Iroquois, in order to denote allies and enemies in the conflict (3). Pownall showed a similar interest in the Indians twenty years later; although the *Topographical Description* never delivered such a description, it did promise, for future editions, "a Description of their Nature, their System of Life, and Mode of Subsistence; of the Progress they have made, and of the Point in which they are found as to Society, Communion, and Government; as to their Manners in the Individual, the Family, the Tribe; as to the general Spirit by which they regulate themselves when considered as a Nation" (153). The concern was with more than military security, and in the next paragraph Pownall lamented the incomplete project of "an Account of this Country IN ITS SETTLED AND CULTIVATED STATE, containing an Account of the Mode of Settling, and a Detail of the Nature, Progress, and Completion of these Settlements" (153). In this linkage, we see the overlapping of ethnography and imperial administration: study the Indians, and you will better manage your rural populations.

A favorite reading of geographic projects, inspired by Lévi-Strauss and Foucault, finds in colonial mapping the creation and imposition of a structure of meaning. By this account, the map "is the collective literary 'container' for locating and formulating American politics as well as identity," a means of "tak[ing] possession of the Continent, Nature, Indians, and ultimately, of the American Self."[3] Cartography, crunching the landscape within its epistemological grid, finds structure even as it is created. But such a critical presumption of Enlightenment confidence cedes too much to the geographers, whose maps are not so much sure assessments or impositions of order as projects groping to make sense of their materials. Colonial mapping is indeed about systematicity, and as Pownall undertook his project, the language of systematicity permeates his work: oconomy, hierarchy, society, superintendents, choirs, classes, form, communion, system of life, mode of subsistence, mode of settling: all a "system of community" leading to the still pending "Completion of these Settlements." But Pownall had a keen sense of the messy contexts of war, dissent, and revolution; he was aware of the need for a system, was seeking out the contours and routes, challenges and barriers, examples and resources for possible systems, and appreciated the "Confusion" that might overwhelm other mappers. As Gramsci said in reference to *The Prince*, such work is "not a systematic treatment, but a 'live' work," not "a cold utopia" or "learned theorising" but rather a "concrete phantasy."[4] The Moravians stand out not as a portion of the completed imperial map, but as mappers themselves, an experimental community giving itself a system— one that might, in turn, be incorporated into imperial institutions.

The preceding chapters have attempted to demonstrate not only the tenuous practical and theoretical forms of colonization, but more specifically two great challenges to imperial order: the necessary and problematic seriality of populations and a potentially unsettling group fusion. Each has been implicitly treated in the context of colonial projects of institutionalization. The Land Office's reforms for better settlement and rent collection, juridical treaties with Native Americans, the act to disperse the Acadians, innovations in military organization—these and other manifestations of "institutional proliferation" are attempts to organize, in the apt terms of the Moravians, the "Temporal & Spiritual Oeconomy" of the colonies.[5] In this respect, the focus of this chapter, "institution," is less an alternative, third term than a response to the other two. Institution proceeds on the assumption of seriality and fusion, much as A *Topographical Description* compiles the scattered and clustered elements of the colonies in an attempt to institute— or, to use a related term, *constitute*—a new system of community. We may think of the relationship among ensembles this way: institutions are the form of practical ensemble that deliberately mediates between groups and series.

I will develop this theoretical framework for thinking about institutions with reference to Sartre's account of organizations, but my goal, in this chapter, is not the description of specific institutions so much as an account of the vernacular feeling of structure of institution. Central to my discussion here is the official response to the Native American polities of the Pennsylvania region; in the colonial grappling with tribes, nations, confederations, leagues, and tributaries, we find one of the most explicit and large-scale projects of institutionalization. Relatedly, I examine David Brainerd's understanding of his missionary project among the Indians of eastern Pennsylvania; if backwoods diplomacy highlights the relationship between seriality and institutions, Brainerd's case foregrounds the clash between institutionalization and the group fusion of the pan-nativist movement. My literary guides are Crèvecoeur (again) and two prominent political theorists, Thomas Paine and "Publius." Paine illustrates the agrarian inflection of postrevolutionary reform programs or, better yet, the reformist inflection of agrarian programs. Meanwhile, I read *Federalist No. 10* as a federalist synthesis of the material and cultural dimensions of the institutional project. The related historiographic reference point is the debate over Iroquois Influence, which has been so informed by the republican synthesizers' accounts of value systems that its institutional dimension has been neglected. Through a brief survey of eighteenth-century Indian diplomacy, I hope to suggest a more fruitful account of the much maligned "influence" thesis.

Directed Process

Sartre's study of practical ensembles builds on the polarities of group and series, but the ensembles underlying most social power are forms that in some way incorporate these two extremes. Much of the *Critique* is devoted to a discussion of these intermediate forms (the statutory group, the organization, the institution) that mark gradations in a social process of reification through which a group seeks to extend its praxis by concretizing its most active features (roles, practices, relationships). As such the *Critique* belongs to that largely forgotten moment of bureaucratization theory that developed as the New Left came to terms with advanced capitalism and the history of Stalinism. We can think of the career of Castoriadis, which began with the critique of Stalinist communism and moved to a discussion of capitalist organization and the modern labor movement before focusing increasingly on bureaucratization as the very "transformation of the values and significations that form the basis of people's lives in society."[6] That critical moment now seems a remnant of the last gasps of sociological critique before the turn to discourse analysis, so some effort is required to think about "institution" and related terms as central to the experience of modern culture. It is not my intention to reconstruct Sartre's detailed vocabulary of instituted ensem-

bles: my interest is in a broader phenomenology of institution in early America, the details of which should emerge from the American context.

It may help to start with Sartre's conclusions, with his understanding of
those grand, macrosociological categories—societies, states, and classes—
that he attempted to rethink by resisting the impulse to jump immediately
to the grand scale. Once again, Sartre's primary intellectual adversary is traditional marxism and its distorted perception of the social formation, the
mode of production, and classes. In his discussion of the proletariat, for
instance, Sartre takes issue with the old dualistic view of a class "for-itself"
and "in-itself," or talk of "the working class" doing such-and-such. The working class, he insists, is rather a complex aggregate of series, institutions, and
groups: the series of isolated workers in varying practico-inert fields; the more
limited, institutionalized unions, parties, and trade organizations; the still
more limited fused groups of, say, wildcat strikers. To speak meaningfully of
the working class, one must differentiate these ensembles and then move
toward a complex account of the relations among them.[7] "Societies," too,
are not the organic wholes of sociological shorthand, but are rather aggregates of ensembles in particular relations. Nonetheless, Sartre feels confident
in asserting that "the basic internal relation of the society is *ultimately that of
groups to series*" (635)—that is, of collectives engaged in meaningful praxis
upon collectives of isolated individuals. How, then, do various groups relate
to the various series of a society, or vice versa? "[A]mong the many differentiations of this internal bond," he writes, "one of the easiest to grasp is the
institutional ensemble, . . . in so far as a small group of organizers, administrators, and propagandists take on the task of imposing *modified* institutions
within collectives" (635). The institution is thus defined here as an innovative ensemble deployed upon a serial population, generally by the state, for
the purposes of controlled and directed praxis. The state, he writes, is "*primarily a group* which is constantly reorganising itself and altering its composition by means of a partial, discontinuous or continuous, renewal of its members" (637).

This deployment has its origins in the challenges of group survival. As
the group struggles to continue, it faces the threats of constant dispersal back
into seriality. In response, group members undertake to preserve the powers
of the group by rendering permanent the elements of its praxis. The group
"defines, directs, controls, and constantly corrects the common *praxis*," ultimately rendering praxis itself "a constituted instrument" (447, 446). A series
of "differentiations" occur as "specialised apparatuses" are created; praxis is

broken down into so many *functions* understood as prohibitions ("do not do *anything* else") and creative imperatives ("*do precisely that*") (450). The ever-differentiating ensemble begins to define its members as so many instruments, and power "comes to the third party through the group which produces (or acquires) the tool and defines the function" (453), rather than from all the other members. This distribution of functions will be double-edged. As needs and practical options are concretized, the ensemble increases its chances of survival; at the same time, this differentiation, which follows from expectations of the future, "may limit possibilities," perhaps making it difficult to change course (460). Institutionalized goals may "become destinies" (663), and the individual will fashion herself as a "common objectification" (460), a "capacity" (462), or a "directed process" (549) of everyone else in the ensemble. As a result, an "inert reciprocity" develops and the relations within the ensemble become "*centrifugal:* instead of being a lived, concrete bond, produced by the presence of two men (with or without mediation), it becomes *the bond of their absence*" (470). Such are the "contradictory tensions of freedom and inertia" (480), as the institution is "both *praxis* and thing" (600). This contradiction hearkens back to the problem of seriality: for, "to combat a re-emergence of seriality," the ensemble "strengthen[s] inertia," creating, in comparison with the group, a "degraded form of community" (591). In this account, the group has, then, imposed upon itself certain dimensions of seriality for self-preservation. For the institution defines itself in terms of "powers, tasks, a system of rights and duties, a material localisation, and an instrumentality" (603) to which new members must conform. In such a way, the institution "produce[s] individuals who will perpetuate it" (600), and the inertia of the directed practice imposes itself to the extent that the original group "becomes powerless to change it without completely disrupting itself" (602). The group, to prolong its existence, has ceased to be a group, but now cannot change its institutional dimensions without further endangering its activities. The institution is somehow vaguely empty and separated: its activity becomes "*the praxis as other*"—praxis separate from the agents in question, what Sartre also calls "passive activity" (603). *This* is where we typically experience the sharpest sense of reification, in the impotence that makes possible "the ossification of the ossified *praxis*" (606).

Sartre's exemplary institution is the army (604), and with this in mind we may think back to the Highlanders described by James Smith, whose own celebration of Black-Boy group fusion hinged on a comparison with British military rigidity. Committed to the "passive activity" of established tactics and procedures—"praxis as other"—the British troops are unable to adapt to changing conditions and find themselves defeated by the smaller, more adaptable group. Or perhaps a better example would be the American military experience during the War for Independence. The conflict was, as Mark Kwasny calls it, a "partisan war," partisan troops here defined, in the terms of eighteenth-century military theory, as ensembles of troops between one hundred and two thousand men in size, separated from the main army to conduct the actions of patrolling, raiding, reconnoitering, foraging, and protection of that main army.[8] Not all of these partisan corps were militia units—some were detachments of regular soldiers—but most were, and, in Washington's correspondence, the problem of central army coordination is almost always described in relation to the state militia or a related ensemble, the short-term enlistees from the states. Kwasny claims that, "[d]espite the traditional view, the militia's duties and the operations of the main armies were not two separate wars but one combined and chaotic conflict fought on many levels," and he gives an image of armies surrounded by "swarms of small detachments consisting of militia and regular soldiers maneuvering around the massed formations and creating a swirl of activity through which the armies moved and fought" (xii). Not surprisingly, Washington's writings from early in the war repeatedly stressed the challenges of imposing order upon this chaos. He complains about the short enlistment times, which undermine the "subordinate way of thinking as is necessary for a Soldier" because short-termers will view themselves as citizens passing through the army rather than as functions within the army.[9] Officers, to motivate reenlistment, become too familiar and indulgent with their troops, who thereby "have the Officers too much in their power" (210). Fluctuating enlistments mean that "instead of having Men always ready to take advantage of Circumstances you must govern your Movements by the Circumstances of your Inlistment" (208). By September 1776, Washington was offering this painful assessment of the army: "The Dependance which the Congress has placed upon the Militia, has already greatly injured—& I fear will totally ruin, our Cause—Being subject to no controul themselves they introduce disorder among the Troops you have attempted to discipline while the change in their living brings on sickness—this makes them impatient to get home, which spreads universally & introduces abominable Desertions" (247). What we find in these reflections is the active theorization of the army as institution. Washington is concerned less with the reenlistment of militia troops, or even their quality, than he is with their impact upon the feeling of structure of the Continental Army itself: they undermine its strict division of duties and functions, its possibilities for certain actions, its general cohesiveness.

He is aware, in other words, that the weaker institutionalization of the auxiliary troops can have a determinate effect, cultural and practical, on the
organized structures of the army. Washington's apprenticeship in institutionalization, it should be added, became crucial to his views about government:
it wasn't that a strong central government was necessary to support the army,
but rather that a strong national government *is* an army of sorts, and needs
to be regulated so that it can engage successfully in the campaign known as
History. In a 1780 circular to the state governments, he made this parallel
explicitly: "Every motive which can arise from a consideration of our circumstances, either in a domestic or foreign point of view calls upon us to
abandon temporary expedients and substitute something durable, systematic
and substantial. *This applies as well to our civil administration as to our military
establishment.* It is as necessary to give Congress, the common Head, sufficient
powers to direct the common Forces as it is to raise an Army for the War."[10]

As the situation of Washington and the army suggests, the institution
faces the serious problem of leadership, which must be the "permanent living structure of coercion" for "sovereignty as authority" to work (608). The
institution needs a regulator, for it can no longer regulate itself as the group
did: "the existence of a sovereign is based negatively on the impossibility of
every third party becoming directly regulatory again" (613). So the role of
leader emerges. Specifically, "the function of the sovereign is to ensure the
mediation of all the mediations and constitute himself as such as a permanent mediation between the common individuals" (613). Leadership necessitates centralization as the "negation of direct reciprocity" as found in groups;
the sovereign must be "*other than all* because he cannot become a *regulated
third party*" (614–15).

And to return to the macrosocial level, an institution may itself become
"sovereign" in relation to other ensembles. As Sartre observes, "among the
many differentiations of this internal bond one of the easiest to grasp is the
institutional ensemble, cloaked and reunited by the sovereign institution,
by the State, in so far as a small group of organisers, administrators and propagandists take on the task of imposing *modified* institutions within collectives" (635).

This summary blurs many of the distinctions emphasized by Sartre in
the passage from *group* through *statutory group* and *organization* to the full-
blown *institution*—a path of the gradual withdrawal of agency and the progressive reification, as process overtakes praxis. But this development is,
after all, a narrative fiction: as Sartre's summary of the state implies, institutionalization may be imposed by institutions and need not result from the

inevitable degeneration of the pristine group, while, at the same time, groups may work with institutions upon serial collectives. By this point in the *Critique*, Sartre no longer speaks of pure ensembles in isolation, and now describes the inevitable and uneven relations between and among ensembles. What this suggests for the cultural critic is that the most productive account of institutionalization comes not from the application of some precise definitional taxonomy, but through the exploration of the relations between ensembles in which institution is a force of mediation and preservation. This framework suggests, as well, that we cannot simply condemn the *institution* as inherently "bureaucratic," as Sartre felt it to be in postwar France. From a different postwar moment in Italy, Antonio Gramsci, struggling for institutional leverage, complained that "[p]ermanent passion is a condition of orgasm and spasm, which means operational incapacity.... [I]t is impossible to conceive of a passion being organised permanently without its becoming rationality and deliberate reflection and hence no longer passion."[11] Not that Gramsci was arguing that institution is as bad or as good as the passion it seeks to preserve: Gramsci was attuned to the dangers of institution per se, as potentially authoritarian. Central to a future "science of organisations" would be matters of "democratic" rather than "bureaucratic" preservation of culture, the links between organization and common sense, the development of tactics that might keep an institution fluid and responsive, and so on. From this perspective, the analysis of the antidemocratic institution was imperative to the preservation of an alternative.

Plough and Sail

If the vernacular concepts linked to seriality and group fusion were not exclusively linked with the backcountry, they were nonetheless deeply associated with the agrarian dimensions of colonization: yeoman farmers and Native Americans oscillated between long spells of dispersal and spontaneous eruptions of fusion. But was there a vernacular sociology of *agrarian* institutions? And what was the role of the institution when it came to the backcountry? American colonization was fundamentally a metropolitan project undertaking the political and commercial management of agricultural labor and peoples; to put it another way, colonial American modernity was not a purely urban phenomenon, but a particular relationship between the urban and the rural. As the British North American understanding of organizational modernity developed, most particularly in the discourse of "federalism," the understanding of the institution (or the association, constitution, or sodality) would commonly imply management of the backcountry, that vast space of land and resources, of large serial populations and dangerously unruly groups. Institution was the answer to the dual problems (seriality and fusion) of the agrarian sphere, the site at which the city met (or hoped to meet) the backcountry.

A powerful illustration of this is found in the last major political pamphlet of that erstwhile Philadelphian, Thomas Paine. The work in question, *Agrarian Justice, Opposed to Agrarian Law, and to Agrarian Monopoly*, was written in France during the winter of 1795–1796, and eventually published in Paris and London in the first half of 1797. Best known today as a remarkable and prescient proposal for an earlymodern social security system, the pamphlet ostensibly proposes land reforms for France and England. In many respects it would seem far from the American context, and recent biographers have helpfully written about the European contexts, political and intellectual, of the tract: the philosophy of Rousseau, the conflicts between Babeuf and the Thermidoreans, the financial crisis in England, and so forth.[12] But Paine's essay was equally informed by the American country–city opposition, and should be read as a powerful illustration of his deeply urban and liberal-capitalist views on agriculture, as well as an argument for state regulation of the countryside informed by the proliferation of urban associations.

Paine's essay begins with a definition of "reformed legislation," the goal of which is to "preserve the benefits of what is called civilized life, and to remedy, at the same time, the evils it has produced."[13] To illustrate this distinction, Paine resorts to a further dichotomy, between civilization and "the natural and primitive state of man." This last state is best illustrated by "the Indians of North America," for whom life "is a continual holiday, compared with the poor of Europe," though "abject when compared to the rich" (397). The Indian "requires ten times the quantity of land to range over, to procure himself sustenance, than would support him in a civilized state, where the earth is cultivated" (398). So "reformed legislation" must figure out how to make "every person born into the world" as happy as an Indian, but without the loss of civilization (398). At this point, Paine shifts from the image of serialized Indians to a different agrarian terminology, insisting that all land once was and now should still be "the COMMON PROPERTY OF THE HUMAN RACE"; in fact, every person should ideally be viewed as "a joint life-proprietor" of the earth (398). Surely, he insists, "the Creator of the earth" never "open[ed] a land-office, from whence the first title-deeds should issue" (399). What about the "improvements" made on the land by cultivators? As a liberal defender of private property, Paine aggressively upholds one's right to the value of one's improvements. Hence his titular condemnation of "Agrarian Law," a reference to the French revolutionary program for the equal division of land inspired by the *lex agraria* of the Roman Gracchi. But, in a slight departure from his earlier total insistence on property rights, he distinguishes (following Locke, Ogilvie, Spence, and Babeuf) between "two kinds of property: the bounty of nature, especially land, . . . and property created by the labor of men."[14] Consequently, every present-day proprietor "owes to the community a *ground-rent*" (398), which Paine will later calculate to be one-tenth the value of the improved land (403). Paine then proceeds, through bureaucratic details and statistics, to outline his plan for a "National Fund" that will pay £15 to every person reaching the age of twenty-one, and £10 per year to everyone reaching the age of fifty (400). The fund will be financed by a 10 percent tax upon land, to be levied, over thirty years, upon all land inheritances. This fund will gradually effect a redistribution of wealth such that the poor youthful majority will earn something like a citizen's coming-of-age stipend and the elderly poor will receive a pension. We see here the refiguring of the old colonial proprietary, collecting quit-rents from its Land Office, as society at large: the citizens of the republic are the new proprietors to whom rent is due.

So why is an essay about a nationwide citizens' pension called "Agrarian Justice" when so much of Paine's interest elsewhere is in urban commerce? To ask this differently, what is the connection between a utopian fantasy of revolutionary rationalization and land occupation? The allusions to the American backcountry are revealing, as if America contained within its history the full rural–urban trajectory. The Indians represent primitive humanity, wasteful ownership of undeveloped land (tenfold what a farmer needs), and the absence of social labor; they are the uncolonized and unmastered backcountry, the source of the raw materials from which civilization will develop, at once a utopian ideal of relative prosperity and freedom and the savage absence of capital and civilization. Paine has in mind the "white Indians" of the frontier, as well: from his experience in Pennsylvania (largely as an advocate of the Bank of North America) Paine developed a notion of white settlers as Indian-like—distinguishing "settlers" and "farmers," the former simply occupying land and subsisting, the latter producing social wealth and engaging in commerce. "The frontier parts of the state are called settlements, and the improved parts farms," he writes: "A settler is not yet a farmer; he is only in the way of being so. In the stage of a settler, his thoughts are engrossed and taken up in making a settlement. If he can raise produce enough for support of his family, it is the utmost of his present hopes. He has none to bring to market, or to sell, and therefore commerce appears nothing to him.... Therefore, when a back county member says that the Bank is of no use to the farmer, he means the settler, who has yet no produce to sell, and knows nothing about the matter."[15] And then the original crime of imperial colonization occurs, presented in Paine's account by the ironic reference to a tyrannical God issuing land grants. Rather than the rational and planned distribution of land suitable to a deist economy, there occurs the irrational and superstitious appropriation of land by a grand proprietor (e.g., the Penns) who arbitrarily distributes and accumulates the profits of nature. American colonization thus contains the fundamental distortions of property—common property both underdeveloped and overappropriated—that must be overcome by "reformed legislation." The 10 percent tax on land may be read as the "reformed" tactic for dispossessing the "Indians," white and Native, though Paine may have set his sights on the big urban land speculators as well. Since undevelopment keeps the value of land at the "natural" stage where it has only 10 percent of its potential value—since Paine calculates social improvements to account for 90 percent of the value of civilized land—his taxation plan essentially takes undeveloped land and redistributes it to the citizenry as a whole. The irrational system of colonization and land distribution becomes systematized, as citizens become "joint life-proprietors" collecting ground-rent from the backcountry.

"Reformed legislation," then, amounts to the seizure and total administration of the backcountry by the urban revolution. This is why the justice is "agrarian": there can be no reform touching on urban capital, which is sacrosanct. The malleable sector of society, in which justice and reform might be undertaken, is precisely the agrarian region, the region that consistently provided trouble for revolutions. Paine reiterates this point, which developed from his Philadelphia political career, throughout his writings. In a 1786 essay, "Common Sense" wrote:

> the interest of the farmer and the merchant, the one being employed to raise the produce and the other to export it, are as naturally connected, as that of sowing the grain is connected with reaping the harvest; and any man must be held an enemy to the public prosperity, who endeavours to create a difference, or dissolve the mutual interest existing between them. The Plough and the Sail are the Arms of the state of Pennsylvania, and their connection should be held in remembrance by all good citizens. (362)

Paine is speaking here of the *producing* backcountry, but his analysis still exemplifies his urban-managerial perspective. He insists upon the interconnectedness between backcountry and city, but in a relationship in which antagonism is treasonous and in which the merchant effectively realizes the wealth of the backcountry. This is nowhere more evident than in the creeping analogies Paine uses: farmer is to merchant as raising is to exporting, *as sowing is to reaping*.

Backcountry and City, Plough and Sail: Paine asserts their connectedness in the Pennsylvania state arms, but what exactly is the nature of the link? In a 1793 policy letter to Citoyen Danton to address the "despair" felt in France during Year 2 of the Revolution, Paine addresses three major problems, the first being the danger "of a rupture between Paris and the departments" (393). Paine explicitly compares the French threat with an earlier American context, and "the exceeding inconvenience that arose by having the government of Congress within the limits of any Municipal Jurisdiction" like Philadelphia or New York. In the American context, municipal authorities developed antagonistic relations to national authorities, and "the people of each of those places expected more attention from Congress than their equal share with the other states amounted to" (393). Consequently the backcountry-city divide sharpened. Second, Paine reflects upon the challenges of price-fixing and currency regulation, as the "People of Paris" attempt to set prices for provisions. But Paine insists the Parisians "cannot compel the country people to bring provisions to market" and in fact will simply make prices soar (393); such was the case with salt and flour in revolutionary Pennsylvania, and a similar chaos resulted from attempts to increase the money supply (394). Finally, Paine takes issue with the "spirit of denunciation that now prevails" in France, largely originating in Paris and directed toward the less radicalized countryside, noting that "[t]his denunciation will injure Paris in the opinion of the departments because it has the appearance of dictating to them what sort of deputies they shall elect" (394–95). French revolutionary despair, then, is deeply connected with the country-city divide understood in political, economic, and cultural terms. Although Paine clearly views the countryside as a drag on revolutionary reform—this is his position throughout the Bank of North America writings, too—he recognizes the dangers of an exacerbation of the country–city split when municipal forces are too explicitly heavyhanded.

When it comes to urban management, then, Paine is clearly on the side of the commercial, capital-driven cities, but seeks a kind of purification of that urban control. Thus Paine counters the municipal manipulation of the national government with government as a national municipality, celebrating the "building [of] a Town not within the limits of any municipal jurisdiction for the future residence of Congress" (393)—a town Paine liked to call "Federal City" in his correspondence. Economically, Paine envisions a similar distillation, the overt and shortsighted manipulation of the economy to be replaced by a permanent system. This is the essence of "reformed legislation," to return to *Agrarian Justice*. There Paine insists that, if a revolution is to succeed, "it is necessary, as well for the protection of property, as for the sake of justice and humanity, to *form a system*" (409, emphasis added). He maintains there is "but little that any individual can do when the whole extent of the misery to be relieved be considered," and proposes "organizing civilization upon such principles as to act like a system of pullies" (406). Society is to be "the treasurer" of human wealth "in a common fund," for "only in a system of justice" can the property owner "contemplate security" (409). *System*, then, is the key to reform—rendering principles institutionally secure and neutral, apart from the agency of groups or individuals.

We should see in this utopia of "the system" a sublimation of urban mercantilism and national administration, one that replaces the temporal antagonisms of faction with the perpetual motion of rational organizing. Related in an interesting way is an 1801 letter from Paine to Jefferson titled "On the Means of Generating Motion for Mechanical Use." Paine begins with the unreliability of natural power sources (water and air) and the need for a human-made system for generating power; he also assumes an alternative to the steam engine is necessary, given the expense and resource demands of the latter. What he proposes is a wheel with small cartridges for gunpowder, to be discharged by barrels. This would make the apparently unruly explosive power of gunpowder more manageable: "as an ounce of gunpowder, or any other quantity, when on fire, cannot be detailed out so as to act with equal force through any given space in time, the substitute in this case is, to divide the gunpowder into a number of equal parts and discharge them in equal spaces of time on the wheel, so as to keep it in nearly an equal and continual motion. . . . Every separate stroke given to the top acts with the sureness of explosion, but produces as to continual motion the effect of uninterrupted power."[16] A systematic regulation of the explosive power behind firearms . . . as this example shows, surely Paine's architectural and mechanical experiments were informed by his practical political experience.

If the political and economic dimensions of the revolution are to be purified and systematized, the same must be true of its cultural dimensions— namely, the overt antagonisms implicit in "the spirit of denunciation" and despair. Such concerns may sound ironic coming from the pen of the "Founding Father" most frequently dismissed as a crank. But in *Agrarian Justice* and contiguous writings we find in Paine a cultural theorist committed to suppressing overt postrevolutionary antagonisms, specifically the dual forces of motivation and resistance. On the one hand, Paine writes, "it ought not to be left to the choice of detached [that is, serialized] individuals, whether they will do justice or not" (406)—an assessment of the difficulties of politically motivating serially isolated citizens. On the other hand, the great obstacle to revolutionary change is the "dread" and "apprehension" felt, perhaps unjustly, by property owners; it is the perceived "*hazard* and not the principles of a revolution that retards their progress" (409). Given the weakness of revolutionary culture, and the strength of its conservative counterpart, cultural values must be institutionalized. "An army of principles will penetrate where an army of soldiers cannot," concludes Paine at the end of *Agrarian Justice* (411). With this privileged metaphor for structured, hierarchical, institutional power, to which Paine gives his cultural twist, an "army of principles"—an institutionalized culture—will carry out the revolution of agrarian justice in a secure and regulated manner.

Does this conclusion make Paine more of an eighteenth-century Walter Lippmann than the firebrand of popular mythology? He's actually somewhere in between. His understanding of political, economic, and cultural conflicts was thoroughly shaped by the backcountry-city split he had first seriously encountered in Pennsylvania, and his reform proposal may be read as an attempt to end the perennial conflicts along this important divide. The solution was to be found in neither a democratically self-governing citizenry nor in the machinations of an elite urban junto. "System" was what Paine sought, and one could no more expect merchant elites to act systematically than one could George III or the Roman Catholic Church. What was required was a level of institutionalization that made citizens simple taxpayers and beneficiaries, while, on the other end of the spectrum, oversight would also become a passive activity of a specialized apparatus in a rationalized Federal City. The most revealing connection, perhaps, might be with *The Age of Reason*, which had argued for a depersonalized and systematized Deity. God, it will be remembered, was associated with the large arbitrary landlord collecting rent and antagonizing the agrarian population. The new pension system, like the deist universe, would require enacting a systematization that would forever depersonalize agrarian relations, transforming the active Agrarian Law into the more passive Agrarian Justice, in a society in which each citizen knows his or her appropriate function under an impersonal sovereign. The sectarian factionalism, petty tribalism, economic narrow-mindedness, and culture of resentment, despair, and sullen resistance—all these features of backcountry life, with their analogues in the fractious denominations of Christianity, would be streamlined into impersonal institutions in a purified deistic city. In this framework, a national pension plan could sensibly be developed under the rubric of "agrarian justice"—a justice taken from, imposed upon, and purifying the backwards chaos of the backcountry.

Administering the Ordinance

This brief discussion of Paine may suggest that the vernacular sociology of institutions was confined to the explicitly governmental or macropolitical sphere, but such isn't the case. As historians of federalism have long noted, the theory of organized sodalities was heavily informed by the feeling of structures expressed in Protestant theology, much as Paine's own approach to systems was related to his radical deism. So our understanding of institutions will be enhanced by the examination of a context in which the praxis of organization took shape at some remove from explicit political reform: the missionary experience of David Brainerd, the Connecticut protégé of Jonathan Edwards.

After expulsion from Yale ruined his chances for a clerical position in Congregationalist New England, Brainerd turned to a missionary career that took him through three distinct kinds of Indian settlement. The first, his apprenticeship at Kaunaumeek on the New York–Massachusetts border, brought him to the New England "praying towns," which began with John Eliot's Natick and found contemporary manifestation in Stockbridge. These institutions were part of the "second phase of the Puritan conquest of New England . . . a phase based not on immediate military force but on the utopian organization of social detail."[17] We have little record of Brainerd's missionary praxis at Kaunaumeek. Edwards, who edited Brainerd's diary, deleted any specifics of Brainerd's labor, leaving a subjective narrative that nearly rendered Indians invisible: "It appears by his diary, that while he continued with these Indians he took great pains with them . . . but the particular manner how, has been omitted for brevity's sake."[18] But from the materials that have survived, it seems that, at this already institutionalized setting, Brainerd was uninterested in his work, paid little attention to the Indians, and repeatedly linked his experience with Biblical exile and the serial dispersal codified in the Old Testament. Such was Brainerd's career from 1743 to 1744, but he soon found himself assigned to Crossweeksung, in central New Jersey close to the Pennsylvania border, to create a Christian community among a group of Delaware Indians. Brainerd's transfer marks the moment when he leaves the established "praying" institutions of New England and at last faces the problem of Indian organization on his own, in a context of extreme Indian dispersal. Where Brainerd had before thought of "Abraham's pilgrimage in the land of Canaan" or "Joseph's sufferings" in captivity (141), he now reflects on Nehemiah and Ezra "reforming his people and re-establishing His ancient church" (167). "Last year," he writes, "I longed to be prepared for a world of glory and speedily to depart out of this world; but of late all my concern almost is for the conversion of the heathen, and for that end I long to live" (170). Brainerd's new concern can be explained, I think, by a transformed and dialectical perception of Indian practical ensembles: transferred from the praying towns, he now perceives Indians through their *disorganization*, the absence of institution; not surprisingly this means an increased perception of *seriality* and *fusion*.

Brainerd is initially shocked and disappointed, for instance, at how "much scattered" the Jersey Delawares are (161). As he writes back to Scotland, "I found very few persons at the place I visited, and perceived the Indians in these parts were very much scattered, there being not more than two or three families in a place, and these small settlements six, ten, fifteen, twenty, and thirty miles, and some more, from the place I was then at" (203). Living lives of serial isolation, the Jersey Delawares are the more greatly influenced by neighboring "nominal" Christians, as Brainerd notes in a reflection upon the Quakers: "There were sundry persons of the Indians newly come here, who had frequently lived among Quakers. Being more civilized and conformed to English manners than the generality of the Indians, they had imbibed some of the Quakers' errors, especially this fundamental one: That if men will but live soberly and honestly, according to the dictates of their own consciences (or the light within), there is then no danger or doubt of their salvation." These Indians, notes Brainerd, were "much worse to deal with than those who are wholly under pagan darkness" (259). Of course, this is a critique of liberal Christianity, but it is more fundamentally a diagnosis of a dangerous social arrangement, one in which Quakers do not fuse with or organize Indians but instead encourage isolated and reciprocal living "according to the dictates of *their own* consciences." This is a Christianity of Crèvecoerian tolerance, the slow sharing not only of "English manners" but of "Quakers' errors" as well, as all are brought to the least common denominator of spirituality. With the dangers of seriality in mind, Brainerd moved to congregate the Indians, and by the end of 1744 could write, "The Indians are now gathered together from all quarters to this place, and have built them little cottages, so that more than twenty families live within a quarter of a mile of me" (267). Yet this is not enough, as Brainerd now turns his attentions to "discharging their debts and securing these lands, that there might be no entanglement lying upon them to hinder the settlement and hopeful enlargement of a Christian congregation in these parts" (271). By March, the concentration is gaining momentum, with the Delaware "clearing some of their land... in order to their settling there in a compact form" with public worship and schools. Brainerd notes this "design of their settling thus *in a body*" is "of such *necessity and importance to their religious interest*" (286, emphasis added). In this new community, dispersal is overcome, and potential converts "can scarce go into a house now but they will meet with Christian conversation, whereby it is hopeful they may be both instructed and awakened" (277). A fundamental enemy of conversion under a Christian federalism, then, is the seriality of lax, isolated belief, a nominal and comparative Christianity searching for a spiritual and ideological mean.

But *fusion* poses its own problems, and primarily receives an analysis with reference to the third type of Indian community encountered by Brainerd: the trans-Native communities of Pennsylvania's Susquehanna Valley. Brainerd makes two local trips, to Shamokin and Juniata, both Indian communities on the Susquehanna. In these, he finds mass groups engaged in drinking binges and indigenous rituals, "near a hundred of them" dancing "around a large fire, having prepared ten fat deer for the sacrifice," or "gathered together... and acting their frantic distracted postures" in "all the wild, ridiculous, and distracted motions imaginable; sometimes singing; sometimes howling" (233–34). Brainerd admits "[t]heir monstrous actions tended to excite ideas of horror" (234), horror at the cultural impenetrability of the group. It is in Juniata, too, that Brainerd meets the Delaware prophet (mentioned in the last chapter) building a new religion and searching "to find some that would join heartily with him in it" (237). Although the prophet terrifies Brainerd, Brainerd must admit "there was something in [the prophet's] temper and disposition that looked more like true religion than I ever observed amongst other heathens" (238). Such religious figures pose the greatest threat to his missionary work, as he later notes in reference to a "conjurer." Heathen beliefs aside, the conjurer's worst sin "was his conjuration," calling away Brainerd's potential converts into a group formation. Brainerd even fantasizes the Indian's death, for he "often thought it would be a great favor to the design of gospelizing these Indians if God would take that wretch out of the world" (298). Conjuring, in this view, amounts to the formation and reformation of the Indian community as a contained unit to which Brainerd and his Christianity have no access.

So the institutionalization of Christianity must counter serial dispersal and group fusion by managing both tendencies. Just as Paine sought systematicity in an imposed seriality unifying the nation, Brainerd seeks a combination of serial belief and congregational union. His solution is an individuated conversion process signaled by repeated narratives of specific conversions, mostly by women. The result is the congregation of isolated believers, together yet also apart, powerfully captured in a description of an August meeting:

> They were almost universally praying and crying for mercy, in every part of the house, and many out of doors, and numbers could neither go nor stand. Their concern was so great, each one for himself, that none seemed to take any notice of those about them, but each prayed freely for himself. And, I am to think, they were to their own apprehension as much retired as if they had been, individually, by themselves in the thickest desert; or, I believe rather, that they thought nothing about any but themselves, and their own states, and so were *everyone praying apart, although all together.*
>
> It seemed to me there was now an exact fulfillment of that prophecy, Zechariah 12: 10, 11, 12; for there was now "a great mourning, like the mourning of Hadadrimmon"; and each seemed to "mourn apart." (217, emphasis added)

Universally joined *and* separated, none noticing the others, each one retired, everyone praying apart though all together.... The reference to Zechariah and the restoration of Judah after the exile is telling as well, specifically in the allusion to the ritual worship of the pagan god of thunder, Hadadrimmon, now reworked, legitimized, and purified. "And the land shall mourn, every family apart," reads Zecharaiah 12:12, concluding a few verses later, "All the families that remain, every family apart, and their wives apart."

Here is one moment blending seriality and fusion, and we get another, related episode in Brainerd's account of the conversion of his translator, Moses Tattamy, who at first "seemed to have little or no impression of religion upon his mind" (208). In the account of Tattamy's conversion, the flash point seems to come when he witnesses Brainerd preaching "to an assembly of white people, with more freedom and fervency than I could possibly address the Indians with" (208). Similarly, "[s]ome of the white people who came out of curiosity to 'hear what this babbler would say' to the poor ignorant Indians were much awakened, and some appeared to be wounded with a view of their perishing state" (218): the "white heathen found they had souls to save or lose as well as the Indians" (222). What is happening in these instances? Brainerd is clearly attuned to the racial dynamics of his work: if liberal whites earlier proved an obstacle to the unified conversion of Indians, now the gatherings of Indians challenge the spiritual seriality of whites, as whites yearn enviously for the same cohesive rebirth that the Indians have apparently achieved. It's as if seriality and fusion dialectically interact, canceling each other out: the isolated sinner is drawn to the congregation by the perception of the *racially other* group. With Moses Tattamy a similar awareness takes shape. As Brainerd preaches hellfire to the assembled white people, his missionary work is universalized; he is a white man not only badgering Indians, but entreating the damned white settlers, as well. To this point, the Indians, including Tattamy, have perhaps practiced a spiritual version of quiet possession, resisting the attempts at conversion, but in Tattamy's desire for transformation he seems to have perceived the inequality of equality. If Indians are as resistant to preaching as the whites, they are weaker than whites, but when they are born again, they will achieve the organization that the whites will not or cannot achieve; equality will then become inequality, as the Indians achieve a higher spiritual state than the whites. Witnessing the damnation of the whites provides the critical inspiration for Tattamy.

This racial dialectic is of course inseparable from the related feelings of structure. Tattamy, like the other converts, comes to a profound sense of his individual sinfulness: "He was brought under great concern for his soul... so that his mind was burdened from day to day," observes Brainerd. "It was now his great inquiry, 'What he should do to be saved?'" He begins to perceive an "impassable mountain before him," and he thinks "if he could but make his way through these thorns and briers, and climb up the first steep pitch of the mountain, that then there might be hope for him" (209). The mountain seems related to his perception of serial isolation, for from it he "saw the world around him... in the same perishing circumstances, notwithstanding the profession many of them made of Christianity, and the hope they entertained of obtaining everlasting happiness" (210–11). Then, "sensible of the impossibility of his helping himself by anything he could do," he hears the individual voice telling him "There is hope, there is hope" (211). He is saved, becomes a more fervent translator-preacher, and now has a sense of "the absolute sovereignty of God" (212). It is the internalized sense of God, the unifier of the dispersed, the organizer, the institutional manager, that marks the change, and allows Tattamy to feel distinct from the whites who remain the mass of scattered sinners. We may sense that Tattamy, like many of his fellow Delawares, comes to feel his serial isolation through his contact with white people. But whereas some Delawares responded with the cultural nationalism of the fused group, Tattamy, the hired translator, elects a different route. At Crossweeksung group fusion is not an option, in part due to the established seriality, in part due to the strong presence of Brainerd. So Tattamy accentuates his seriality, now understood within the discourse of sinfulness, and transforms it with reference to God's sovereignty and grace, the latter visited upon sinners when they most acutely perceive their weakness, isolation, and helplessness. He cannot overcome his seriality, so he will relocate it within the institutions of Christianity, where he will find at least some form of ensemble to answer the seriality of the more powerful white settlers of the area.

Something akin to this dynamic happens from the other side, so to speak. The conjurer that Brainerd had wished dead also undergoes a conversion experience, one of Brainerd's most "remarkable instance[s] of divine grace" (298), and becomes his Paul at Crossweeksung. His strong spirit of conjuration is shaken when he "murdered a likely young Indian," probably, Brainerd implies, from drunkenness (298). Then, witnessing the "awakening" among his fellow Delawares, the conjuror declares "his spirit of conjuration left him entirely" and is plunged into individual despair (299). He now understands his distinct function within the community to be damnation, telling Brainerd "I would have others come to Christ, if I must go to hell myself" (301). And when his conversion finally comes, unexpectedly, he emerges as defender of the Christian community against other conjurers, including "an old Indian at the place where I preached who threatened to bewitch me and my religious people who accompanied me there." The reborn conjurer "challenged him to do his worst, telling him that himself had been as great a conjurer as he, and that notwithstanding as soon as he felt that Word in his heart which these people loved (meaning the Word of God), his power of conjuring immediately left him" (302). The protection of this anticonjuration amounts to the declaration of a different form of cohesion, the unity of institution, more lasting than the chaotic fusion of the group experience. In this way the conjurer, like Tattamy, reworks one feeling of structure, that of group fusion, within the context of another: a new form of power and union that will emerge from the congregated settlement, as the sovereign word in the heart replaces the word of the group.

Somewhere between group and series, then, the *institution* takes shape. And Brainerd's final days are devoted to systematizing his mission's achievements. At the end of 1745, confident in the individual experiences of his converts, he finds "it proper to set up a catechetical lecture among them" (258), to culminate, in April 1746, with the "administration" of "the ordinance of the Lord's Supper" (290). After he has "catechized those that were designed to partake of the Lord's Supper... upon the institution, nature, and end of that ordinance," the sacrament is given. Again, Brainerd's descriptive language is revealing:

> The ordinance was attended with great solemnity, and with a most desirable tenderness and affection. It was remarkable that in the season of the performance of the sacramental actions, especially in the distribution of the bread, they seemed to be affected in a most lively manner, as if Christ had been really crucified before them. The words of the institution, when repeated and enlarged upon in the season of the administration, seemed to meet with the same reception, to be entertained with the same full and firm belief and affectionate engagement of soul, as if the Lord Jesus Christ Himself had been present and had personally spoken to them. The affections of the communicants, although considerably raised, were notwithstanding agreeably regulated and kept within proper bounds. So that there was a sweet, gentle, and affectionate melting, without any indecent or boisterous commotion of the passions. (293–94)

The overtly institutional language—ordinance, distribution, institution, administration, communicants, regulated—is clear enough, but more interesting is Brainerd's outline of the *feeling* of the institution. Its components, with reference to "the *author*, the *nature*, and *design* of the Lord's Supper" (292), are carefully described: a solemn and full "engagement of the soul" that comes from the invocation of the invisible sovereign who provides order to the ensemble; the repetition of the spoken communication of the institution, so that the institution not only reproduces individually but among others, while pointing to its continuation in past, present, and future; and the regulation of affections "within proper bounds," so that a "melting" occurs that does not become "boisterous commotion." In this way, communicants are reminded "to discharge the relative duties incumbent upon them respectively" (292). Subsequent conversions will now happen through the workings of the institution, "in a more silent way," as the instituted converts "communicate" with their peers (304–5).

At the end of his journal, Brainerd writes, "How are morose and savage pagans in this short space of time transformed into agreeable, affectionate, and humble Christians, and their drunken and pagan howlings turned into devout and fervent prayers and praises to God!" (307). From the bad seriality of sullenness to the good seriality of agreeable humility, from the bad fusion of massed howlings to the good fusion of fervent prayer—the transformation has been effected by the establishment of "a compact settlement, in order to their more convenient enjoyment of the gospel and other means of instruction, as well as the comforts of life" (297). The community is now organized around the sacrament, which will perpetuate the new centralized feeling of structure, a feeling of administration that will keep complete dispersal and unification at bay. Brainerd has achieved the cultural equivalent of Paine's large-scale reform: the scattered agrarian population has been brought together and regulated in the establishment of new spiritual ordinances. The Indians will now give and receive in orderly fashion within this "spiritual Oconomy," as a solution to the scattered state of weakness revealed to them by the missionary. They take their place in an institution that, on the Pennsylvania-Jersey border, seems to provide them the greatest security and power against their white agrarian counterparts.

We should be clear, too, that Brainerd's success and the Delawares' election hinges upon the sovereignty essential to the feeling of the institution. With Brainerd's arrival, the Indians sense, at worst, the absence of sovereignty in their serial existence, or, at best, the fleeting fusion of their pow-wows. Brainerd's initial one-on-one encounters with the Indians emphasize the need for sovereignty, and the eternal preexistence of the sovereign: in this respect, he plants the seeds of the desire for institution: once a sovereign is acknowledged, a corresponding order must follow. Paine cast the sovereign as the impersonal state-city, countering a politics of parties and classes and factions; Brainerd, like most of the preachers of the white Great Awakening, casts the sovereign as a personal omnipotent abstraction, countering a sociality of dispersal and scattered groups. We should compare Brainerd's approach with that embodied in Edwards' "Sinners in the Hands of an Angry God," a sermon framed around a similar structure of feeling, seeking to move the isolated sinners while breaking apart the clusters of unmanaged believers taking shape during the revival movement. Edwards, too, sought to have his series and unify it too, and his primary rhetorical emphasis was likewise upon *sovereignty*. Edwards' sovereign, it may be added, was a quasi-Indianized power terrifying and unifying his congregants: "The bow of God's wrath is bent, and the arrow made ready on the string, and justice bends the arrow at your heart, and strains the bow, and it is nothing but the mere pleasure of God, and that of an angry God, without any promise or obligation at all, that keeps the arrow one moment from being made drunk with your blood."[19] By contrast, Brainerd's sovereign, as he notes repeatedly, is a welcoming and inviting one, the God of the "dying Saviour," a sovereign appropriate for the disorganized Delawares seeking political power. In a final nasty irony, the "dying Saviour" was literally appropriate as well: the result of Brainerd's institution was the death of most of his converts. Assembled in this compact settlement, they received not only the greater communication of the Gospel, but Brainerd's tuberculosis as well.[20]

Paths and Campfires

The plans of Pownall, Evans, and Paine were grand and largely unfulfilled; David Brainerd's small-scale project of institutionalization had a fleeting local success. But I turn now to what may be eighteenth-century Pennsylvania's most ambitious and large-scale institutional project prior to independence: the attempt to build a structured British–Native American empire centered in the middle colonies. This occurred within the sphere of white–Native American relations, understatedly called "backwoods diplomacy," which was radically transformed from the 1720s to the 1750s as Pennsylvania went from being a minor region of diplomatic chaos to the cornerstone of British-Native relations. In use throughout the period was a template of sorts that William Penn had encountered in his initial dealings with Native Americans. I cite here the example of a treaty from the late 1720s:

> 1st. That all William Penns People or Christians, and all the Indians should be brethren, as the Children of one Father, joyned together as with one Heart, one Head & one Body.
>
> 2nd. That all Paths should be open and free to both Christians and Indians.
>
> 3rd. That the Doors of the Christians Houses should be open to the Indians & the Houses of the Indians open to the Christians, & they should make each other welcome as their Friends.
>
> 4th. That the Christians should not believe any false Rumours or Reports of the Indians, nor the Indians believe any such Rumours or Reports of the Christians, but should first come as Brethren to enquire of each other; And that both Christians & Indians, when they hear any such false Reports of their Brethren, they should bury them as in a bottomless Pitt.
>
> 5th. That if the Christians hear any ill news that may be to the Hurt of the Indians, or the Indians hear any such ill news that may be to the Injury of the Christians, they should acquaint each other with it speedily as true Friends & Brethren.
>
> 6th. That the Indians should do no manner of Harm to the Christians nor their Creatures nor the Christians do any Hurt to any Indians, but each treat the other as their Brethren.

7th. But as there are wicked People in all Nations, if either Indians or Christians should do any harm to each other, Complaint should be made of it by the Persons Suffering that Right may be done, & when Satisfaction is made, the Injury or Wrong should be forgott & be buried as in a bottomless Pitt.

8th. That the Indians should in all things assist the Christians, & the Christians assist the Indians against all wicked People that would disturb them.

9th. And lastly, that both Christians and Indians should acquaint their Children with this League & firm Chain of Friendship made between them, & that it should always be made stronger & stronger & be kept bright and clean, without Rust or Spott between our Children and Childrens Children, while the Creeks and Rivers run, and while the Sun, Moon, & Stars endure.[21]

In this Chain of Friendship (as it was termed), we find, between links 1 and 9, which look to the past of William Penn and to the future of Pennsylvania, roughly three moments. The first (links 2 through 4) stresses the matrix of cooperation, compellingly expressed in language metaphoric *and* metonymic. Paths, houses, campfires, and reports denote not only the real things, but more broadly the *infrastructure* of cooperation (mobility, hospitality, and communication) and the concomitant politicoeconomic relations of trade, land dealings, and security. The second moment, that of the middle links, moves to counter possible disruptions in or threats to that cooperation in the form of rumors, ill news, and harm, by emphasizing *procedures* within the just-outlined infrastructure: there should be regular surveillance and established protocols, negative and positive, for communication and punishment. Together, these two moments express the spatiotemporal dimensions of a confederated Chain of Friendship between the Pennsylvania executive and the Indian polities: the chain will be realized and renewed in houses at moments of need and hospitality, through cautious reports that provide the community of information, and on the paths that connect the member polities in moments of crisis. This is an imagined community, to use the preferred native metaphor, linking elite council fires across wildernesses of loosely monitored plebeian activity. These two moments lead to the final one, which unites the leaders of the polities against "wicked People in all Nations." This last moment revealingly assesses the greatest danger to cooperation in the serial actions of the respective masses, while insisting on a "firm Chain" of institution to unite elites against the popular forces of anarchy. All parties have their duties in "this League," and these must be passed on as passive activity with the spatial and temporal regularity of the flowing rivers and the circling stars.

What is most notable about such treaties, however, is the combined theoretical sophistication of the imagined league, and its practical ineffectiveness. At the moment in question, the late 1720s, the proprietary's diplomacy was muddling its way, in great confusion, through treaties with a number of small polities. In May 1728, there was a treaty with the Conestogas, the Brandywine Delawares, the Conoys, and the Shawnees; this was followed by another with the Delawares in June, a third, with the Delawares and the Brandywines, in October, and a fourth, with Conestogas, Conoys, Delawares, and Shawnees, in the spring of 1729. As an index of the confusion, the "Brandywines" *were* Delaware Indians, and, although the first and third treaties implicitly acknowledged divisions among the Delawares, the second and fourth assumed that the Tulpehocken "King," Sassoonan, spoke politically for all Delaware Indians.[22] If such negotiations reflected wishful thinking—on the part of Pennsylvanians, but also on the part of the Tulpehocken Delawares—about the political cohesion and therefore regulation of the Delawares, references to the Shawnees were even more fantastic. Records suggest that only one Shawnee was present at the second treaty, none at the third (where Sassoonan claimed to speak for them), and none at the fourth (where the Conestogas claimed to speak for them). Francis Jennings has observed that "Colonials often recognized particular Indian authorities for the colonials' convenience,"[23] and this was certainly the case in the late 1720s, when treaties were conducted with Indians of scattered settlements (the Brandywines, the Conestogas, the Conoys) imaginatively reconceived first in terms of broader ethnic communities (the Delaware, the Shawnee) and finally in terms of a bloc denoted "the four Nations."[24]

"Nations" is a revealing term, then, not because it denotes a stable political body but because it reveals the conflicted and confusing uses of the term in white diplomacy with the Indians. A contemporary New York expert on the Iroquois, Cadwallader Colden (a correspondent, incidentally, of the great classifier Linnaeus), reveals the extent of the confusion in his "Short View of the Form of Government of the Five Nations," writing that the "Five Nations (as their Name denotes) consist of so many Tribes or Nations joyn'd by a League or Confederacy." In the next few paragraphs, he insists that "Each of the Nations are distinguished into 3 Tribes or Families," that "Each Nation is an absolute Republick by itself," that the Oneidas, Cayugas, and Tuscaroras were "adopted or received into this League" in a relation of children to "Fathers," and that "the present state of the Indian Nations exactly shows the most Ancient and Original Condition of almost every Nation."[25] What we find, in these brief and quasi-scientific remarks, is the chaotic blurring of ethnic and political terms, with "Nations" here synonymous with "Tribes," there made up of Tribes, here equated with equivalent Republics, there defined as uneven partners in a League or Confederacy. In other words, this is the same terminological confusion we find in today's scholarship about Native America, in which an ethno-linguistic definition of nation-as-folk blends into a politico-juridical definition of nation-as-polity. It is the confusion we find even in the simple eighteenth-century term for the Iroquois, "the Six Nations," which casts them simultaneously as multiple nations and as one political unit. And it is the confusion, theoretical and practical, of the treaties with "four Nations" who were actually scattered settlements hoping, or assumed, to be speaking for other scattered settlements.

To make sense of the change in strategy of the Pennsylvanians, we need to undertake the same work that the proprietary did, and make some sense of the native polities occupying Pennsylvania in the eighteenth century.[26] The Delawares, as noted earlier, suffered serial dispersal in this period, as they were often politically divided according to settlement location. "[E]ach Delaware village was an independent community, having its own chieftains. . . . Often the people living in villages along the same stream constituted what can best be described as a band, and the most influential village chief may have functioned as the nominal head of the band."[27] Anthony Wallace estimates that there were about thirty or forty such communities along the Delaware in 1600, each autonomous, "at one juncture entering into a military alliance with its neighbors, and at another pursuing its own way independently."[28] Weslager lists the significant geopolitical subgroupings of the Delawares that must be kept in mind when studying the treaties of the eighteenth century: for instance, when the Brandywine Delawares made reference to the Minisinks; both groups were "Delawares" but remained politically distinct.[29] Weslager and Wallace both suggest that the divisions of the Delawares were largely the result of decentralized, precontact modes of production reinforced and exacerbated by encounters with both Iroquois and Europeans. By the Seven Years' War, these external forces, combined with economic duress, contributed to a unifying militancy (discussed in the last chapter). But fragmentation and dispersal would be the rule through the early eighteenth century.

The Shawnees, meanwhile, developed a different political organizational structure, related to a more mobile, and at times military, mode of production.

Callender describes Shawnee bands or divisions, which "were linked together at the tribal level by an overall organization, including a council composed of the divisional officials as well as a tribal chief, and were further integrated by specific political or ritual functions for which each division was responsible when tribal action occurred. . . . No other tribe in the [Great Lakes–Riverine sociopolitical] series had such a formal system of political subdivisions."[30] The Shawnees are designated as unruly, anarchistic renegades in most colonial documents, but this caricature reflects a political independence borne of internal unification, and a mobility that consistently placed them beyond easy contact with colonial and Iroquois officials. Caveats about regional distinctions among the Shawnee, then, are less relevant than for the Delawares. The same holds, during this period, for many nations of the Ohio region, such as the Miamis/Twightwees, the Wyandots, and the Ottawas.

A third pattern, of small multicultural conglomerations, also proved significant in Pennsylvania—a recurrent destination for refugees and migrants from New York and the wartorn South, not to mention local polities, like the Susquehannocks, irrevocably dispersed by warfare. The Conoys and Nanticokes moved from the Chesapeake and Potomac regions, passing through Pennsylvania before ultimately being settled by the Iroquois near Chenango in the 1750s.[31] Both groups were fleeing colonial encroachment and warfare, as were the Tutelos of the Virginia-Carolinas region who passed through Pennsylvania before being settled near present-day Ithaca. So were the Tuscaroras, who gradually relocated from the Carolinas to become the sixth nation of the Iroquois League.[32] From the east came Mahicans, as well as scattered Housatonics, Mohegans, Montauks, and Narragansetts, among others.[33] Out of these crossed paths emerged a number of multicultural clusters throughout Pennsylvania. They were: settlements established by colonial land grants (like Conestoga, on the lower Susquehanna, originally composed of a group of Susquehannocks defeated by the Five Nations, later absorbing Delawares, Cayugas, Senecas, and Conoys); mission towns (Gnadenhütten, on the Lehigh, a Moravian settlement home to Delawares, Mahicans, and Wampanoags); settlements under Six Nations supervision (like Catawasse, Nescopeck, Wyalusing, Shesheguin, Tioga, or Shamokin, home of Delawares, Shawnees, Mahicans, Conoys, Nanticokes, Cayugas); and trading outposts (Logstown, on the Ohio, eventually home to Senecas, Shawnees, Mohawks, Cayugas, Mahicans, Delawares, Onondagas, Ojibwa, Wyandots, Fox, Nipissings, Ottawas, Oneidas, and even Abenakis).[34] It was in these multicultural settlements that the pan-Nativist movement thrived.

Finally, we find a fourth type of polity in the League of the Iroquois, also known as the Haudenosaunee, or the Five– (from about the 1710s on, Six–) Nations.[35] The Six Nations—from west to east, the Senecas, the Cayugas, the Onondagas, the Oneidas, and the Mohawks, with the later addition of the Tuscaroras—were regionally distinct and relatively unified culturally, although languages varied slightly among the six member nations. The League also actively assimilated, as a matter of population policy, Indians from different communities. Although the League was fairly unique in the Pennsylvania region, there were somewhat analogous polities elsewhere in eastern North American (the so-called Seven Nations of French Canada, the Creek Confederacy, the nations momentarily united in Pontiac's Conspiracy, and so on). Many Iroquois migrated from the upstate New York region to settle in multicultural communities to the south and, more significantly, to the west, where they were known as Mingos. Non-League Iroquois maintained tenuous links with the League under "Half-Kings," but became more and more autonomous as they attempted to establish hegemony in the Ohio region.[36]

Dispersed homogeneous settlements, mobile unions, unique geographical aggregates, and coordinated confederation—these four types of polities were the Native American constituents of Pennsylvania's diplomatic practice in the mid-eighteenth century, constantly overlapping and shifting beneath the wishfully indiscriminate label "nations." Pennsylvanians were gradually coming to understand this, through the 1720s. At a 1720 treaty between James Logan and representatives of the Conestogas, Delawares, Shawnees, and Conoys, Logan learned that these four nations were caught in the middle of a war between the Five Nations and southern Indians, the results of which included high casualties among Pennsylvania Indians, reduced commerce with Philadelphia, actual warfare in Pennsylvania itself, and (to Logan's eye) the strengthening of the French. A Conestoga leader told Logan privately that the Five Nations were hostile toward Pennsylvania, due to recent settlements on the Susquehanna, and the proprietary promptly complained to the governor of New York about "your five Nations."[37] At this moment, the League was perceived as disrupting the economy, security, and political order of the local Indians, while constituting the major opposition to land settlement.

But, in a decade's time, Pennsylvania elites had figured that the major disruptive force could likewise become, logically enough, the major regulatory force. In August 1731, James Logan articulated this new vision in a Provincial Council meeting, having informed the board that the Shawnees were allegedly engaged in negotiations with the French. He "Moved that to prevent or putt a stop to these designs if possible a treaty should be sett on foot with the five Nations, who have *an absolute authority* as well over the Shawanese *as all our Indians*, that by their means the Shawanese may not only be kept firm to the English Interest, but likewise be induced to remove from Allegheney nearer to the English Settlements." He concluded "that such a treaty becomes now the more necessary, because 'tis several years since any of those Nations have visited us, and no opportunity ought to be lost of cultivating & improving the Frindship which has always subsisted between this Government & them."[38]

Between this government and them—the implication clearly being that *they* are a real government, like us. And to some extent this was a valid approximation, given the unique, and for some time dominant, political position of the Iroquois League.[39] Geographically, the Six Nations had strategic access to major trade routes and occupied a crucial buffer zone between the competing imperial powers of France and Britain. They were also relatively distant (unlike the Massachusetts, Mohegans, or Delawares) from white colonial expansion, and thus not only primarily encountered the colonials as traders but maintained a political and military advantage over other, more battered Indian nations. Socially, the Six Nations' policy of absorbing captives from other nations helped them offset population depletion; economically, their agricultural base kept them from the intensive dependence on colonials normally related to the fur trade. Finally, the Six Nations had developed a network of military and political relations which gave them a relatively flexible cohesion and force, and within which they actively worked to integrate other, smaller Indian groups, as strategic defensive props. Taken together, these factors meant that the Six Nations both had a great interest in the Indians of Pennsylvania—they would provide a buffer against war and settlement, and a resource pool for labor and trade—and were in a position to exercise political control over these Indians. By the middle of the eighteenth century, contact with Euro-Americans, challenges from other Native Americans, and the contradictions of their political economy began to undermine the Six Nations' privileged position; by century's end, the Iroquois suffered tremendous disintegration, responding in part as had the Delawares and Shawnees, with a political and religious movement of fusion.[40]

But the elites of Pennsylvania did not perceive the decline until the 1750s, and in a sense pursued contact and coordination with an idealized Iroquois League of the late seventeenth century. From the League, they sought a military alliance and, from its tributaries, a military buffer to, as well as information about, the western French; this was particularly important for a colony hostile to military development and concerned to maintain a thriving Indian trade.[41] There were concerns, too, expressed in the treaties of the late 1720s, with squatting yeomen and land titles, with random and incendiary violence, with unpredictable or openly renegade Indian groups. The Iroquois League "would police Pennsylvania's woods in return for Pennsylvania's recognition of their sole right to do so."[42] From Pennsylvania, the Iroquois in return sought tighter oversight of land treaties in the Susquehanna Valley area and beyond—in other words, help in maintaining their geopolitical advantage. Their aim was to prevent non-Iroquois Indians from ceding territory claimed by the Six Nations; this could in turn prevent white settlement, native flight, and the consequent loss of an important defensive buffer.[43] Relations with Philadelphia also entailed economic advantages, as the Iroquois sought to ride the economic wave of Pennsylvania's booming growth. Further, Pennsylvania provided the hard place against which the Six Nations' rock wedged some tinier nations, as the two larger polities functioned as paired superpowers.

Such was the union pursued at a series of major treaties from the early 1730s to the mid-1750s: Philadelphia in 1732 and 1736, Lancaster in 1744 and 1748, Albany in 1745 and 1754. At the first, the Iroquois reasserted control over wayward Shawnees, recounted detailed information about French imperial maneuvering, and claimed to have added to the "chain of friendship" five westward nations (the Twightwee/Miamis, the Ottawas, the Altoomatte, the Onichkarydyo, and the Seysaghe).[44] If the Provincial Council did not completely believe such claims, it nonetheless supported the League's imperial project, Thomas Penn advising the chiefs "that you should bring over as many Nations of Indians as you can into your Interest, and make firm Leagues with them." By these means, he concluded, "you will make yourselves greater and Stronger."[45] By the 1736 treaty, the Seneca speaker Kanickhungo declared "our earnest Desire this Chain should continue & be strengthned between all the English & all our Nations, & likewise the Delawares, Canayes, & the Indians living on Sasquehanna, & all the other Indians who now are in League & Friendship with the Six Nations." He then updated the Council on relations with *six* nations to the west, said to "acknowledge us for their Elder Brethren, & [to] have promised to join with us as one People, & to act altogether in Concert with us."[46] By the 1742 treaty, the Onondagas, Oneidas, Cayugas, Senecas, Tuscaroras, Shawnees, Fork Delawares, Tulpehocken Delawares, and Conestogas were in attendance, with Iroquois speaker Canasatego confidently mapping a coordinated strategy against the French while promising links with "a Vast many Nations" to the west.[47] War against France was officially declared around the time of the 1744 Lancaster Treaty, where again Canasatego stressed League ties with the English while claiming to "have put the Spirit of Antipathy against the French" in the western nations.[48] The next three years saw numerous alarms of "a defection of the Six Nations through the Intrigues and Artifices of the Enemy," and by 1748 the "four nations" of the Ohio region Twightwees were meeting at Lancaster, admitted to the Chain of Friendship under the aegis of the Six Nations, with hopes of future treaties with *twelve* nations of that area.[49]

As importantly, the Shawnees were apparently back in the fold. In 1742 there had been rumors of Shawnee warriors parading white scalps, and in 1745 Conrad Weiser reported that the Onondaga expected war with the Shawnees, but, by 1748, delegates were confessing to League officials that "We the Shawonese have been misled, & have carried on a private Correspondence with the French without letting you [the Six Nations] or our Brethren the English know of it. We travell'd secretly through the Bushes to Canada, and the French promis'd us great Things, but we find ourselves deceived. . . . We earnestly desire you wou'd intercede with our Brethren the English for us who are left at Ohio, that we may be permitted to be restored to the Chain of Friendship and be looked upon as heretofore the same Flesh with them."[50] The Delawares, too, seemed managed in the new League. The 1730s had seen the great expropriation of the Delawares under Thomas Penn's rationalized Land Office and the notorious "Walking Purchase" of 1737, after which white settlement proceeded full force.[51] At the 1742 treaty, the Iroquois promised the forced relocation of the Delawares, Canasatego publicly scolding the Delaware "King" Sassoonan: "You ought to be taken by the Hair of the Head and shak'd severely till you recover your Senses and become Sober. . . we charge You to remove instantly. . . . You may go to either [Wyoming or Shamokin], and then we shall have you more under our eye, and shall see how You behave."[52] Relocation occurred accordingly in the 1740s, the Delaware shifting to the refugee towns of the upper Susquehanna Valley visited by Brainerd and others.

It was not only the Indian tributaries who were reaffirmed in, or added to, the Chain of Friendship. Iroquois wars with Catawbas and other southern groups had created a series of backcountry flashpoints in the 1730s, including Iroquois complaints about land encroachment by Virginians and Marylanders, the 1742 jailing of Pennsylvania Nanticokes in Maryland, a major clash between an Onondaga war party and Virginia settlers in 1743, and a conflict between the Shawnees and the Tutelos. In the face of these crises and recurrent European conflicts, Maryland and Virginia were brought into the Chain of Friendship in 1744. It was at this treaty that Canasatego gave his famous unification speech. After stressing Iroquois control over the "Conestogoe" and "Susquahannah" Indians, he proceeded to "heartily recommend Union and a Good Agreement between you our Brethren." He continued, "Never disagree, but preserve a strict Friendship for one another, and thereby you, as well as we, will become the Stronger." He concluded, "We are a Powerfull Confederacy; and, by your observing the same Methods our wise Forefathers have taken, you will acquire fresh Strength and Power; therefore whatever befalls you, never fall out one with another."[53] By the next year's gathering in Albany, colonial delegates were in sharp disagreement about Indian policy—the New Englanders wanted the Iroquois to fight the Abenakis, and the Pennsylvanians wanted Iroquois neutrality—but they were nonetheless calling for a "joint Speech, as what would show our Union, and consequently have the greater weight with the Indians."[54]

By the famous Albany Congress of 1754, the colonies seemed to have taken this advice, the Chain of Friendship now including Connecticut, New York, and Massachusetts. It was at this congress that Franklin drafted and circulated the Albany Plan, often considered the first proposal for union among the mainland colonies.[55] The "Proposed Union" sought to guarantee "Mutual Defence and Security," but added an express concern with "Extending the British Settlements in North America" (378). The new union of colonies would be structured around a President General and a Grand Council, and as in the Six Nations the eleven colonies of the mainland would cohere around dominant colonies of the north, center, and south (Massachusetts, Pennsylvania, and Virginia).[56] The new union would have its central campfire in Philadelphia, from which it would "hold or direct all Indian Treaties in which the general Interest or Welfare of the Colony's may be Concerned; And make Peace or Declare War with the Indian Nations" (380). Additionally, it would regulate "all Indian trade" and land deals, and undertake "New Settlements on such Purchases," centrally "regulating and Governing such new Settlements, till the Crown shall think fit to form them into Particular Governments" (380). Subsequent references to raising soldiers and paying taxes were subordinate to the initial matters of Indian relations (380). In sum, the Chain of Friendship would be consolidated longitudinally among the colonies, and latitudinally between the English and the Indians coordinated by the Iroquois Confederacy.

Some have identified the Albany Plan as an "attempt at organic confederation," a prototype of the American nation. But the Albany Plan was a tremendous failure, in actuality an index of the tremendous divisions within and among colonies and within and among Indian polities. The Mohawk leadership was in conflict with other Iroquois groups, Connecticut had its eye on land in Pennsylvania, Virginia refused to send commissioners, and, in Pennsylvania and New York, the delegations embodied deep conflicts within state institutions. The congress was a practical failure, and what it "showed very clearly to the board of trade in London was that the Covenant Chain system had ceased to be viable as previously operated." Rather than announcing a unified beginning, "Albany was the *end* of a system."[57] In response, the Board of Trade would restructure Indian administration by centralizing it under royal superintendents of Indian affairs. These centralization schemes notwithstanding, Indian diplomacy remained a cobbled affair, with Johnson reactively attempting to orchestrate events. The Grand Chain collapsed, while the more improvised collection of minichains persisted.

Iroquois Influence

Assessment of the Albany Plan poses serious methodological challenges for the cultural historian. On the one hand, it demonstrates a fairly remarkable organizational creativity worthy of analysis. On the other, it was a practical failure that never bore fruit. What are we to make of the plan? The question puts us squarely amid the recently simmering debate over Native American influences upon American political culture.[58] To date, arguments about Indian influence have largely emphasized the political values and constitutional systems of Native Americans, "the legacy and influence of the Iroquois Great Law of Peace and other genuine Indian constructs on the United States system of government and on the general philosophy of democracy in America."[59] Donald Grinde, for instance, stresses "the way of democracy" white colonials learned from the Iroquois, and how it "would live on even within the new governments that the white colonists would create." Bruce Johansen's work similarly oscillates between ideals and political structures, arguing that colonials discovered "life, liberty, and happiness" among Native Americans and sought to "mold the political life of the colonies" from such encounters.[60]

Attention to institutions and cultural values—this seems the kind of analysis we should pursue with the Albany Plan. But the arguments of the Influence school reveal some distorting tendencies in this appeal. In considering the Native–colonial engagements through social and political practices, narratives of influence consistently highlight the "journey of ideas."[61]

The paradigmatic moment of cultural transmission is the political oration, most famously Canasatego's Lancaster speech exhorting the colonists to unite. There, Canasatego purportedly formulated the essence of Iroquois institutions—motivating principles like unity, democracy, and representation—reworked in Franklin's Plan of Union at Albany a decade later.[62] Institutions, in this view, are synonymous with, and translatable as, ideas, which then make the transition back to institutions. Additionally, most accounts of influence refuse to differentiate the meaningful conflicts between and among Euro-Americans or Native Americans. On the one hand, the goal has been to stress native influence upon the Founding Fathers (particularly Franklin and Jefferson), who are then cast as the greatest representatives of thinking society. Johansen, for instance, argues that "American Indians (principally the Iroquois) played a major role in shaping the ideas of Franklin (and thus, the American Revolution)"—in one fell swoop eliding class, institutional, and provincial divisions in an erasure of history from below.[63] Although he makes a decisive case for Iroquois influence on Franklin, his uncritical admiration, combined with a one-dimensional view of the American Revolution, leads him to reductive conclusions about Franklin's concerns (unity) and political interests (freedom and democracy). Equally troubling is the extreme bias toward the Iroquois, which reduces consideration of other Indian nations to acts of lip service, while depicting Iroquois society as unproblematically unified. Grinde describes a number of significant conflicts and divisions among the Iroquois—among nations, between sachem and warriors—but these are attributed to the influence of "warring whites" and do not complicate the general claim that "Unity, not only in a political sense, but also in a spiritual and environmental sense, was the binding force in Iroquois life."[64] This is a pro-Iroquois version of the republican synthesis, which in its emphasis on vaguely shared values neatly parallels republican accounts of Anglo-America. Just as the dissenters and insurrectionaries are shut out of the republican synthesizers' accounts of early America, the Delawares, Shawnees, and other tributary groups never seriously intrude on the Influence argument.[65] Great sachems of the great Indian nations influence great Founders with great ideas for great values with great results.

The response to such arguments has been cold, a methodological conservatism answering the idealist conservatism of Influence proponents. Anti-Influence historians consistently reaffirm a constellation of empiricist tenets associated with the quantitative conventions of evidence: context, frequency, scale, consistency. The Mohawk influence on John Adams, argues one critic, can best be gauged by the proportions of references in *A Defence of the*

Constitutions of Government of the United States of America: "The distribution of his pages strongly suggests that he believed Anglo-Americans could learn more, for better or worse, from Athens, Sparta, Mycenae, Argos, Thebes, Corinth, Rome, Siena, Genoa, Milan, Florence, Padua, San Marino, Biscay, Appenzel, Underwald, Glarus, Bern, Lucerne, Zurich, Geneva, Poland, and Neuchatel than from the Indians."[66] Ignored is the possibility that a proximate touchstone might serve as a lens for other references. The same kind of argument is used in assessing the institutional details. Responding to the observation that the Albany Plan provided for forty-eight delegates, a number close to the fifty of the Iroquois Confederacy, the same historian insists "forty-eight is not fifty."[67] Limited textual evidence of the flow of ideas, and the paucity of empirical similarities in the respective institutions, prove the quantitative weakness of the Influence thesis. Further, whatever signs of contact with Indians may exist are negated by the racism that kept the two groups apart; bigotry cancels modeling. Thus Francis Jennings has condemned the "Iroquois propagandists," wondering how Franklin's "contempt for 'ignorant Savages' can be twisted into praise for them."[68] Yet Franklin's reference to "ignorant savages" comes from a 1751 letter to James Parker in which Franklin writes, "It would be a very strange Thing, if six Nations of ignorant Savages should be capable of forming a Scheme for such an Union, and be able to execute it in such a Manner, as that it has subsisted Ages, and appears indissoluble; and yet that a like Union should be impracticable for ten or a Dozen *English* Colonies, to whom it is more necessary, and must be more advantageous; and who cannot be supposed to want an equal Understanding of their Interests."[69] The letter was written for public consumption and printed in a 1751 pamphlet, "The Importance of Gaining and Preserving the Friendship of the Indians to the British Interest, Considered," before being reprinted the following year in London. One would think that any reader of Franklin would be able to recognize the irony behind this common rhetorical strategy; in the context of Franklin's letter, the argument is that the Six Nations have developed a diplomatic confederacy and we surely can do the same. But even if we acknowledge a deep racism in a Franklin or a Jefferson, Jenning's argument—that an object of antipathy cannot also be a source of influence—remains astonishing.

The debate over Iroquois Influence seems fruitless, as it stands. Although the questions it raises are worthy of a central position in contemporary scholarship, the debate remains marginal, with sharply divergent camps often arguing crude positions. At its heart, the conflict concerns not just the influence of the Iroquois, but the very notion of influence. Assessed solely in terms of ideas or organizational specificities, the case for Iroquois influence seems tenuous, but a richer and more accurate picture emerges once we consider the practical encounters between whites and Native Americans, and the feeling of structures engendered in this contact. The Imperial School historian Randolph G. Adams noted that in the aftermath of the Seven Years' War, there was a growing concern with how "the structure of the empire [was] to be reorganized to meet a situation in which the overseas dominions were no longer 'inconsiderable and distant parcels' to be ruled through absentee Boards of Trade or negligent Colonial Offices, but were to be given a share and a place in the empire commensurate with the dignity which the late war had demonstrated that they possessed." In such a context, "the British Empire [was] not a nation, but a league of nations, for which some suitable machinery [was] to be devised."[70] This was the case on the eve of the Seven Years' War as well, when the organizational solution was sought in the terminology of empires, leagues, and nations united in a hierarchical chain. Numerous political scientists have described the significance of the chain metaphor for aristocratic Europe, as "the metaphoric embodiment of the hierarchical ideal": as Isaac Kramnick writes, "This metaphor of the chain serves two functions. It describes infinite interconnectedness, the continuous linkage of each gradation in creation. It also described the fixity of God's creation. Social ranks are held in place; they are chained to their assigned place."[71] As the Indian treaties illustrate, this was not only a metaphor for British civil society but also for the Britanno-American empire and its constituents, whether other polities (the Shawnees are taken "into your Protection . . . that they may be usefull to and assist you, on all Occasions" and "to secure them from others") or classes (unruly League Warriors are to be strictly controlled).[72] The feudal echoes are particularly strong in the colonials' request "That if any Negroes should run away from their Masters, and the Warriors or Hunters should find any of them in the Woods, they should take them up, and delivering them to the Sheriff of some County in the nearest English Government, when their Masters come for them they shall be paid whatever can be received from their Masters, for the Indian's Service and Trouble."[73] It is thus misleading to compare, as some historians have, the League's chains with the United Nations on the assumption that constituent members were sovereign nations. "Nation" in these treaties served as a loose category, now drawing on racial theory, now touching geohistory, now expressing political theory. Together these meanings may bear "family resemblances," to use Wittgenstein's term,[74] but their kinship is derived from the parent cluster of concepts—nation, league, chain, empire—

that conceptualize a hierarchical union of disparate polities. The Six Nations claim, and are imagined, to exercise hegemony over four nations to the east and five or six nations to the west. Specifically, then, a League exists at the center of a chain of nations, nations being brought into the chain, often in a tributary status of dependence, in order to make the core "greater and Stronger."

The military context is critical here, for colonial security was not significantly challenged by French troops so much as by Indians acting on their own or in alliance with the French. Governor Clinton of New York had called on the British governors to prevent "our losing the Indians and with them a very valuable Branch of Trade" and to "greatly encourage the Indians to be steady to the British Interest."[75] The Albany Plan was decisively and fundamentally about British-Indian union, and we should pair the old name for the ensuing conflict, the "French and Indian War," with its imagined solution, the British and Indian Chain of Friendship. In this respect, the Albany Plan cannot be compared to the Articles of Confederation or the Constitution, which were plans for the permanent legislative and executive unification of the English colonies. The Albany Plan proposed no comparable union, instead narrowly emphasizing only Indian affairs and the related matter of land settlement. It was a fundamentally diplomatic document aiming to unite colonial councils for consistent coordination of security, land transfers, and trade with Indians coordinated by the Iroquois. Although the Board of Trade dismissed the plan as granting too much power to the colonies, Franklin clearly envisioned the Plan as a means for consolidating the British empire in the New World. In 1789, he reflected that if the Albany Plan "or some thing like it, had been adopted and carried into Execution, the subsequent Separation of the Colonies from the Mother Country might not so soon have happened, nor the Mischiefs suffered on both sides have occurred." With a solid defense, the Stamp Act would never have been proposed, the resulting conflicts never have erupted, and "the different Parts of the Empire might still have remained in Peace and Union."[76] Two points follow from this. First, the Albany Plan is an incomplete document, for its unwritten half was without a doubt the similar system already in place among the Indians; this system could not be dictated, nor was it even described by Franklin, possibly for fear of too strong an association with the "ignorant savages" he admittedly sought to copy. Second, the invisible Indian half of the plan was not the Six Nations, but the more extensive tributary system, including the Shawnees, the Delawares, the western "nations," and possibly additional populations to the north and south, over whom the Iroquois were or could be the masters. There should be no doubt that the Iroquois profoundly influenced the Albany Plan of Union, particularly if we accept that they were key members of the union itself. But the opponents of the Iroquois influence thesis are equally correct in challenging the claim that the Albany Plan was a protonationalist document of democratic values. In fact, the plan, as a diplomatic document informed by a racialized concept of the nation, affirmed the separation of polities even as they were unified: peoples were to be the discrete "specialized apparatuses" of the new system, each managing their own "bad People." The Iroquois values embodied in the plan were imperial and hierarchical, whatever the values of Iroquois society itself.

By midcentury, as Pennsylvania became the keystone of British-Native relations, "Pennsylvania's Indian policy had taken on the aspect of international diplomacy."[77] And the Albany Plan, which grew out of this experience, is a diplomatic, *para*national plan, not a national one. It grew out of the institutional feeling of structure of paths and campfires, and it was *in reaction to* this imperial feeling of structure that a colonial nationalism took place. As I suggested earlier, a protonationalism of fusion took shape in the revivals of the dispersed Delawares and the racist violence of the Paxton Boys. As we have situated the Paxton Boys, we might further situate the Delawares in relation to the history of diplomatic relations outlined above. With the turn to the Iroquois in the early 1730s, the Delawares were relocated to the upper Susquehanna Valley to resettle among other refugee groups. Here the "eastern Delawares" were temporarily removed from colonial encroachment, but by the mid-1750s they found themselves in a vise: from the east came speculators, settlers, and missionaries from Connecticut's Susquehannah Company; to the north was the League of the Iroquois; to the south were the settlers of the Paxton area, interested in moving northward; to the west were numerous breakaway Indian groups. When hostilities broke out in 1754, there were many killings in the region, with the first major episode (twenty-two white settlers killed, eleven taken captive) occurring at Penn's Creek, just miles south of Shamokin. In November the mission at Gnadenhütten was raided and ten Moravians killed. By the end of the month, the Shamokin Indians (the same described by Brainerd) had moved north to Nescopeck, where they were dancing "a perpetual war dance"; by December Wyoming Indians were participating in attacks, and by January they were initiating attacks.[78]

We should view this warpath as the Indian parallel to the yeoman march, for it seems likely that the violence from the west and the south forced them to recognize and overcome the danger of their own dispersal much as the farmers around Paxton did. A November 17 message from the Wyoming Indian community to the Gnadenhütten Moravians declared, in words echoing the farmers' petitions, "We are in danger of being attacked on all sides by [Indian] enemies, who are much enraged. We are no less afraid of the white people, who suspect us of having been accessary to the murders, committed in various places. We wish to speak of these matters to the governor of Philadelphia. But we cannot go thither without a proper passport. We are in danger of being murdered by the white people. Tell us therefore what to do." A similar message to Philadelphia declared, "We believe, that We are in great Danger. For We hear the Hatchets fly about our Ears, & we know not, what will befall Us, and therefore We are afraid."[79] No responses came from Philadelphia, Gnadenhütten was turned into ashes, and the only "answer" seemed to come from the militant Shawnees, the Western Delawares, and the "French" Indians: *Fight!* This message was seconded in the spring when the government of Pennsylvania declared war on the Delawares and issued scalp bounties—$130 each for the men, $50 each for the women and children.[80] This is another dimension of the Delaware fusion described earlier, in which military and spiritual cohesion sought to end serial isolation. But it should now be clear that this serial dispersal was imposed institutionally by the Great Chain of Friendship, and most specifically by the Iroquois and their proprietary allies. The petitioning Delawares clearly understood this, as their plea for "a proper passport" suggests. Their ultimate counterreaction was thus also an anti-institutional reaction, a repudiation of their position within the Great Chain, which had made them vulnerable without providing protection. In this case, "Iroquois Influence" proved profoundly negative, as the Delawares sought an anti-Iroquois solution, defined against the Great Chain. We might at this point speak of a "Delaware influence" answering the Iroquois influence of the Albany Plan.

The Spirit of Federalists

In the remainder of this chapter, I want to move toward a definition of federalism as an institutional response to the rural challenges of colonization. We commonly define federalism in one of two ways: in the upper case, in relation to the Federalist Party of Washington, Adams, and Hamilton and the specific programs of 1788–1800; in the lower case, as a broad political philosophy of divided, structured governance between nation and states. How we define the term will determine how we consider its relation to "republicanism," but we generally assume that the latter is an umbrella term for a dominant cultural discourse, while "federalism" denotes a mechanics of government or, narrower still ("Federalism"), a party movement. But we might consider the relation between these terms differently, keeping in mind Thomas Jefferson's claim "that the mass of our countrymen, even of those who call themselves Federalists, are republicans," and the remark of Publius that "according to the degree of pleasure and pride, we feel in being Republicans, ought to be our zeal in cherishing the spirit, and supporting the character of Federalists."[81] Of course, these assessments are partially rhetorical attempts to downplay differences between two competing parties, particularly in the aftermath of such conflicts as the 1800 election, but they also express a truth that federalism and republicanism are more like apples and oranges than ideologies in opposition. And the assessments may even hint that "federalism" is the broader term, encompassing republicanism, as republican synthesizer Gordon Wood suggested when he observed that the "Federalists helped to foreclose the development of an American intellectual tradition in which differing ideas of politics would be intimately and genuinely related to differing social interests."[82] The federalist achievement was the appropriation of the "rhetoric of the Revolution," but reworked, redirected, and redefined within an institutional frame, as if republicanism was the water to be contained in the most appropriate federalist vessel. By this account, federalism is more fundamentally a theory and project of institutional framing than a fleeting political ideology soon to be subsumed by the Whigs; and republicanism is a conceptual subset.

Of course, even these preliminary complications of federalism still identify it as a revolutionary or postrevolutionary phenomenon, but this feeling of structure did not take shape suddenly with the American Revolution. Federalism was constitutive of colonial modernity and the attempt to manage white agrarian settlement and Indian populations, to counter and manage seriality and fusion. The colonial charters, the land offices and rent systems, the posses and militias, the dispersal acts and treaties, the missions and trading delegations and tradeposts—these were all institutional gropings toward some more centralized coordination of the tremendously challenging chaos of the colonial backcountry. The Albany Plan, despite its spectacular failure, marked a significant turning point in this development, inspired as it was by the real or perceived federalism of the Six Nations and the crisis of the pending global military conflict. The Seven Years' War initiated the most concerted drive yet toward federalism as the coordination of the multiple colonial enterprises, and if we are to note any significant shift from the properly colonial period to the national period, it is in the opportunities afforded by the Revolution for still more centralization. These realizations partly developed in reaction to the Articles of Confederation, which appeared alarmingly ineffectual in the face of rural insurrections like the Massachusetts Regulation of 1786. A proper narrative of federalist development would have to take into account the myriad attempts to regulate the serial inactions and group actions of the Revolution's *military* crisis. One of the conventions of Sovietology has been to speak of "War Communism," the crisis of civil war and invasion that reshaped and deformed Bolshevik policy and practice. What came to define communism, according to this analysis, were the specifically military exigencies of 1918–21, which in turn reshaped Bolshevik administration and theory. It is worth considering what it might mean to offer an analogous assessment of eighteenth-century America, in which one could speak of the profoundly military influences upon crucial political formations from the Seven Years' War to the War for Independence. An account of "War Federalism" might extend from the early 1750s' attempts to manage Indian populations through the popular resistance actions of the 1760s and early 1770s, to the attempts to wage war, fund and order an army, and suppress mutinies.

But here I would like to focus on a key cultural dimension of the federalist project: the suppression of group mobilization, or more specifically the serial dispersal of groups. The classic account of this project is *Federalist No. 10*, penned by "Publius" in November 1787. Publius, not James Madison—for, as Albert Furtwangler suggests, the *Federalist Papers* should be viewed as a collaborative project producing an author figure united by a complex compromising outlook and effect.[83] The tenth essay begins by stressing the supreme advantage of "a well constructed Union," namely "its tendency to break and control the violence of faction" (*Debate* 1: 404). Publius clearly has in mind the phenomenon of group fusion, citizens "who are united and actuated by some common impulse of passion, or of interest, adverse to the rights of other citizens, or to the permanent and aggregate interests of the community" (405). Specifically, the dangerous instances of fusion concern class divisions: "the most common and durable source of factions," he writes, "has been the various and unequal distribution of property.... A landed interest, a manufacturing interest, a mercantile interest, a monied interest, with many lesser interests, grow up of necessity in civilized nations, and divide them into different classes, actuated by different sentiments and views" (406). Publius notes, at the outset, the alarm "our most considerate and virtuous citizens" experience at the realization that "our governments are too unstable," with political decisions made with reference to "the superior force of an interested and over-bearing majority" (404). And he concludes that the "*regulation of these various and interfering interests forms the principal task of modern Legislation, and involves the spirit of party and faction in the necessary and ordinary operations of Government*" (406, emphasis added). This last statement is the conceptual breakthrough of Publius's essay, for whereas the established administrative practice was proactively to prevent, or reactively to suppress, fused factions, Publius concludes that factions must always exist and therefore must be *integrated* into a system of administration, rather than be seen—wishfully, naïvely—as external to the system. Publius immediately drives this point home with some surprising analogies of factions and components of the federal system: factions are of course like "legislators," who are "advocates and parties to the causes which they determine" (407). In such a context, "It is vain to say, that enlightened statesmen will be able to adjust these clashing interests, and render them all subservient to the public good," for statesmen *are* parties, and enlightenment in the sense of impartiality is impossible in a context in which "interest would certainly bias his judgment" (407, 406). From this we must conclude that "the *causes* of faction cannot be removed; and that relief is only to be sought in the means of controlling its *effects*" (407).

In thinking about the regulation of effects we encounter a major short-coming of republicanism. "If a faction consists of less than a majority, relief is supplied by the republican principle, which enables the majority to defeat its sinister views by regular vote" (407). But when "a majority is included in a faction"—a reference to the farmers, the class of debtors—"republican principle" no longer provides a safeguard; now republican values become a problem in themselves, justifying the "sacrifice to its ruling passion or inter-est, both the public good and the rights of other citizens" (407–8). This is an interesting insistence on the abstraction of republican ideology, here implicitly acknowledged as a guiding force of the terrifying Shaysites. A complementary and more fundamental *system*—federalism—is needed "to preserve the spirit and the form," if not the results or specific agendas, "of popular government" (408). Once again, Publius insists that faction must be integrated into the system, for it is impossible to prevent majority factions: "neither moral nor religious motives can be relied on as an adequate control," for, weak as they already are in influencing individuals, within the group they "lose their efficacy in proportion to the number combined together" (408).

We might pause here to note that Publius, far from simply defending a par-ticular institutional system, is formulating a rich theory of structure, agency, and culture. He is envisioning a social network threatened by factional attempts to seize certain institutions and transform the whole. Other moments in the *Federalist Papers* develop this theoretical project differently, as in the later papers (conventionally attributed to Hamilton) that explore the social dynamics of judgment through an account of the new juridical sphere. But here Publius focuses specifically upon legislative praxis in a representative government, where "[m]en of factious tempers, of local prejudices, or of sinister designs"—conspirators—"may by intrigue, by corruption or by other means, first obtain the suffrages, and then betray the interests of the people" (409). It is for this reason that a larger, more extensive republic is a good thing—not because the representatives will be better, but because in the larger institution their effects may be better regulated. But this brings us to the heart of *Federalist No. 10*'s insights regarding size. In the small republic, "the fewer probably will be the distinct parties and interests composing it," and "the more frequently will a majority be found of the same party," with the result that "the more easily will they concert and execute their plans of oppression" (410). In a large republic, by contrast, the number of representatives will be raised to a certain level "to guard against the cabals of a few," but the number will be low enough "to guard against the confusion of a multitude" (409). At issue is the *cognitive* dimension of politics, for Publius aims for an objective complexity in the institutional apparatus that will provide just the right perspectival murkiness. "Extend the sphere, and you take in a greater variety of parties and interests," Publius writes; "you make it less probable that a majority of the whole will have a common motive to invade the rights of other citizens; or if such a common motive exists, *it will be more difficult for all who feel it to discover their own strength, and to act in unison with each other*" (410, emphasis added). In other words, the republic must be large enough to make it difficult for the group to "discover" its strength, in both senses of the word—to perceive or to achieve political power. At the same time, the republic must be small enough to offer the "big picture" of the system, and thus to prevent the chaos accompanying seriality, "the confusion of a multitude." In sum, the republic must be of such a size that we can see the system but not see ways of disrupting it.

Let's be clear: the point here is not that federalist totalizers will be smarter or have a better vantage point than the group factionalists. Publius is not crafting a system in which the elites will be all-controlling masterminds, as in the crude caricatures of conspiracy theory. Rather, the goal is an institution that will delimit any political "enlightenment" by imposing the grand vista (which will always favor capital) while obscuring perceptions of immediate factional projects (of farmers, say, but also of specific groups of capitalists). If we situate *Federalist No. 10* in the late eighteenth-century tradition of conspiracy theory, what Publius offers is a plan to *end*, decisively, all conspiracies. And in connecting Publius's observations with conspiracy theory, we can remember Albert Furtwangler's justified skepticism about reading *Federalist No. 10* as a programmatic statement of political philosophy—for example, as an attempt "to defeat Montesquieu by revitalizing Hume."[84] We may better read the essay, he insists, as a situational work of "shifting contexts," at some remove from narrowly theoretical musings. For all that, a situational approach need not imply the absence, or purely contingent use, of theory, and we may discern in Publius's writing the vernacular traditions of certain feelings of structure. Hume and Montesquieu may be legitimating touchstones, but the essay is most deeply concerned with the structures of feeling—the serial field, the explosive group faction, and the drive to institutionalize—that define American politics in the eighteenth century. In theorizing how the series may be affirmed and groups strategically hamstrung, Publius outlines the institutional culmination of colonial federalism.

The analysis by Publius further highlights the challenges posed for antifederalists, who needed to develop a countermovement of decentralized, more or less consistent organizing that could simultaneously overcome seriality, draw on the energies of groups, and resist the permanent dominance of institutions. But as has been observed by the recent historians of antifederalism, the "movement" barely deserves the name, consisting instead of scattered, reactive tendencies that not only failed to cohere but ultimately never articulated a meaningful countersystem. As Saul Cornell notes, "No group in American political history was more heterogeneous than the Anti-Federalists," and even earlier accounts, like Jackson Turner Main's, which adopted the fiction of a unified movement, defined antifederalism as a reactive formation.[85] But this is not to suggest that federalism was (or is) an all-powerful enclosed system. The overreaching and abuses of the Washington and Adams administrations initially weakened federalism by blocking Democratic-Republican participation, and we might read the Pennsylvania Regulation (the Whiskey Rebellion), with its local movements in various central states, as a *potentially* successful attack on early federalism.[86] In the event, however, the federalist response to the insurrection greatly strengthened the federalist system, which consolidated its properly political institution-building with a military-cultural response. As Alexander Hamilton wrote at the outset of the military conflict, "the insurrection will do us a great deal of good and add to the solidity of every thing in this country." In the aftermath he noted, "Our insurrection is most happily terminated. Government has gained by it reputation and strength, and our finances are in a most flourishing condition."[87] The only major yeoman insurrection to follow in the eighteenth century was the Fries Rebellion, the farcical repeat of the Whiskey tragedy. And, although the governmental reaction to the two rebellions was a factor in the Democratic-Republican victory of 1800, the result of that triumph was the absorption of a potentially antifederalist opposition in the federalist system.

The Federalist Synthesis

This and the preceding chapters have suggested that a continual interplay of seriality, fusion, and institution offers an initial sense of "what is colonial about colonial America." Implicit in this presentation has been a narrative overview of colonial culture as well, an overview that should now be presented more explicitly. This reframing is of course open to revision and would need to account for the differing white–Native relations in New England and the South, as well as the powerful presence of chattel slavery. Nonetheless, I hope to sketch a framework that may accommodate, focus, and redirect the republican megasynthesis summarized in the opening chapter.

The starting point is simple. Anglo-American colonization demanded specific forms of rural and urban development: rural for the production of necessities and trade staples, with the reward of land for immigrants, and urban for the empire's local management and administration of that agrarian development, which of necessity included (to different degrees in different regions) the related mercantile activity, relations with the indigenous populations, and forced assimilation of slave labor. Although this development was initially carried out in modest form in seaport settlements and surrounding agricultural areas, migration and entrepreneurial investment quickly fostered what may accurately be called a country-city opposition. Conflicts of varying kinds, typically concerning security and rent, arose, and these were particularly evident in areas where oversight of rural development was strained or inadequate: it is here that we can begin to speak of a *back*country beyond the better-managed country of the littoral periphery.

In this field of conflicts, a vernacular vocabulary quickly developed, focusing on two seemingly opposed areas of social and cultural organization. A vocabulary of *seriality* emerged to address the problems of dispersed settlement, including vulnerability to indigenous peoples, management of property and rent, and cultural cohesion and control, whether political or religious. Given the relatively small-scale and dispersed social patterns of indigenous peoples in eastern North America, which knew no counterpart to Tenochtitlán, the vocabulary of seriality was applied to Native Americans as well, to guide programs of land acquisition, mercantile conquest, cultural conversion, and imperial competition. At the same time, a colonial vocabulary of *fusion* emerged to address the problems of group resistance, whether cultural or violent. Special attention was again given to indigenous peoples and their periodic ability to resist the frequently less unified colonizers. Increasingly, analyses of fusion were applied to acts of group resistance in the backcountry, though of course the analyses had urban and maritime applications as well. That these vocabularies of fusion and seriality developed in tandem suggests that dispersal and cohesion were the two extreme divergences from orderly manageable populations. Each had its European antecedents; neither was a phenomenon unique to the New World. But settler colonization in North America involved extreme degrees and forms of seriality with no parallel in the English countryside, and, in the context of nascent and feeble administrative institutions and procedures, a qualitatively different vulnerability to group fusion. For these reasons, talk of a postcolonial situation—in which colonials and new citizens struggle with and against an imperial culture—focuses too much on the urban-imperial elites at the expense of the rural populations. A more serious cultural challenge was faced in the seriality of the countryside (what Marx was describing with the term "rural idiocy") that resisted the backcountry's integration into the imperial fold, and, at times, in a resistant fusion against urban-colonial administration.

The polarities of fusion and seriality additionally had strong racial inflections, given the dangers and necessities imposed by chattel slavery, which sought to isolate slaves and prevent rebellions, and given the antagonisms with Native Americans, who were simultaneously coded as dispersed squanderers of America's riches and as primitively fused peoples. The contradictions are evident in the concept of the *tribe* (applied to Native Americans *and* Africans), which simultaneously connoted nomadic dispersal and a loose form of protocivilization, and conversely an alien clan-based cohesion. A Mary Rowlandson could simultaneously deride the chaos of savages wandering through the woods while lamenting her own isolation amid the fusion of undifferentiated hellhounds. Or a Crèvecoeur could celebrate the serial freedoms of Native Americans, who could evade the worst horrors of imperial politics, while a James Smith could celebrate the cultural and practical unity of Indian groups, which became models for American freedom. In sum, the Euro-American vernacular of seriality and fusion emerged through specific encounters with racial others, who, in the crises of colonization, were likewise developing vernacular lexicons of seriality and fusion. These lexicons are most obviously evident in the vocabulary of Indian treaties, not to mention in the pan-nativist movements, which foregrounded the serial isolation and dispersal of the smaller Indian polities while advocating forms (typically religious and military) of cultural fusion.

The nexus of this colonially specific understanding of seriality and fusion in turn shaped the development of a colonial vernacular of the institution. Although European institutions and their vocabularies existed in abundance, they could not be seamlessly transferred to the New World: political and religious ferment and experimentation combined with the unique demographic and economic situation of colonial life to prohibit any easy transfer, whatever the minor achievements of Boston or Williamsburg. The result was an explosive and innovative proliferation of institutional forms, and a correspondingly acute interest in the interplay between culture and structure, most evident in conspiracy theories and the framing of colonial charters and state constitutions. During the earliest moments of colonization, while settlements were still small and the rural-urban division negligible, institutionalization was undertaken with some confidence. The situation changed profoundly with the major colonies' "Glorious Revolutions" of the late seventeenth century, with the increasing occurrence of provincial border conflicts and acts of yeoman resistance, and with the growing prospect of indigenous fronts against colonization, from Metacom's to Tecumseh's.

The appearance of new spin-off colonies, a massive increase in immigration and economic production, increasing unrest among Native Americans in the face of further encroachment and past betrayals, and rising tensions between imperial competitors all contributed to a growing sense of administrative crisis. In Pennsylvania, for instance, land management and rent collection were in disarray, with squatting rampant, borders challenged first by Maryland and later by Connecticut, and unrest growing among shabbily overseen Indian populations, for whom the passage from Teedyuscung's Delawares to the refugee settlements like Shamokin may serve as illustration. Meanwhile, competing economic and political agendas among Philadelphia's elites made provincial governance feeble in many spheres. By the middle of the eighteenth century, growing colonial prosperity was accompanied by the sense of a looming crisis brought to a head by the Seven Years' War. The perceived threats of colonial disunion, uncoordinated diplomatic programs, conflicts from London, and threats from Paris were realized by the war's end:

Indian relations were under severe stress, with Pontiac looming large to the west and the Iroquois confederacy showing signs of possible disintegration; a violent insurrection from Paxton promised not only a shift in political power but a bloody sequel in the Wyoming Valley; and the metropole began to turn its administrative eye to colonial confusion, imposing new policies of settlement and taxation.

It is at this moment that we witness the emergence of the colonial genre which may usefully be called the *imperiography*, first emerging in the 1730s and 1740s, blossoming in the 1750s and 1760s. An initial catalogue includes the following: Cadwallader Colden's *History of the Five Indian Nations* (1727 and 1747), Joseph Morgan's *Temporal Interest of North America* (1733), William Douglass's *Discourse Concerning the Currencies of the British Planta- tions* (1739), Franklin's "Proposal for Promoting Useful Knowledge among the British Plantations in America" (1743), Douglass's *Summary, Historical and Political . . . of the British Settlements in North America* (1749–1751), Aaron Burr Sr.'s *Discourse . . . on Account of the Late Encroachments of the French, and Their Designs against the British Colonies in America* (1755), Lewis Evans' *Essays* (1755), Stephen Hopkins's *True Representation of the Plan Formed at Albany for Uniting all the British Northern Colonies* (1755), John Mitchell's *Map of the British and French Dominions in North America* (1755), Franklin's *Interest of Great Britain Considered with Regard to Her Colonies* (1760), James Otis's *Rights of the British Colonies Asserted and Proved* (1764), Thomas Pow- nall's *The Administration of the Colonies* (1764), John Dickinson's *The Late Regulations Respecting the British Colonies on the Continent of America . . .* (1765), Richard Bland's *Enquiry into the Rights of the British Colonies* (1766), John Morgan's *Four Dissertations on the Reciprocal Advantages of a Perpetual Union between Great-Britain and Her American Colonies* (1766), and so on, up to James Adair's *History of the American Indians* and Pownall's *Topographical Description of Such Parts of North America . . .* (1776). If an earlier tradition had developed the *ethnography*, the detailed account of the cultural "nation," as the colonial genre *par excellence*, the eighteenth century witnessed a tran- scendence of these local mappings in the outlines of empire. The character- istic triple focus of such works is revealing: in the continued concern on geog- raphy and agrarian settlement, the rural–urban problem remains central; in the interest in the developing history of Indian nations, Native American diplomacy implicitly emerges as a model or template; and in the transcolonial grandeur of mapping and organizing, the proper extension of the imperial system is brought to America. In a crude sense, these foci combine utopian

ideals of seriality (ordered dispersal), fusion (ordered tribes), and institution (administrative omnipotence). Coordinating a range of aspirations—
management of large populations, oversight of trade, systems of military security, and cultural exchange and assimilation—the imperiographs envisioned
a carefully differentiated hierarchy of "nations," and a cadre of initiated ex-
perts piecing them together. Such is the coalescence of a federalist synthesis
committed to the ambitious administration of the colonies, from the urban
trade centers to the yeoman producers and the indigenous populations. It is
here that we must locate the "creole functionaries," to use Benedict Anderson's term.[88] For in British North America, these functionaries were not
confined to specific provinces but were, rather, circulating among the
colonies: Pownall administering New Jersey and Massachusetts, working for
Loudoun's transcolonial military, and serving the empire at Albany; Franklin
representing Pennsylvania, Massachusetts, and the empire in the royal colony
campaign; Sir William Johnson, overseeing Indian affairs from the New York
frontier. The list could go on and on. Behind this group of imperiographers,
we find a frequent driving force of the federalist syntheses: land speculation,
for which a centrally administered synthesis would provide the needed stability and order to invest in the western lands and reap a profit. We must remember, too, the Native American "functionaries" who played central roles
in this emergent federalist synthesis—agents like Canasatego and the
Mingo "half-kings" overseeing the six Iroquois groups and a host of tributary
peoples. And finally, we should remember the religious federalists, the David
Brainerds, Eleazar Wheelocks, and Charles Chaunceys constructing shad-
owy federalist parallels in the kingdom of God.

The initially abortive practical achievement of this moment was the
Albany Plan, an anglified revision of the Six Nations' confederacy undertaken by a range of imperial placement, colonial functionaries, and land
speculators. By the 1770s, however, the break with Britain offered a new
outlet for institution and the federalist synthesis, in the formation of state
constitutions and the gradual groping toward a federal unification of the
United States of America. Yet the Revolution was hardly the culmination
of the process; it was more a stage along the way, in which the federalists
achieved a stunning victory in the 1780s with the framing of a Constitution
determined to regulate seriality and to cramp, once and for all, provincial
fusion. For all its long-term successes, however, the consolidation was incomplete. The Massachusetts Regulation found a more serious sequel in the
1790s with the Whiskey and Fries Rebellions (two Pennsylvania Regula-

tions), not to mention separatist conspiracies along the borders and the persistent resistance of western Indian populations. The federalist synthesis was an ongoing process in which the Revolution was never the ultimate moment. Despite the common cliché of literary explorations of a triumphant nationalism by century's end, many writers were exploring the persistence of backcountry insurrections, trying to imagine the institutional means for coordinating the continuing colonization of the American backcountry.

Conclusion
Toward an Antifederalist Criticism

Urbane Bifocals

An excellent narrative of the eighteenth-century federalist synthesis may be found in Franklin's 1760 pamphlet, "The Interest of Great Britain with Regard to her Colonies," familiarly known as "The Canada Pamphlet."[1] In this imperiography, written at the winding down of the Seven Years' War, Franklin enters the imperial debate over whether Britain should keep Guadaloupe or "Canada" as its spoils. And, in arguing for the possession of Canada, he develops detailed analyses of the colonial feelings of structure summarized in the preceding chapters. The "bulk of the inhabitants of North America are landowners" (72), and live in a serial isolation:

> The English inhabitants, though numerous, are extended over a large tract of land, 500 leagues in length on the sea-shore; and although some of their trading towns are thick settled, their settlements in the country towns must be at a distance from each other: besides, that in a new country where lands are cheap, people are fond of acquiring large tracts to themselves; and therefore in the out settlements, they must be more remote: and as the people that move out are generally poor, they sit down either where they can easiest procure land, or soonest raise subsistence. (67)[2]

The political economy of colonial land acquisition (note Franklin's restrained reference to "sit[ting] down," or squatting) means that yeoman dispersal in the "out settlements" is a (perhaps the) fundamental reality of colonial life,

although Franklin concedes that differences among the colonies can esca-
late to the fusion of violence. Perhaps with a memory of the Maryland–
Pennsylvania border conflict of the 1730s, he notes "even the people of our
own colonies have frequently been so exasperated against each other in
their disputes about boundaries, as to proceed to open violence and blood-
shed" (66). Indians, meantime, are similarly dispersed by *their* economy (cari-
catured as hunting-and-gathering), though they remain capable of sudden
acts of fusion: "Although the Indians live scattered, as a hunter's life requires,
they may be collected together from almost any distance, as they can find
their subsistence from their gun in their travelling" (67).

Under such circumstances, the institutional binding of the colonies is
extremely weak. The fourteen continental governments "are not only under
different governors, but have different forms of government, different laws,
different interests, and some of them different religious persuasions and different manners," and are not only unable "to effect such an union among
themselves" but cannot even "agree in requesting the mother country to
establish it for them" (90). And here we see the interesting institutional
twist of Franklin's pamphlet, for one of its central points is that the American colonies will never achieve independence given their institutional disorder. The pamphlet thus insists that the colonies will remain part of the
British empire unless "the most grievous tyranny and oppression" intervene
(90). We might view this line of argument as at once an admission of the historic difficulties of colonial federalism—surely there is a soreness at the failure of the Albany Plan of six years earlier—but at the same time an expression of utopian optimism for the future institutional development of North
America upon the acquisition of Canada. The dangers of seriality and fusion
will be minimized, and institution will increase with an equal number of new
colonial governments "on the inland side" (90)—that is, in a more secure
backcountry as it fills with new settlements. One gets the sense that the institutional cohesion of America may at last be achieved with the aggressive
administration and colonization of the "out settlements," the backcountry.

I cite Franklin's "Canada Pamphlet" not only to demonstrate the vernacular presence of the analysis I've been developing, but also to highlight
a very different Franklin than the one we've canonized. The "Canada Pamphlet," with its vocabulary of practical ensembles and its anti-independence,
imperial ambitions, was "one of [Franklin's] most important publications in
pamphlet form," his "first large-scale attempt to influence the British on a matter of major public policy" in the tradition of "broad imperial interests" (53,
59). Yet it is not part of our Franklin canon, which by and large buries the

writings of the 1750s, 1760s, and 1770s between the early prose pieces of the 1720s and 1730s and the stylistically different postrevolutionary writings, of which the *Autobiography* is the most important.[3] My goal in this chapter is to present Franklin as an archfederalist in a broader colonial tradition, but I intend to do this not through an excavation of the imperiographic writings of the "middle Franklin" but via a rereading of that most canonical of texts, the *Autobiography*, which I shall locate squarely in the federalist tradition. Not only do I argue that the *Autobiography* is best read as a masterful, if cagey, guide to early America's feelings of structure, but I stress that the long-established critical resistance to such a reading sheds more light on this federalism than on the more obvious imperial content of works like the "Canada Pamphlet." It is through an engagement with the *Autobiography*, and its progressive movement toward a grand federalism, that we best consider the necessary moves of a critical antifederalism.

Franklin at times lamented never writing his planned volume on "the ART *of Virtue*,"[4] but with the *Autobiography* he gives us a work deserving the title "the ART *of Practical Ensembles*." Further, as preceding references to Franklin have implied, the *Autobiography* can be more carefully situated, not as the classic of "America" but as an urban masterpiece—skipping across Boston, New York, Philadelphia, and London (and written in Paris), but also a bit constrained, defensive, at odds with the surrounding countrysides. It's an underappreciated fact that the narrative breaks off in 1757, which means we lack not only Franklin's account of the war for independence but—more important here—Franklin's analysis of, and outrage at, the Paxton Riots and the Black-Boys, his related miscalculations concerning the Stamp Act and the efforts to achieve a royal governorship, his massive investments in land speculation, and his notorious comments about the rural "*Palatine Boors*" ("swarm[ing] into our Settlements" and "herding together"), which likely cost him reelection to the Assembly in 1764.[5] In other words, Franklin ends his story just before the harshest conflicts with the backcountry, clashes that made this confident master of irony gasp with outrage. Had the narrative continued beyond the scraps of part 4, our portrait of this American icon would perhaps be very different. But we have to deal with what we have, and find the urban Franklin amidst the interplay of parts 1, 2, and 3. There, we find not only a guide to practical ensembles, but also a primer for finding and reading them. The *Autobiography* is, to think of another early American genre, the history and secret history of Franklin's work in one volume. And it is imperative that we figure out how Poor Richard has directed our thinking—how he invited, encouraged, planned a certain reading of his autobiography that has succeeded surprisingly well.

We have to be clearer, from the outset, what readings of Franklin we must avoid. For decades, criticism of the *Autobiography*, often indistinguishable from commentary on the author, has oscillated fairly predictably. On the one hand, Franklin is cast as the ultimate self-made man, the supremely self-reflective philosopher, America's first great canonical writer, a Founding Father in culture as well as in politics. The *Autobiography*, in this view, is the success manual, the uncanny revelation, the sociopolitical manifesto, and literary classic in one. The correlate of Louis K. Wechsler's view of Franklin as "the archetype of the self-made American" is his declaration that the "living words of the *Autobiography* had the power to perform . . . the elusive goal of true education, to change men for the better."[6] Another crew of critics, on the other hand, has found Franklin the typical Enlightenment man, the exemplary rational capitalist, the paradigmatic American. Max Weber famously outlined in Poor Richard the "spirit of capitalism," "the social ethic of capitalist culture," the *Autobiography* specifically capturing a "conversion" to capital's utilitarian virtues.[7] Russel Nye stresses Franklin's position as "true son" of the "Age of Reason," while locating in the *Autobiography* the "essence" of "eighteenth-century America"; more recently, Michael Warner has found in Franklin "the exemplary figure of modernity" who, with his "exemplary modern subjectivity," becomes "the republican man of letters, the citizen of print."[8]

Franklin as exceptional individual—or is it Franklin as embodiment of the system? Franklinologists have creatively worked to have it both ways—Franklin as Supermodel—making a recurrent critical exercise of neatly formulating "the dialectic of the 'simple separate person' and the democratic mass."[9] There are exceptions, but most readings give us this bifocal Franklin: one can either peer down one's nose at the incomparable particulars of the busy hero or, with a slight tilt of the head, gaze upon the imposing horizon of history and nation. What is virtually impossible, though, given the way the two lenses are fitted together, is to focus upon the intermediate terrain of practical ensembles, those energetic clusters midway between personal details and the big picture. Poor Richard once wrote that "*Blame-all* and *Praise-all* are two blockheads."[10] The same could be said for *Individu-All* and *Structur-All*, though this charge shouldn't be taken too ungenerously. It's not that such interpretations are unintelligent or uncreative, but that readings of Franklin are effectively *blocked*, in both senses of the word. These readings have an oppressive, immovable density, like flagstones, and divergent readings—of Franklin as class agent, as booster, as local organizer, as practical revolutionary and/or reactionary—seem impossible, inaccessible, or hopelessly secondary.

Such bifocal readings should be linked to what Walter Benjamin called "the state of emergency" in which the text was written, and are certainly inculcated by the *Autobiography: a federalist reading, stressing individuals and impersonal systems, is written into the text itself.*[11] Central here are the complementary rhetorical achievements of the text's *sincerity effect* and its *analytical frontloading.* The former has critics claiming that the *Autobiography* speaks honestly, revealingly—an ironic perception given Franklin's reputation as master manipulator (what other Founding Father is commonly tagged as "clever," "sly," and "crafty"?). But it is precisely this renown, contrapuntally performed in endless evasion and confession, that enables and magnifies the effect in most of its permutations. Carl Van Doren gives the simplest rendition of the sincerity effect when he says that Franklin "had investigated his own mind till he knew it and was at home there."[12] From such psychology, it is a short step to calling the *Autobiography* "that masterpiece of memory and honesty" (v) or to speak, as does Weber, of its "really unusual candidness" (53). More common is the double-layered, modernist take on sincerity, which stresses not deep realities but performance. Zuckerman speaks of Franklin's "proliferating public images," arguing that Franklin "did not *become* those parts. He *was* his roles.... His life and his account of his life alike affirmed the reality of appearances."[13] Here the autobiography is not the baring of the (serial) sole but its literary-existential constitution. Yet another version of sincerity, loosely structuralist, traces Franklin not through the bared or performed self but via the tactics and interpretive strategies revealed in the text. Michael Warner's reading of the *Autobiography,* for instance, immanently extrapolates Franklin's method of thinking and writing, his attitude toward rationality, and his understanding of the self from some privileged anecdotes, above all those of Young Ben's education. When Franklin "seems only to be recommending a rhetorical tactic," he is in fact presenting "a principle of social discourse" that provides a key to Franklin's actual subjectivity; in this Foucauldian analysis, then, we can learn what "Franklin thought of his own life" through discourse analysis (81, 89).

The second technique, *analytical frontloading,* invites critics to focus unrelentingly on parts 1 and 2, roughly the first half of the text covering Franklin's childhood to his establishment as an independent printer. R. Jackson Wilson, for instance, says that "our attention is... firmly riveted on parts one and two, on the searching and inquisitive boy, the anxious and ingenious young man," these parts telling us "not about how Benjamin Franklin became great" but "about how he became good."[14] Leonard W. Labaree and his coauthors, whose frontloading sets part 1 against parts 2, 3, and 4, concur that the first section of the text offers "an highly personal account" of Franklin's youth before turning to "Franklin's external, rather than his inner, life."[15] Leibowitz says that Franklin "siphoned off most of the emotional power of Part I from the remaining three parts" (55), and Warner cites all the basic anecdotes of part 1, then focuses upon part 2's "Plan of Conduct," which provides the touchstone for "Franklin's career of public involvement"—that is, for parts 3 and 4 (90). The review of most American literature anthologies will confirm this frontloading bias; most reproduce part 1 and most of part 2, with only scraps of part 3, if any.[16] Such bias is far from surprising. In the early sections of the *Autobiography*, we learn (in part 1) about Franklin's view of the autobiographical project; his family and childhood; his early educational experiences of reading, writing, speaking, and printing; his move to Philadelphia, and his search for meaningful employment; his first encounters with women and with politicians; his musings on reason, persuasion, and religion; his travels to London; his long-term moral and business plans; his establishment of the Junto and library. And we discover (in part 2) some reflections on morality, religion, and self-examination. Compare these thematics with those of parts 3 and 4: general reflections on political history; observations on the Great Awakening and specific religious sects; extension of the printing business and the Junto; establishment of a reformed city watch, fire departments, a militia, the Philosophical Society, an academy, a hospital, paved and lit streets, a reformed postal system; inventions and scientific experiments; the beginnings of a political career and its arcane institutional conflicts; and details of the Seven Years' War. Not only does the division conform to Franklin's own distinction between "the necessary close Attention to private Business in the early part of Life, and public Business since,"[17] but the "public Business" seems a systemic extension of "private" reflections, expressive of the first half's foundational analyses of rationality, strategic communication, moral programs, psychological self-examination, intellectual influences, literary experimentation, political manipulation, and cultural organization. In short, Franklin's public career seems to proceed organically from his private development, his politics from his psychology, his adult projects from his childhood and adolescent formation. It goes without saying that this critical frontloading—with its valorization of the overtly formative, emotional, moral, personal, interior, energetic, and powerful—reinforces the sincerity effect and vice versa, and each in turn sharpens the bifocal perspective framed above. Frontloading magnifies the individual, then gives the impression of established systems as the text tapers off, while the sincerity effect directs our attention away from the parochial details of part 3 back to the revelatory, personal anecdotes of parts 1 and 2. Each, in other words, diverts us from practical collectives.

I want to suggest at the outset that these two features of Franklin's *Autobiography* embody a social tactic: they are *not* the result of a naturalized new subjectivity's "accession to language," but a strategy developed for a certain class politics, that of the petty bourgeoisie. No term will seem uglier, more anachronistic, to many Early Americanists than "petty bourgeoisie," combining the alien and inappropriate class vocabulary of Europe with a demeaning adjective. But no term seems better suited for Franklin, particularly when we give it its dialectical meaning: it refers less to a static set of descriptors (ownership of a business but with few employees, some kind of moderate income—that is, the early Franklin of the printshop) than to a relational position between the bourgeoisie and the wage-earning working class: "Aspiring to the position of the first, the least adverse turn of fortune hurls the individuals of this class down into the ranks of the second."[18] Franklin's *Autobiography* of course reads as the comic version of the petty bourgeois position, clearly (and retrospectively) on the rise. And to appear universal, it must not only conceal the means by which the bourgeoisie keeps its special position, but also conceal the means by which the petty bourgeoisie establishes security. It is no surprise, then, that the internal template for the autobiography is the apprenticeship, through which one graduates—if he follows the rules and gets his education—to a high class position: what we're given here is an apparently accessible and obvious manual for a similar apprenticeship to language and culture, one that we might all follow in our own American pursuit of success. The punchline is that Franklin violated his own apprenticeship contract (with his brother James), and, as I show below, used and described unconventional and only partially accessible tactics to rise to the bourgeoisie. So we might revise Weber's argument and suggest that Franklin had to write, if not follow, a program describing the mythical "work ethic" and "spirit of capitalism," and crucial to this was an emphasis on basic individual principles (via the sincerity effect and analytical frontloading) to make the system seem a logical extension open to all. This Weberian fantasy was spelled out in parts 1 and 2, while the details of Franklin's class mobility are tucked away, in plain sight, in part 3.

But this view is still too abstract, focusing on "the petty bourgeois" removed from his particular contexts. We also need to consider the very particular political coordinates of Franklin's career, evident in the different contexts of the *Autobiography*. Part 1 (August 1771) was written by Franklin the British Whig factotum unsure where his career was heading, part 2 (mid-1784) by the American in Paris at the end of the Revolution unsure where America's career was heading, and part 3 (August 1788 to May 1789) by a postrevolutionary Federalist.[19] This identification of political context is important not because Franklin's political outlook changes radically between parts 1 and 4, that he went from being a Whig to being some kind of "conservative." Rather, Franklin's participation in the constitutional convention and his affiliation with the new political system meant that his institutional and discursive position shifted radically: he came to occupy an "anti-Whig" position, upholding, in the context of Pennsylvania, the centralized urban republic against confederal rural democrats. More exactly, part 3 was written immediately after the great strategic battle for ratification of the U.S. Constitution had essentially been won (by August 1788, eleven state conventions had ratified), and as Franklin was finally withdrawing from institutional politics (service as president of Pennsylvania's Supreme Executive Council until 14 October 1788). The first portion of part 3, written in August 1788, came on the heels of a period of aggressive Antifederalism in Pennsylvania and before the final bursts of that resistance in September.[20] If the Franklin of part 1 wrote quietly from the left of the imperial system, that of part 2 from the hazy moment of national construction, the Federalist Franklin of part 3 was fully parrying attacks from the left in a new national system in which the discourse of competing political positions was much more open. But this later Franklin was carefully veiled behind the comic individualism of the early, stealthier Franklins.

To counter the *individu-all* and *structur-all* readings of Franklin, to challenge Franklin's petty bourgeois myth-making, to unpack the shifty political positions of Franklin's career, to crack the seeming system of the *Autobiography*, we need an Antifederalist reading of the text, one that commences by taking issue with the operations of this federal text. And in fact some guidelines for such a counterreading can be found in part 3, in its opening "OBSERVATIONS on my Reading History in Library" (dated from 1731 by Franklin). Here we're offered a new twist on the platitude that history is driven by "Parties." Young Franklin had blasted this cliché to atoms with a hard methodological individualism, maintaining that all parties are gatherings of individuals driven by self-interest and therefore ever fragmenting into "Divisions." Is this a confirmation of the "individualist" readings of Franklin? Not quite, for Franklin's solution to this endless atomization is the vision of a qualitatively distinct collective: "There seems to me at present to be great Occasion for raising an united Party for Virtue, by forming the Virtuous and good Men of all Nations into a regular Body, to be govern'd by suitable good and wise Rules, which good and wise Men may probably be more unanimous in their Obedience to, than common People are to common Laws" (1395). Franklin proceeds to explain that this "Party" would first cohere covertly in "Sect" form under the name of "the Society of the *Free and Easy*," a gathering of "young and single Men only," recruiting further members from "ingenuous well-disposed Youths" (1396). The "Sect" would "be begun & spread" and adopt a deist creed and a moral self-examination program, but "the Existence of such a Society should be kept a Secret till it was become considerable"—at which point, presumably, it would blossom forth as the United Party for Virtue. Meantime, "the Members should engage to afford their Advice Assistance and Support to each other in promoting one another's Interest Business and Advancement in Life" (1396). We catch here one of Franklin's proleptic fantasies of federalism, and in strongly petty bourgeois terms: a sect that at last will transcend "Division" in the definitive establishment and management (at the crucial yet undefined moment of revelation) of a moral, political, and economic system of order.

Franklin immediately downplays the significance of this scheme, saying first that he planned to undertake it "when my Circumstances should afford me the necessary Leisure" (1396), then that his "narrow Circumstances, and the Necessity I was under of sticking close to my Business, occasioned my Postponing the farther Prosecution of it at that time, and my multifarious Occupations public & private induc'd me to continue postponing, so that it has been omitted till I have no longer Strength or Activity left sufficient for such an Enterprize" (1397). Given that this historical program follows from and builds upon Franklin's "bold and arduous Project of arriving at moral Perfection" (1383), elaborated in part 2, readers are invited to dismiss the United Party scheme—as a youthful utopian fantasy, as a gag to be read ironically, as an index to the author's general political commitments (virtue beyond party). But two motifs of part 3, sects and boosterism, demonstrate that Franklin never left the project behind, and even indicate that his early career, as mapped in part 3, is the practical application of the "OBSERVA-TIONS." In tracking Franklin's understanding of these two phenomena, we find a theory of culture and language that leaves behind the facile self-nation correspondence. What emerges, in short, is a federalist theory of culture that, brought to light, might serve as the foundation for an antifederalist methodology.

The Joy of Sects

Part 3 abounds with the discussion and analysis of sects and their operation, commencing with Franklin's discussion of the 1735 controversy surrounding Irish Presbyterian Samuel Hemphill. Hemphill, Franklin tells us, "delivered with a good Voice, & apparently extempore, most excellent Discourses, which drew together considerable Numbers of different Persuasions, who join'd in admiring them" (1399). But the nascent sect forming around the reverend collapsed when orthodox Presbyterians arraigned Hemphill on charges of heterodoxy; shortly thereafter it was discovered that Hemphill had plagiarized his sermons, which "Detection gave many of our Party Disgust" (1400). Still, while Hemphill was under assault, Franklin "became his zealous Partisan, and contributed all I could to raise a Party in his Favour; and we combated for him a while with some Hopes of Success" (1400). In the end, Hemphill was defeated and expelled from the church, and a defeated Franklin left institutionalized religion for good. Most readers of the *Autobiography* have passed over this single-paragraph episode as a minor, passing clue to Franklin's *religious* views.[21] But the clash surrounding the Hemphill affair was, as Merton A. Christensen observes, of great importance to Franklin, for it was one of his first conflicts with an established institution as well as his first serious—and ultimately unsuccessful—foray into that vital field of pamphlet warfare (422–23). Of the twelve or so essays written during the trial, Franklin wrote three, perhaps four, raging polemical pamphlets, which together reveal a certain education regarding the use and power of "Discourses."[22]

Theologically, Hemphill stressed exterior norms of good works and moral behavior over doctrinal inner experiences. Franklin gave mildly hyperbolic expression to the contrast in his first essay on the affair, the "Dialogue between Two Presbyterians" printed in the *Pennsylvania Gazette*, writing that "Morality or Virtue is the End, Faith only a Means to obtain that End: And if the End should be obtained, it is no matter what Means."[23] Such a pronouncement immediately extends the Weberian commonplace that utilitarian and instrumentalizing principles permeate Franklin's thought, here colonizing even his theology. But more striking is the insertion of this utilitarianism into cosmology; as with the Society of the Free and Easy's deist creed, the resulting blend yields an interesting sociology. In summing up the spiritual universe in "A Defense of Mr. Hemphill's Observations," Franklin described "the End and Design of the Christian Revelation, or what View the Author of it had in coming into the World," by asserting that "the main Design and ultimate End of the christian Revelation, or of Christ's coming into the World, was to promote the Practice of Piety, Goodness, Virtue, and Universal Righteousness among Mankind, or the Practice of the moral Duties both with Respect to God and Man, and by these Means to make up happy here and hereafter." He concluded, "All the Precepts, Promises, Threatnings, positive Institutions, Faith in Jesus Christ, and all the Peculiarities and Discoveries in this Revelation tend to this End."[24] God, then, is every bit as utilitarian as Franklin, making a tool of himself (called Jesus) and creating a number of "Means to make us happy." Left to function according to plan, such godly tools and methods could create a spiritual unity in Christian society, a godly Constitution of a federalist hue. But as is often the case, heavenly Ends and Designs get mucked up by human factions. Thus Franklin laments about Philadelphia what God no doubt bemoans as well, that "[e]ven in this City we have half a Dozen, for aught I know half a Score, different Sects; and were the Hearts of Men to be at once opened to our View, we should perhaps see a thousand Diversities more." "Creeds or Confessions may perhaps bring upon some small Christian Societies, an external Show, and outside Appearance of Unanimity in religious Sentiments," he continues, but "this is the very best Effect they can produce. A poor, an inconsiderable, a bad one indeed!"[25]

This assessment of Philadelphia's religious community—with Sects wildly proliferating into a world of One Man, One Creed—clearly echoes concern with endless fragmentation from the 1731 "Observations." But now, instead of advocating a transcendent United Party, public pamphleteer Franklin apparently opts for the familiar liberal position: "I cannot help thinking, that allowing Christians as much Liberty as is here contended for, is the likeliest Means to produce that very Unity, or Uniformity, so much recommended. . . . [A]t least an inward Unity, a Unity of Affection, which is infinitely preferable, would in all Probability soon spring from Liberty."[26] What distinguishes this credo from garden variety liberalism is Franklin's delineation of the necessary preconditions for, and limitations to, unity-producing liberties. Religious freedom leads to "Unity of Affection," yes, but only in the context of the clever "Designs" of the Almighty, who quietly slipped us Precepts, Promises, Threatnings, positive Institutions, Faith in Jesus Christ, and other such goodies.

It would be a mistake, then, to focus on Franklin's vaguely whiggish philosophy of religion here or on its corollary, the condemnation of partisan, factional sects. For Franklin is outlining a proto-federalist theory of salvation, in which higher powers *draw upon and use* sects to establish the ordered framework and mechanisms within which puny mortals find the truth, seemingly on their own. The crucial point to be gleaned from the Hemphill affair, then, is that Franklin undertook to engineer the institutional framework for Pennsylvania's famous religious liberalism—in other words, that he attempted to actualize his prospectus for the United Party of Virtue. The connection between the two becomes even clearer when we trace the parallels between the hypothetical and secretive United Party of Virtue and Hemphill's ministry. For the latter, according to Franklin, was a more or less ecumenical sect devoted to "the Practice of Virtue," bringing together arduous followers from "People of all Persuasions,"[27] and to which Franklin, as he recalls in the *Autobiography*, allied himself not as a devotee or member or follower but as a "Partisan" seeking to "raise a Party" through combat (1400). What's more, this ministry was to avoid and supersede the cardinal limitation of sects and parties ("Divisions") here manifest in the doctrinal disputes of the Presbyterian Church and the dozens of sects "in this City." In short, it was to be a Party encompassing Parties, a Sect incorporating Sects.

In part 2 of the *Autobiography*, Franklin tells how, having been raised Presbyterian, he at first "regularly paid my annual Subscription for the Support of the only Presbyterian Minister or Meeting we had in Philadelphia" (1382–83). But this minister, Jedediah Andrews, who would lead the charge against Samuel Hemphill, was a poor preacher in Franklin's eyes, for "his Discourses were chiefly either polemic Arguments, or Explications of the peculiar Doctrines of our Sect, and were all to me very dry, uninteresting and unedifying, since not a single moral Principle was inculcated or enforc'd, their Aim seeming to be rather to make us Presbyterians than good Citizens" (1383). The "Discourses" of Andrews—confirming Franklin's sober "Observations"—can be contrasted with those of Hemphill, which were not "dogmatical" but "inculcated strongly the Practice of Virtue, or what in the religious Stile are called Good Works" (1399–1400). We seem to be firmly in the world of part 1, in which Franklin contrasts an older, rigid approach to language (Andrews) with the newer, more constructive, and dynamic view of discourse (Hemphill). In fact, however, the lesson of the Hemphill affair has to do less with competing rhetorical strategies (pragmatic vs. dogmatic) than with *cultural infrastructure*. For, though Hemphill promotes his views, even seems popular and successful to a certain degree, Andrews, with the church around him, triumphs. In this way, part 3 alludes to an important lesson about language carefully omitted from parts 1 and 2. For the Synod Commission crushed Hemphill through a range of tactics documented by Franklin in his denunciatory pamphlets. They packed the tribunal with hostile judges, waged an indirect campaign in local congregations, and restricted testimony at Hemphill's trial. To these maneuvers, Franklin and his man responded naïvely. Hemphill refused to cooperate with the commission's inquiry on the principled grounds that it was unjustly stacked against him, while Franklin adopted the naïve Enlightenment fiction of the apocalyptic critical dialogue. In detailed and sophisticated textual analysis, he explained how Hemphill's sermons had been decontextualized, misinterpreted, and distorted, how they were in fact sensible and incontrovertible, how the tribunal's positions were inconsistent, contradictory, outrageous. Like an early Habermasian committed to communicative rationality, Franklin sought to lay bare the public sphere and to offer a purely discursive (and metadiscursive) defense of Hemphill. This, despite a basic assumption of his 1731 "Observations": one needs a solid party structure, base, and vanguard to utilize discourse effectively, to inculcate values and beliefs.

The problem, in 1734–35, was that Andrews, the Synod, and the Commission firmly commanded the institutional framework Franklin sought to exploit. In adopting the enemy terrain, Franklin, as much as Hemphill, may have had no choice but to respond "naïvely." The alternative would have been to outflank the church institutions from the start, as the itinerant George Whitefield and others would do a few years later in the Great Awakening. That Franklin recognized the difference comes across in the *Autobiography*'s unsettling assessment of Whitefield. Franklin first notes that Whitefield was forced out of the pulpits and into the fields, where he preached to "Multitudes of all Sects and Denominations"—that is, where he transcended the limitations of sects. What most impressed Franklin, however, was the "extraordinary influence of [Whitefield's] Oratory on his Hearers, and how much they admir'd & respected him, notwithstanding his common Abuse of them, by assuring them they were naturally *half Beasts and half Devils*" (1406). Franklin remarks how "wonderful" it was "to see the Change soon made in the Manners of our Inhabitants" (1406), and later (in his correspondence) compares Whitefield to "Confucius, the famous eastern reformer" who managed the careful top-down transformation of society in contrast to "[o]ur more western reformations [which] began with the ignorant mob." Actually, Franklin dreams of a reformation combining "both methods," "eastern" and "western," the guiding masters harnessing those ignorant mobs—a beautiful insider's description of federalism.[28] Whitefield, then, succeeds for a time where Hemphill could not; he inculcated good values into the masses without the interference of partisan churchmen.

Of course this circumvention also hindered Whitefield when he was later charged with corruption and graft and exposed to criticism because of his extensive "Writing and Printing": "Unguarded Expressions and even erroneous Opinions del[d] in Preaching might have been afterwards explain'd, or qualify'd by supposing others that might have accompany'd them; or they might have been deny'd; But *litera scripta manet*" (1409). The written word remains . . . but this is not a naïve lapse into pure discourse analysis. Franklin maintains that Whitefield's opponents cynically "attack'd his Writings violently, and with so much *Appearance* of Reason *as to diminish the Number of his Votaries, and prevent their Encrease*" (1409, emphasis added)—i.e., they wrote not to correct or contradict his doctrine, not to set the doctrinal record straight, but to weaken his sect. Had Whitefield been more cautious, "his Reputation might in that case have been still growing, even after his Death," for "his Proselites would be left at Liberty to feign for him as great a Variety of Excellencies, as their enthusiastic Admiration might wish him to have possessed" (1410). The question of Whitefield's actual virtues suddenly becomes moot as the printer imagines the United Party that might have been: taking shape from Whitefield's powerful inculcations, it assumes a regularity, a systematicity, of its own, the charged proselytes rallying around the absent, idealized master. But the Whitefield sect needed an infrastructure of something other than discourse.

As Franklin proceeds to diagnose other Pennsylvania sects throughout part 3, he speaks most approvingly of the Dunkers (the Church of the Brethren). Dunker leader Michael Welfare complained to Franklin that "they were grievously calumniated by the Zealots of other Persuasions, and charg'd with abominable Principles and Practices to which they were utter Strangers" (1416). Franklin advised Welfare that "this had always been the case with new Sects; and that to put a Stop to such Abuse, I imagin'd it might be well to publish the Articles of their Belief and the Rules of their Discipline" (1416). Another lapse into the discursive strategy of the Hemphill affair—though Franklin had learned better in the meantime, as I will show below. Welfare was not so naïve and explained that the Dunkers did not want to write down their doctrine for fear of inhibiting change: "we fear that if we should once print our Confession of Faith, we should feel ourselves as if bound & confin'd by it, and perhaps be unwilling to receive farther Improvement; and our Successors still more so, as conceiving what we their

Elders & Founders had done, to be something sacred, never to be departed from" (1417). Franklin lauds the modesty of the Dunker sect, but does not follow up on the Dunker conflict, does not openly assess Dunker strategy. Clearly, though, the Dunkers had adopted a sound tactic (*shut up and organize*) that might be read as a corollary to that of the Presbyterians (*shut up, we're organized*).

One more sectarian example: perhaps the most important sect to receive extended treatment, throughout part 3 is the Quakers, although the emphasis is no longer upon internal organization and expansion but upon the maintenance of power. By the time of Franklin's arrival in Philadelphia, the Quakers had become established colony leaders, dominating the legislature, the courts, the loan office, and the municipality of Philadelphia. (The proprietary faction, around which gathered most prominent Anglicans, maintained control of the Land Office and Indian affairs, but was on the defensive until the 1750s and 1760s. Quaker hegemony, largely consolidated around the end of the seventeenth century, continued with little interruption until the march of the Paxton Boys.) Franklin's discussion of the Quakers focuses on Pennsylvania's defense during two military crises, King George's War (1744–48) and the Seven Years' War (1756–63); each involved public panic over defensive preparations, as well as a quandary for Quaker politicos—they largely controlled the political institutions and the provincial infrastructure, yet were immobile in these crises.[29] Their dilemma afforded Franklin incredible political opportunities, which I discuss in more detail in the next section. Here my interest is in the lessons learned from the Quakers as they passively and tacitly supported the defense movement. Uncertain how to respond to the war crises, the Quakers developed "a Variety of Evasions to avoid Complying, and Modes of disguising the Compliance when it became unavoidable" (1415), three of which are discussed by Franklin. The first concerned a proposal whereby Franklin's local fire department would spend £60 of its stock on a lottery to finance a riverside battery. Of the thirty members, twenty-two were Quakers, and votes on expenditures had to take place at the meeting *following* any proposal. The eight non-Quakers arrived at the next meeting to vote for the expense, but only one Quaker pacifist appeared; meanwhile Franklin was informed by two other Quakers that a party of eight Quakers stood ready at a nearby tavern to support the non-Quakers, but only "if there should be occasion, which they hop'd would not be the Case" (1414). As many as twenty-one Quakers, then, cast invisible votes and left the non-Quakers to take charge of their dues. The second instance, a macrovariant of the first, concerned the Assembly's evasion-of-choice, voting funds "under the Phrase of its being *for the King's Use* . . . never to enquire how it was applied" (1415). The third mode, a variation of the second, concerned requests specifically for military provisions. When a demand arose for funds for gunpowder, the Assembly granted £3,000 "for the Purchasing of Bread, Flour, Wheat, *or other Grain*"—the last a veiled reference to gunpowder (1416).

The cultural lessons here concern three interrelated "modes of disguising": (a) hide your actions by making others seem responsible; (b) speak generally and don't outline the details; and (c) if you have to get into details, distract with the particulars. Critics often note (in reference to part 1) that when Franklin outlines a principle of language, he proceeds to give an example in the text. For example, when he criticizes "abrupt Contradiction" in part 1, opting instead for "the Habit of expressing my self in Terms of modest Diffidence," Franklin immediately gives a demonstration of this principle in the text: "This Habit I believe has been of great Advantage to me. . . . This however I should submit to better Judgments" (1321–23). The same routine is evident here, as Franklin camouflages the unenergetic details of the "modes of disguising" (typical of part 3) with several witticisms (typical of part 1). After describing the Quakers' lottery maneuver, Franklin recounts an anecdote in which William Penn was traveling by ship with his secretary James Logan; when the ship sighted what appeared to be an enemy warship, Penn retired below decks. Logan "chose to stay upon Deck, and was quarter'd to a Gun." After the discovery that the other ship was friendly, Penn rebuked Logan for taking up a weapon: "This Reproof being before all the Company, piqu'd the Secretary, who answer'd, *I being thy Servant, why did thee not order me to come down: but thee was willing enough that I should stay and help to fight the Ship when thee thought there was Danger*" (1415). Logan's response, like all good Franklin punch lines, distorts the question at hand. In the midst of this appreciative yet prosaic documentation of Modes of Disguising, we are thrown a gag that evokes an antithetical affect. The joke stings Penn, whose actions are cast as cowardly and ungracious, as it praises Logan, who, though a Quaker, responds forthrightly. Yet the surrounding, "serious" exposition makes *the opposite point:* careful evasion is laudable, forthright action naïve. The decisive clause in the joke is "being before all the Company": Penn was indiscreet, embarrassed Logan, blew his cover, invited the harsh punch line. In fact, then, the joke *narrative* masks, by inversion, the joke *function:* seeming also indiscreet and embarrassing, blowing the Quaker cover, the gag discreetly veils Franklin's insight and preserves his cover—hiding his actions, distracting with particulars. The other joke of this segment operates similarly. In a play on the "grain" pun, Franklin quips to a fellow volunteer fireman, "if we fail [in getting a Battery], let us move the Purchase of a Fire Engine with the Money; the Quakers can have no Objection to that: and then if you nominate me, and I you, as a Committee for that purpose, we will buy a great Gun, which is certainly a *Fire-Engine:* I see, says [my friend], you have improv'd by being so long in the Assembly; your equivocal Project would be just a Match for their Wheat *or other Grain*" (1416). Again the joke's directed affect distracts us from the immediately preceding lesson of an effective, admired, and approved Mode of Disguising. We are invited to find the wordplay farcical or preposterous, to share the muted disapproval of the sly, scheming politician exposed by Wry Old Ben. But the parody not only distances Franklin from the Quakers, it distances him from himself; by mock-acting the Quaker tactic, he distracts us from his lower-key approval, his later adoption of related tactics, and his use of these methods in the very text we're reading.

Boosterism

One could further document the joy of sects, out of which Franklin began to *theorize* organizations, thinking carefully about the relationship between institutional infrastructure and language. What emerges is not just a simple theory of secrecy, but more accurately a sectarian hermeneutics: *interpretation requires a sociological mapping, meaning emerges from the lay-out of practical ensembles.* To appreciate the development of this point in Franklin's narrative, we pause to situate the "sect" in the context of the practical ensembles discussed earlier. Franklin adopts a definition of the sect close to what Sartre characterized as "statutory groups," roughly meaning groups making the transition from ephemeral fusion to institutional permanence. Franklin's sects, whether scientific, religious, or political, are mostly newborns struggling to move from ideological and discursive commitment to an established place in the institutional domain.[30] They figure prominently in part 3, insofar as they parallel Franklin's apprenticeship: he too is trying to move, as a character, from youthful philosophical beliefs to practical power, as his "OBSERVATIONS" fully attest. The lessons of sects are somewhat basic when not cursorily read as extensions of the false individualism of part 1: *Ideology is not the same as infrastructure. Don't fight organizational battles with fervor and discourse. Battles over words are rarely about words.* What this view ultimately suggests is a fatal division in the very concept of the "sect," a concept that (like "party") implies both an ensemble and a belief system. The specifically sectarian danger is that an abstracted ideology will become a joy in itself, and distract one from the necessary practical details.

This implicit critique of sects explains the shift, in part 3, from sects to civic enterprises, the boosterism of Franklin's practical efforts to implement the United Party for Virtue. Denials notwithstanding, Franklin had already, four years before the "Observations," inaugurated a Society of the Free and Easy. This was of course the Junto, established in 1727, passed over by most Franklinologists as a "Club, for mutual Improvement" or, more grandly, Franklin's "benevolent lobby for the benefit of Philadelphia."[31] The aptly named Junto is initially discussed as more or less a cultural club in part 1 of the *Autobiography*; members would discuss and debate "any Point of Morals, Politics or Natural Philosophy," read essays, and the like (1361). Franklin mentions only matter-of-factly how the club helped him procure business (1362–63). But such accounts are typical of the Modes of Disguising of part 1, and an examination of the standardized club rules, proposals, and queries reveals the economic impetus driving the club.[32] Of the twenty-four standard questions to be asked at every meeting, only the first was "cultural" in the belle-lettristic sense. Questions 3, 4, and 5 immediately plunge into business analysis, before the questions move on to others' personal behavior (questions 6–8, 12, and 13) and to practical mutual assistance (questions 9 and 10). Still, the striking characteristic of the queries is not so much their thematic emphasis upon prosperity and material improvement as their *strategic furtiveness*.

It's illuminating to compare the Junto questions with their alleged model, the standard queries of Cotton Mather's "Reforming Societies," also called "Societies for the Suppression of Disorder." Mather's questions may date back to the late 1670s and were finally published in his long essay "Bonifacius" (later known as "Essays to Do Good") in 1710.[33] In 1784, Franklin wrote Samuel Mather that "Essays to Do Good" "gave me such a turn of thinking, as to have an influence on my conduct through life,"[34] and re-publication of the questions in Samuel Mather's *The Life of the Very Reverend and Learned Cotton Mather* (1729), around the time Franklin formed the Junto and prepared his questions, certainly suggests an influence. The common claim in Franklin studies is that the Philadelphian secularized, humanized, and/or further developed the program of Boston's stern societies—transforming them, in effect, from cudgels into clubs (Levin, 75; Van Doren, 75). But this reading obscures more than it clarifies. Cotton Mather's "REFORMING SOCIETIES" were to be "an incomparable and invaluable blessing to a town, whose welfare shall become the object of their watchful enquiries," serving as moral *"garrisons"* engaged in surveillance of the frontiers of sin.[35] Another of Mather's metaphors casts the societies as lamps that could "soon irradiate a place," and the imagery elsewhere presents the societies as aggregate ministers in the pulpits of society.[36] Each of these metaphorics—garrisons, lamps, pulpits—asserts a strategic visibility. But Franklin seems to have gleaned something very different from Mather's societies. Instructive here (although in a typically oblique way) is Franklin's anecdote about Cotton Mather recounted (in the letter mentioned above) to Samuel Mather. "The last time I saw your father was in the beginning of 1724," writes Franklin, "when I visited him after my first trip to Pennsylvania. He received me in his library, and on my taking leave showed me a shorter way out of the house through a narrow passage, which was crossed by a beam over head. We were still talking as I withdrew, he accompanying me behind, and I turning partly towards him, when he said hastily, *"Stoop, stoop!"* I did not understand him, till I felt my head hit against the beam. He was a man that never missed any occasion of giving instruction, and upon this he said to me, *"You are young, and have the world before you; STOOP as you go through it, and you will miss many hard thumps."*[37] The little narrative sounds just like the folksy fable two septuagenarians would share, and Franklin's supplementary moral, like the morals of Aesop, nearly ruins the story: "This advice, thus beat into my head, has frequently been of use to me; and I often think of it, when I see pride mortified, and misfortunes brought upon people by their carrying their heads too high."[38] Better to strip away Franklin's pushy reading, his moral atop the moral, and read the tale as a creatively indirect prose poem. The young man, after initiation into the intellectual world of his elder, exits via a narrow shortcut; not watching his way, not grasping the older man's advice, talking too much, he cracks his head against a hard structure. And we'll crack our heads too if, babbling appreciatively, we turn to listen to Franklin's bland moralizing, ignoring the complexities of his private passage. Yes, Franklin may adequately paraphrase Mather, this fable may have been a commentary on pride. But the "stooping" that Franklin seems to have learned from Mather concerns not so much modesty as stealth, not so much bowing one's head as keeping one's head low.

Mather's first question asks, "Is there any REMARKABLE DISORDER in the place, that requires our endeavor for the suppression of it, and in what good, fair, likely way may we endeavor it?" Compare this with the closest parallel in the Junto series: "Hath any citizen in your knowledge failed in his business lately, and what have you heard of the cause?" Mather's second question asks, "Is there any PARTICULAR PERSON whose *disorderly behav-*

iors may be so scandalous & so notorious that we may do well to send unto the said person our charitable *admonitions?* Or, are there any *contending persons*, whom we should admonish, to quench their *contentions?*" But Franklin's seventh question, the closest analogue, inquires, "What unhappy effects of intemperance have you lately observed or heard of? of imprudence? of passion? or of any other vice or folly?" Mather: "Do we know of any Person languishing under sad and sore AFFLICTION; and is there anything that we may do, for the succor of such an afflicted neighbor?" Franklin: "Hath any body attacked your reputation lately? And what can the Junto do towards securing it?"[39] With the "Reforming Societies," then, the emphasis is upon suppression and correction, admonition and assistance; we strengthen the society so as to strengthen Society, to consolidate the existing order of things. For the Junto, the stress is upon observation and analysis, security and retaliation: we strengthen the cell so as to strengthen the Sell, to extend slowly and furtively a new social and economic network.

To such an end, the Junto, around 1736, secretly extended itself from its core group of twelve. "We had from the Beginning made it a Rule to keep our Institution a Secret," Franklin explains early in part 3, but now there was a drive by some to increase membership. How to have it both ways, to expand while maintaining the secret core? "I was one of those who were against any Addition to our Number," Franklin responds, "but instead of it made in Writing a Proposal, that every Member separately should endeavour to form a subordinate Club, with the same Rules respecting Queries, &c. *and without informing them of the Connexion with the Junto*" (1402; emphasis added). Thus the Junto takes a step toward systematizing itself, creating a network of subordinate units that do not realize they are subordinate—Federalism again. Five or six auxiliary clubs were in fact formed and given different names (the Vine, the Union, the Band). The "Advantages" they offered were tremendous:

> [T]he Improvement of so many more young Citizens by the Use of our Institutions; Our better Acquaintance with the general Sentiments of the Inhabitants on any Occasion, as the Junto-Member might propose what Queries we should desire, and was to report to Junto what pass'd in his separate Club; the Promotion of our particular Interests in Business by more extensive Recommendations: and the Increase of our Influence in public Affairs & our Power of doing Good by spreading thro' the several Clubs the Sentiments of the Junto.... [T]hey were useful to themselves, & afforded us a good deal of Amusement, Information & Instruction, besides answering in some considerable Degree our Views of influencing the public Opinion on particular Occasions. (1402–3)

The subjuntos, thriving within their own domains, serve the master Junto well with business connections, information, entertainment, transmission, and, via the inculcation of "the Sentiments of the Junto," mechanisms for influence, for transformation and "Improvement." In a nutshell, they are masterful, compact apparatuses of hegemony. And we might also find here, rather than in the examples, in part 1, of written communication, a model for Franklin's text: might not the *Autobiography* be a textual form of subjunto, promoting the Junto's particular interests, increasing influence in public affairs, spreading the sentiments of the Junto?

That these subjuntos serve their organizational and political purpose becomes clear throughout the *Autobiography*'s third section, starting with Franklin's discussion (a few pages later) of the 1737 centralization of the City Watch, "one of the first Things that I conceiv'd to want Regulation" (1404). Before the Junto's intervention, the watch was managed by constables elected in city wards—and believed by Franklin to be venal, corrupt, and vulgar: springing from the anarchy of decentralized neighborhoods, constables would ally themselves with "such Ragamuffins" as "reputable Housekeepers did not chuse to mix with" (1404). Concerned, Franklin "wrote a Paper to be read in Junto, representing these Irregularities" and complaining about the "Inequality" of the watch's financing such that "a poor Widow Housekeeper" would have to pay as much as "the wealthiest Merchant" to protect much less property (1404–5). Franklin claims to have proposed fulltime, professionalized watchmen financed by a graduated property tax, to have discussed the idea in the Junto, then to have disseminated the idea throughout the various subjuntos "but as arising in each of them" (1405). He comments that this tactic, "by preparing the Minds of People for the Change, . . . paved the Way for the Law obtain'd a few Years after, when the Members of our Clubs were grown into more Influence" (1405). It is tempting to focus upon the progressive, civic features of this scheme; these are, after all, what Franklin emphasizes. But the fire company scheme discussed in the very next paragraph operates on the antithetical and just-condemned principles of regressive funding that favor "Men of Property" (1405), suggesting that the more significant features of the City Watch plan are the mode of implementation and the organizational strategy, used again and again with slight variations.

Most revealing in these accounts, particularly as regards the *Autobiography*'s method, is Franklin's view of writing and publishing. In his account of "the Affair of establishing an Academy," he gives this recipe for boosterism:

The first Step I took was to associate in the Design a Number of active Friends, of whom the Junto furnished a good Part; the next was to write and publish a Pamphlet intitled, *Proposals relating to the Education of Youth in Pennsylvania*.—This I distributed among the principal Inhabitants gratis; and as soon as I could suppose their Minds a little prepared by the Perusal of it, I set on foot a Subscription for Opening and Supporting an Academy. (1418)

Design, publish, institutionalize. The scheme is an almost perfect inversion of Eugene Debs's famous slogan, "Organize! Educate! Agitate!": for Franklin the desired end is not emancipatory hell-raising but the creeping extension of organization. Given the diametrically opposed goals, the middle term will have a different inflection: the point is not to illuminate and expose structures from the distinct vantage point of the exploited, but to draft presumably benign structures from the elusive and evidently universal vantage point of society. Thus "[i]n the Introduction to these Proposals," Franklin "stated their Publication not as an Act of mine, but of some *publick-spirited Gentlemen*; avoiding as much as I could, according to my usual Rule, the presenting myself to the Publick as the Author of any Scheme for their Benefit" (1418). Michael Warner aptly summarizes the Franklin effect, albeit from the vantage point of the hoodwinked: "[T]he life most consistent with [Franklin's] model of writing," he holds, "would be the public life, but—and this is crucial—a public life uncontaminated by particular aspirations, party affiliations, dependencies on governments and ministers, influences of powerful men, and the like."[40] Warner takes this model seriously, assuring us that "Franklin explicitly imposed the structure of print rationality on his career from an early date" (89), that the perception of "self-centered cunning" in Franklin's career was an optical illusion (90), and that Franklin's occasional "silence and withdrawal" reflected an "ethic," a "lived form of rationality, a transformation of agon within the structures of print discourse" (94), *not* the scheming one would associate with "particular aspirations, party affiliations, dependencies on governments and ministers, influences of powerful men, and the like." Such is the fantasy Franklin's method aims to promote: the extrapolation, from the "model of writing," of a "consistent" "public life," *not* of a hierarchical network of secret clubs carefully inculcating desires and municipal programs.

The pattern recurs often. One example is Franklin's 1751 support for a city hospital, a program initiated by Dr. Thomas Bond (1422). Bond turned to Franklin, who first "endeavoured to *prepare the Minds of the People* by writing on the Subject in the Newspapers, which was my usual Custom in such Cases, but which [Bond] had omitted" (1423, emphasis added). Most spectacular, though, is the already mentioned "voluntary Association of the People" for defense during King George's War, an enterprise that took advantage of both an institutional vacuum (no extant defensive organization) and an organizational shortcircuit (executive and legislature cancelling out each other). Seizing the moment, Franklin in 1747 wrote "Plain Truth," in which, according to the *Autobiography*, he "stated our defenceless Situation in strong Lights, with the Necessity of Union & Discipline for our Defence, and promis'd to propose in a few Days an Association to be generally signed for that purpose" (1411). The pamphlet, he says, had "a sudden & surprising Effect" (1411). Franklin does not tell us whether or not the plan was hatched in the Junto and disseminated through the subjuntos, but "Plain Truth" certainly evokes the structural and social assumptions of the secret clubs. The similarities are most evident in the pamphlet's class analysis of the "defenceless Situation" of "we, the middling People, the Tradesmen, Shopkeepers, and Farmers," not simply vulnerable to the "*licentious Privateers*" of France and Spain but, closer to home, endangered by "the wanton and unbridled Rage, Rapine and Lust, of *Negroes, Molattoes,* and others, the vilest and most abandoned of Mankind."[41] Further, there is no hope for protection from the quarreling elites, "our Chiefs," "those Great and rich Men, Merchants and others" who are locked in dissension and unconcerned with the middling people.[42] In other words, "the Necessity of Union & Discipline" is specifically urgent for the petty bourgeoisie, which stands defenseless against exterior enemies (the French and Spanish) and, more fundamentally, against interior foes (slaves and lords)—*more fundamentally* because Pennsylvanian society's internal divisions precede, even create, the defense crisis of the middling people. Of course, this analysis repeats, with racist flourishes and hyperbolic urgency, the assumptions of the Junto program, which sought to unite select members of "the middling People" to elevate them above the rabble while also emancipating them from the elites.

There was more than pamphleteering to the implementation of the Association. According to Provincial Council secretary Richard Peters, following the appearance of "Plain Truth," Franklin addressed a meeting of 150 middling people, telling them that they had been "the first Movers in every useful undertaking that had been projected for the good of the City—Library Company, Fire Companys &c." He then read the Association proposal, but when the assembled sought to sign on, "No says he let us not sign yet, let us offer it at least to the Gentlemen and if they come into it, well and good, we shall be the better able to carry it into Execution." There followed a meeting of "the better sort of People"—Franklin called them "the principal Gentlemen, Merchants and others" in his *Gazette* notice—who signed on at the top.[43] We see here two significant maneuvers. First, after rallying the petty bourgeoisie in an inflammatory pamphlet, Franklin drives the point home by equating this civic organization with its predecessors: *organization makes the city exceptional, you have always been the organizers, come on and organize again.* Second, this rally was in fact *staged* to mobilize the bourgeoisie. And the scheme is even more intricate, for from the very beginning, before "Plain Truth," Franklin actively schemed with proprietary merchants

> to assume the Character of a Tradesman, to fall foul of the Quakers and their opposers equally, as People from whom no good cou'd be expected, and by this Artifice to animate all the middling Persons to undertake their own Defence in opposition to the Quakers and the Gentlemen. If this shou'd take effect, Mr. Allen [leader of the proprietary faction] and his Friends might publish a vindication of their Conduct and modestly offer a Junction of their Interest to promote the Publick Good.[44]

In other words, Franklin planned the attack on the anti-Quaker merchants *with the anti-Quaker merchants themselves:* the attack was staged to appear as though the petty bourgeoisie were forcing the merchants to act against their will, when in fact they were providing an opportunity for the merchants to act as they wanted to but could not. This is another formula for federalism, and one that clarifies a third lesson: organize, as much as possible, your own opposition. In publishing "Plain Truth" (and now we can see the deep irony of this title), Franklin facilitated the secret partisan activity of the proprietary forces, for whom the Association also formed a shadow subjunto. In his civic programs, Franklin effectively extended a hermeneutics of sects into a *booster methodology.*

Let's again translate this into the terms of practical ensembles. Boosterism is the corrected opposite of sectarianism: it is the extension of fusion from an institutional framework, the boosting of a system through the creation of peripheral, ephemeral groups. Or, in discursive terms, ideology is now a firmly grounded component of an organizational framework. And we can situate the text as a whole in terms of the sect/booster opposition: the *Autobiography* at first appears a sectarian text promoting Franklin's personal views for new institutions of this program (hence the bifocal split), but is more accurately a booster text offered for an already established infrastructure.

Ship of State

Toward the end of part 3, Franklin recounts an anecdote generally passed over in silence by bored or bemused critics. In 1757, Franklin, appointed the Assembly agent to the Crown, sailed for London aboard the ship of Captain Walter Lutwidge. Lutwidge "had boasted much before we sail'd, of the Swiftness of his Ship," yet "when we came to Sea, she proved the dullest of 96 Sail, to his no small Mortification" (1462). The captain called forty passengers to the back of the ship, which then "mended her Pace," from which he determined the problem: the water supply had been loaded into the ship's head. The ship was accordingly repacked and took sail at unprecedented speeds (1462). The point of this story? "The above Fact I give for the sake of the following Observation," writes Franklin:

> It has been remark'd as an Imperfection in the Art of Ship-building, that it can never be known 'till she is try'd, whether a new Ship will or will not be a good Sailer; for that the Model of a good sailing Ship has been exactly follow'd in a new One, which has prov'd on the contrary remarkably dull. I apprehend this may be partly occasion'd by the different Opinions of Seamen respecting the Modes of lading, rigging & sailing of a Ship. Each has his System. And the same Vessel laden by the Judgment & Orders of one Captain shall sail better or worse than when by the same Orders of another. Besides, it scarce ever happens that a Ship is form'd, fitted for the Sea, & sail'd by the same Person. One Man builds the Hull, another riggs her, a third lades and sails her. No one of these has the Advantage of knowing all the Ideas & Experiences of the others, & therefore cannot draw just Conclusions from a Combination of the whole. . . . Yet I think a Set of Experiments might be instituted, first to determine the most proper Form of the Hull for swift sailing; next the best Dimensions & properest Place for the Masts; then the Form & Quantity of Sail, and their Position as the Winds may be; and lastly the Disposition of her Lading. This is the Age of Experiments; and such a Set accurately made & combin'd would be of great Use. I am therefore persuaded that ere long some ingenious Philosopher will undertake it:—to whom I wish Success—(1463)

The lesson is clear. Ship sailing is not systematic or scientific, because the system of the ship combines (at least) four distinct modes of operation: construction, loading, rigging, and sailing, essentially corresponding to problems of design (hull), differentiation (cargo), internal dynamics (rigging), and general operation (sailing). Because the system of the ship is decentered among different parties, the accomplishments of a successful ship system cannot be predicted, guaranteed, or repeated with certainty. Even the ship captain's knowledge of the system is imperfect. What is needed, then, is a

"Set of Experiments" dealing with exostructure, infrastructure, accumulation, and motion, to create a rational and controllable system. Or, more precisely, what is needed is "some ingenious Philosopher" to oversee such experiments and to manage the system as a whole.

It is no stretch to read this as a political allegory: the ship was a favored metaphor for the state, Franklin wrote numerous pieces like this throughout his career, and the timing of the piece's composition—in the aftermath of constitutional ratification—suggests that system-building was on his mind. And in fact, Franklin's famous comments in defense of the constitutional system strongly echo his remarks about ship construction:

> Sir, I agree to this Constitution, with all its faults,—if they are such; because I think a general Government necessary for us, and there is no *form* of government but what may be a blessing to the people, if well administered; and I believe, farther, that this is likely to be well administered for a course of years, and can only end in despotism, as other forms have done before it, when the people shall become so corrupted as to need despotic government, being incapable of any other. I doubt, too, whether any other Convention we can obtain, may be able to make a better constitution. . . . Much of the strength and efficiency of any government, in procuring and securing happiness to the people, depends on *opinion*, on the general opinion of the goodness of the government, as well as of the wisdom and integrity of its governors. I hope, therefore, for our own sakes, as a part of the people, and for the sake of our posterity, that we shall act heartily and unanimously in recommending this Constitution, wherever our Influence may extend, and turn our future thoughts and endeavours to the means of having it *well administered*.[45]

Note the similarities in the arguments. No matter what the ship, certain precepts hold true: following models doesn't guarantee success; designers are rarely the sailors; one cannot predict how the combination will work; opinions can determine success or failure; the practical administration is ultimately the most important thing. So we may read the ship anecdote as Franklin's version of *Federalist No. 10*, and the final turn of the screw, beyond his analyses of sects and boosterism. If sects amount to the attempt to extend ideology to organization, and if boosterism is the attempt to ideologically extend organization, the ship of state is the detached management, from within, of these organizational and cultural elements. This is a model of supreme confidence, and the original model of the United Party for Virtue, which in Franklin's fantasy sought not a crude establishment of a sect, or rule over and atop other sects, or even the implementation of specific goals, but rather the universalization of virtue as a monitored, self-perpetuating system. And what are the Founding Fathers, from this point of view, if not a crew of ingenious Philosophers drawing upon the "Set of Experiments" of state constitutions, the Articles of Confederation, and republican history, to "determine the most proper Form" of government, "the best Dimensions" for checks and balances, "the Form & Quantity" of liberties, and "the Disposition" of the democratic masses? In the "Ship of State" we have the ultimate Franklinian fantasy—after which the *Autobiography* not surprisingly seems to lose its force, moving briefly, in the few pages of part 4, to the details of a mission to London.

Constitutional ratification is only part of the ship anecdote's context, however, and its significance has much to do with its location in the narrative. Immediately preceding the fantasy of the systematized ship is a critique of Lord Loudoun's incompetent prosecution of the Seven Years' War, and immediately following are accounts of two tyrannical politicos, King's Council President Lord Granville and Proprietor John Penn. In fact, the overall political narrative of the last pages of the *Autobiography* concerns Agent Franklin's quest against the irrationality of the "Proprietaries [who] obstinately persisted in manacling their Deputies with Instructions inconsistent not only with the Privileges of the People, but with the Service of the Crown" (1457). Bad for the masses, bad for the imperial system—so Franklin heads to London "to petition the King" (1457). Clearly he expected to find in the king if not "some ingenious Philosopher" then at least a ship's captain who could appreciate an "ingenious Philosopher": Franklin, of course, who had worked out an imperial system, the Albany Plan of Union, in 1754. The *Autobiography* summarizes the plan, noting "the general Government was to be adminstred by a President General appointed and supported by the Crown, and a Grand Council to be chosen by the Representatives of the People of the several Colonies met in their Respective Assemblies" (1430). And, though the attempt fails, Franklin tellingly states, "I am still of Opinion it would have been happy for both Sides the Water [sic] if it had been adopted" (1431)— a revealing *post-Revolutionary* sentiment, and our best hint of what Franklin considered the scientific-imperial ship of state.

The previous chapter described the Albany Plan as a federalist adaptation of the Iroquois diplomatic system central to British America in midcentury. That influence partly explains a major motivation for the plan, a pressing need to establish a cohesive intracolonial system for land purchases and military security—a motivation that takes us beyond generalizations about colonials' desires for unity. But even here we have only part of the story, and must turn for a moment to a major economic reality driving the plan and Franklin's central participation in it: land-jobbing. Land speculation was a central project of Franklin's later life, and one uniting him with his major rival in the revolutionary pantheon, George Washington. In fact, Pennsylvanians and Virginians frequently eyed the same territories, and Washington and Franklin were occasional competitors for the territories variously labeled Ohio, Indiana, and Illinois. In the early 1750s, Franklin had become acquainted with Thomas Pownall and Lewis Evans, the institutional mappers of the central Atlantic backcountry. They had been interested in the wealth afforded by hundreds of thousands, even millions, of acres of land occupied by the Iroquois tributaries, and had realized that a decentralized colonial system of groups bargaining for land was creating conflicts among the Indians and a dangerous competition among colonial speculators. Franklin had even, for awhile, flirted with investing in the Susquehannah Company, through which speculators and settlers from Connecticut were seeking to extend their boundaries into northern Pennsylvania.[46] This scheme would have pit Franklin against the proprietary Penn family, and his only hope for profit would have been an intracolonial umbrella apparatus adjudicating claims of the specific colonies in favor of investors not linked with specific colonies. Thus the Albany Plan included a provision that "the boundaries of those colonies having extensive Western claims could be curtailed, and a provision that the right to purchase land from the Indians and to provide governments for the same should be restricted to the new central government."[47] What separates the Pennsylvanians from the Virginians here is the political and federalist sophistication of the formers' approach to the problem: rather than battle competing local investment schemes with dubious legal foundations, they sought the creation of an overarching confederal system within which they could pursue land development at a trans- (or para-) colonial level. The difference in strategy partly explains the failure of the Albany Plan (as regional investors, like the Virginians, realized they were being outmaneuvered), not to mention the differing colonial attitudes toward the 1763 proclamation limiting westward expansion: although the Virginians were hostile to the proclamation, the Pennsylvanians were indifferent, as imperial restrictions on the extension of specific colonies coincided with their institutional plans.[48]

Let me be explicit: Franklin entered the field of land speculation with gusto (obtaining land as far north as Nova Scotia, as far south as Georgia), and had a prime economic motivation, the "primitive accumulation" of landed capital, for his federalist plans. The Albany Plan, if enacted, could have helped him pursue major investments in the west—something we must keep in mind as we read his pamphlets touting relocation to America,[49] or as we read his correspondence blasting the unruly westerners; the first targets of the Black-Boys, who caused Franklin such outrage, were his speculating partners sending supplies to the western Indians to encourage the land deal.[50] By 1755 Franklin had drafted a proposal for two western colonies,[51] and in a fascinating 1756 letter to George Whitefield he fantasized "that you and I were jointly employ'd by the Crown to settle a Colony on the Ohio."[52] So we need to challenge the caricature (promoted by Max Weber, D. H. Lawrence, and Franklin himself) of Franklin as a beast of cold economic rationality. Franklin left the printer's shop fairly early in his life, and the major economic pursuit of his mature years was the accumulation of America's great resource, the backcountry. This was not a career for Poor Richard, nor a matter of a new printer making "Industry visible to our Neighbours" to obtain "Character and Credit" (1363). Rather, it was a pursuit requiring an assessment of political systems and the calculation of economic practices. Western speculation was central to Franklin's 1757 trip to England and surely represents a subtext of his account of the "ship of state."

But there are no ships in the Alleghenies. This might be the major unspoken lesson of the incomplete part 4. I've already mentioned the crises of the late 1750s and 1760s that threw the rural–urban conflict into sharp relief: Pontiac's Uprising, the Paxton Rebellion, the first Black-Boys actions, the collapse of the Iroquois diplomatic system, the yeomen's marches on Philadelphia. Several months after penning the pamphlet denouncing the Paxton rioters, Franklin writes that "every thing seems in this Country, once the Land of Peace and Order, to be running fast into Anarchy and Confusion," and in 1764 he went from being the Assembly Speaker (May) to losing reelection (October), having been charged with scheming to become the royal governor. "Our only Hopes," he suddenly cries, "are, that the Crown will see the Necessity of taking the Government into its own Hands, without which we shall soon have no Government at all."[53] Now the ingenious Philosopher doesn't know what to do and calls for outside aid. Ousted from office, he leaves Philadelphia in November 1764 for more than a decade, the idyllic order of his urban engineering critically disrupted by "CHRISTIAN WHITE SAVAGES." The vital point in the context of the *Autobiography* is that an important, modular strain of federalism emerged from the history of backcountry–city conflicts in Pennsylvania, and specifically from the sects, booster projects, and imperial schemes outlined above. The transition from sect to ship toward the end of part 3 marks the moment, in Franklin's career, when his apprenticeship in urban engineering was maximized into a state-level political strategy during the ever-heightening crises of escalating rural–urban struggles.

One further indicator of this theoretical stab at management can be found in Franklin's physiocratic essays on political economy, about which Vernon Parrington was misled enough to suggest that "his economic principles and his views on government . . . both sprang from the same root of agrarian democracy."[54] Nothing could be further from the truth. When, in 1751, Franklin and his cabal tried to organize a hospital, he had to hoodwink the country folks. "The Country Members [of the Assembly] did not at first relish the Project," he writes in the *Autobiography*. They "objected that it could only be serviceable to the City, and therefore the Citizens should alone be at the Expence of it" (1423). Through legislative manipulation, Franklin extracted the necessary funds, and later reflected, "I do not remember any of my political Maneuvres, the Success of which gave me at the time more Pleasure. Or that in after-thinking of it, I more easily excus'd my-self for having made some Use of Cunning" (1424). In fact, Franklin's cunning antipathy to agrarian democracy is fundamental, not simply or even primarily political but rather sociological—that is, concerned with a scientific sense of the organization, operation, and development of social institutions. "Plain Truth" addressed "the Tradesmen, Shopkeepers, *and Farmers*," but more accurate is Franklin's declaration at the public meeting following, when, according to provincial secretary Richard Peters, he praised the gathered as "the first Movers in every useful undertaking that had been projected *for the good of the City*."[55] Farmers and Native Americans are among the raw materials his systems try to (but sometimes cannot) process, their social formation hostile to Junto-like scheming, their problems of organization unmanageable without the city's limits.

Against Ratification

A rereading of the *Autobiography* with greater attention to part 3 and some critical distance from parts 1 and 2 should allow us to situate Franklin's work in a series of overlapping contexts. First, rather than situating the narrative within "le Siècle Franklinien," the Age of Enlightenment, or the Spirit of '76, we should take to heart its culmination—or better yet, arrest—not at the War for Independence but in the Seven Years' War, as white–Native, colonial–imperial, French–English, and rural–urban relations came to increasing crisis, at least in the middle colonies. Second, we certainly see the institutional improvisation discussed in chapter 1, and can connect the

Autobiography to the widespread vernacular examination of practical ensembles. This is less a study in individuality, as it may first appear in parts 1 and 2, than an acute survey of the feelings of structure that make up the moment. Third, Franklin's work can be located within the force-field of tensions between backcountry and city. Skipping across British North America's major cities and the two centers of imperial Europe, there are cautious probings of backcountry life but mostly a careful resistance to its turbulent politics: the investment plan for a western state, Franklin's extensive involvement in Native American diplomacy, and Franklin's links with the traders assaulted by the Black-Boys are ignored, while the text breaks off just before the Paxton Riots. Foregrounding these contexts presents the *Autobiography* as an interesting account of modernity, though not the Weberian rendition of a subjective modernity of rationalized *Kapitalogic*. This is an Anglo-American colonial modernity in which imperial development at various levels, from municipal institutions to backcountry management to the organization of empires, has a definitive impact on culture. Within this broader context, we may locate the "spirit of capitalism," as described by Weber, as a particular moment within the colonial littoral and a rhetorical strategy of Franklin's vernacular sociology.

This brings us to a fourth context, of course—the literary context of Franklin's career, emerging from a self-documented, lifelong experimentation with language. This exploration was much more complicated, not to mention much better documented, than the frontloaded readings of the *Autobiography* would have it. Now we come full circle to Franklin's literary construction of his situation, and more specifically to the tripartite lessons of part 3, for here we find the meeting of Franklin the cultural theorist and Franklin the practical organizer.

First, there is the *sectarian* lesson, that interpretation requires a social mapping and a sense of language's function within particular practical ensembles. This lesson insists that language is not the kind of thing about which one can have a universal theory (language is a utilitarian tool, language is the passionate expression of truth, the essence of language is found in print, the best use of language is speech, etc.). Rather, language must be understood as situational, one component of a practical ensemble, and what it does or means must be understood in terms of the praxis and the relations, external and internal, of that ensemble. Readers who attempt to abstract a theory of language from those celebrated early passages of part 1 miss the further, practical apprenticeship documented in part 3, and the cautiously presented observation that practical political battles are not to be fought *through* dis-

course in some Habermasian sense, but *with* discourse in a more Wittgen-
steinian sense.

The second lesson, which might be termed a *booster methodology*, follows
from the first. For Franklin insists that the effective use of language must be
linked with careful, long-term organization in a planned network of practical
ensembles. The serial, fused, and institutional dimensions of language must
be carefully connected; the sectarian lessons of the Junto must be extended
to subjuntos; public opinion must be planned and laid out as carefully as
paving stones. At this level of Franklin's argument, the sectarian lesson is in
a sense activated. Certainly the frontloading and sincerity effects of parts 1
and 2 create a serializing sense of language, which means that language is
presented in a one-dimensional fashion (with set rules and functions), with
a correspondingly narrow sense of self. It was at this level that Weber stopped
short in his analysis, in a unified assessment of individual-behavioral, discursive, and finally systemic rationality. But in presenting the booster projects,
Franklin has subtly moved beyond this bifocal rationality. Instead of leaping
to the system and a series of conceptual shortcuts (like Weber's unified theories of religion or the bridge of charisma linking leaders and masses), Franklin did the hard and messy work of mapping an intermediate rationality of
ensembles and their cultures. The rationality of the monad isn't the same in
the sect as in the booster movement.

This brings us to the third, most crucial, lesson of the *state secret*—namely,
that for the booster methodology to succeed, the lessons of linguistic complexity are not to be shared. Sharing knowledge of the system significantly
undermines that knowledge: knowing changes doing. So the *state* lesson is
resolutely antidialectical: language works best when its workings are not
clear, and especially when its workings are *seemingly* clear, as when a popular theory of language gives one a ready-made interpretive framework. To
put this another way, the effective use of language should not reveal its situational location, and should in fact provide a kind of cover for that situation. This last point, made again and again in the anecdotes of part 3, provides a metacommentary on the *Autobiography* as a whole, as if warning
selected readers that the printers' analogies and the adolescent debate exer-
cises are not the whole story but serve a specific function within the narrative. Within the situations described by Franklin, the characteristic form of
cover involves the simulation of a serial communicative context: we are all
equal listeners, we are all potentially equal writers, we all develop ideas about
municipal plans at the same time, and so on. The adoption of a serializing
formulation of language, as illustrated by the Junto or Franklin's booster-

pamphleteering, thus greatly aids the working of groups within institutional frameworks, and can properly be called a federalist approach to language.

With this last point, we are close to the linguistic analogue to Publius's analysis of politics in *Federalist No. 10*. The federalist system was to combat the dangers of party power by creating a system so extensive that groups might no longer "discover their own strength," but small enough that factions might perceive the larger political framework without getting lost in the "confusion of the multitude." So, although federalism takes shape in opposition to the group (or party, or faction), its deliberately instituted polarity is one of serialized individual (citizens, "the people") and instituted system (the "frame" of government). The same holds for Franklin's account of language. Although he gives numerous examples, in part 3, of the factional uses of language, he also institutes a linguistic polarity of individuals (I learned these language skills, you can learn them as well) and systems (these are the rules of language use). As I have suggested here, the "lessons" are differentiated: there are to be those in the know and those not in the know. And this is more than an esoteric-exoteric distinction between those (federalists) who understand that language is factional, and those who focus on the individualistic axioms of parts 1 and 2, for the two approaches to language are complementary within a federalist framework: for those in the know to use language situationally, those not in the know must not understand.

A further illustration of this federalist linguistic praxis can be found in Franklin's "Speech in the Convention at the Conclusion of Its Deliberations," called "the literary masterpiece of the Convention."[56] Recall Franklin's standard republican analysis, in which he argued "there is no form of Government but what may be a Blessing to the People if well administered" but any form can fail "when the People shall become so corrupted as to need despotic government" (1140–41). These overtly political sentiments were preceded by two classically Franklinian jokes. In the first, he cites Steele on the difference between Protestants and Catholics: "the Roman Church is *infallible*, and the Church of England is *never in the wrong*." In the second, "a certain French Lady" declares "I meet with nobody but myself that is *always in the right*." The key to the joke is the clause that links them, which observes that "many private Persons think almost as highly of their own infallibility as that of their Sect" (1140; emphases in original). For, in this clause, sectarian differences are reduced to a feminized narcissism—that is, group political positions are individuated. Such is the framework for the subsequent and more ostensibly "political" observations, which simultaneously stress both the systemic impossibilities of a better constitution emerging from an assemblage of individuals *and* the success or failure of the system on "the People" as a whole. So the system–individual polarity is carefully instituted in this, the most popular of all the pro-Constitutional pieces. But then we come to the punchline of the "speech," with which Franklin raised the imperative of unanimous consent: "I cannot help expressing a wish, that every member of the Convention who may still have objections to it, would with me on this occasion doubt a little of his own infallibility, and, to make manifest our unanimity, put his name to this Instrument" (1141). What is interesting about this conclusion is not so much the further insistence on individuality (as in each member's fallibility) and systems (as unanimity strengthens the Instrument), but rather the "secret history" of the resolution itself.

Franklin's resolution was clearly meant to be read as a wise old individual—Poor Richard!—admonishing potential dissenters, and its wide publication clearly means the resolution was intended for ordinary citizens, potential antifederalists, as well. Yet Madison's notes at the convention give a different story. The unanimity resolution was drawn up by the federalist Gouverneur Morris, and read by James Wilson, "in order to gain the dissenting members, and put into the hands of Docr. Franklin that it might have the better chance of success."[57] The stratagem aimed to conclude debate without further substantive objections and to produce a statement with the appearance of unanimous support for the Constitution, since full unanimous support was not forthcoming. Hamilton, as usual, provided the more explicit analysis in the face of a few declarations of dissent: "A few characters of consequence," he noted, "by opposing or even refusing to sign the Constitution, might do infinite mischief by kindling the latent sparks which lurk under an enthusiasm in favor of the Convention which may soon subside."[58] With Madison's account in mind, we can move beyond the rhetorical strategies of the speech and situate it within the well-theorized practical ensembles of ratification. Behind the logic of Franklin's two jokes—groups are vain like individuals—is a deep fear of parties drawing the opposite point: individuals are powerful for groups. Thus the taming of potentially oppositional parties must be achieved by the carefully staged taming of individuals. And this, in turn, must be done by a group (Morris, Madison, Wilson, Franklin) using an iconic Founding Father associated with individuality, and seemingly acting as an individual, to defend an institution.

A federalist linguistic praxis, then, involves a careful assessment of an institutional situation complemented with a rhetorical denial of the same, typically with the imposition of a rhetorical seriality. From this, we might also formulate an ideal federalist *reading* praxis, one that acts as expected, dismissing as unimportant the situation focusing instead on either expressed opinions or assumed systemic rules. In other words, federalist reading is a practice of *ratification*, complicitly accepting its serial location within the institutional framework, dismissing the situational analysis as pathologically conspiratorial. What, then, would an antifederalist criticism entail? For starters, we should resist generalizing theories of language. The eighteenth century is not the century of speech, print, or public sphere, and to speak of the nation being spoken into existence, or of print technologies fundamentally determining citizenship, is to magnify and reify certain dimensions of language use. Although the print-speech debate of the last decade and a half has given us much insight into the dynamics of oratory, publication, and literacy technologies, such technologies need to be situated, in the same sense that literary critics have rightly demanded the institutions of economy, home, religion, or politics be situated with respect to language. Our analyses must be grounded in a hermeneutics of practical ensembles, attuned to the feelings of structure that shape the use of language.

We should keep in mind, too, that a situational analysis should not dismiss any self-theorization of language it encounters, but would instead need to read that theorization as also a situational gesture. Given that a federalist practice of communication is committed to the distortion of its own conditions, this is no minor point: unpacking the situational assumptions within implicit theorizations of language is a crucial dimension of challenging their force. One further example, again illustrative of Franklin's urbane-urban assault on backcountry populations, can be found in the *Autobiography*'s remarks on the Native Americans of Pennsylvania. He writes of "the Design of Providence to extirpate these Savages in order to make room for Cultivators of the Earth," referring here to the "system" of Indian alcoholism that "has already annihilated all the Tribes who formerly inhabited the Seacoast" (1422). Franklin, as an erstwhile diplomat and publisher of Indian treaties, of course knew better, knew that the Delawares, Susquehannas, and Shawnees were not "annihilated" by drink but rather displaced by land fraud, Iroquois-Proprietary diplomacy, imperial warfare, and yeoman violence—in some of which he was implicated. Even as Franklin writes, the supposedly extirpated Delawares are uniting with the Shawnees and other Indians from the Great Lakes to the Gulf of Mexico in an unprecedented effort to halt the American advance: Tecumseh reads the situation differently. But Franklin inculcates in readers the more appealing system trope, even throwing it strategically into the mouth of an Iroquois "Orator" (probably the Oneida

"Half-King" Scarouady) who allegedly says of the "great Spirit" that *when he made Rum, he said,* LET THIS BE FOR INDIANS TO GET DRUNK WITH. *And it must be so*" (1422). Even dumb savages intuit the system, the anecdote suggests, and who can argue with that? In fact, Scarouady not only offered a cogent and antifederalist analysis of imperial politics on the eve of the Seven Years' War, but he also charged white traders with using the alcohol trade to create economic dependency in Native societies and asked for trade regulation. "When these Whiskey Traders come they bring thirty or forty Caggs and put them down before Us and make Us drink, and get all the Skins that should go to pay the Debts We have contracted for Goods bought of the Fair Traders, and by this means," insists Scarouady, "We not only ruin Ourselves but them too. These wicked Whiskey Sellers when they have once got the Indians in Liquor make them sell their very Clothes on their Backs . . . if this Practice be continued We must be inevitably ruined."[59] The response of the commissioners, of whom Franklin was one, was to claim to appreciate the problem and promise to push for regulation.[60]

But careful, explicit, political-structural analysis is not the stuff of Franklinian anecdotes, certainly not in the *Autobiography*, and here the urban writer aims to get the last word.

Now a federalist criticism might read Franklin's remarks critically, foregrounding an imputed systematicity essential to Enlightenment racism, or noting the rhetorical use of the tragic Indian prophesying his own doom. Such analyses miss the careful irony of the passage, and thus neglect the project called for by Dutch historian of cynicism Peter Sloterdijk: exploration of the historic "counteroffensive" *against* Enlightenment whereby "[m]odern elitism has to encode itself democratically."[61] What Sloterdijk most seeks to disrupt is the notion of a "necessarily false consciousness" grounded in a "sociological system theory that treats 'truth' functionalistically."[62] Any form of ideology critique that views an articulation as systemically necessary, or as "correct false consciousness"—for example, that Franklin's expressed racism was part of endemic and ubiquitous beliefs about Native American backwardness—will both miss *and strengthen* the cynicism of that articulation. The critique inadvertently gives greater effectiveness to what is being criticized. Sloterdijk's approach, by contrast, suggests the necessity of a situational reading for any grasping of irony or, more broadly, for a view of language as creative praxis. For an antifederalist criticism should seek not only a debunking of deception and the working of institutions, but also an understanding of situational praxis that seeks creative extensions of freedom. If we read Crèvecoeur, James Smith, Neolin, David Brainerd, Canasatego, or

the Paxton Boys as participants in the same racist and racialized discourses
as Franklin, we miss their very different engagements with Native American situations, and their attempts to craft emancipatory responses that are
not simply normalizations of the current state. At stake here is a critical
practice concerned not with spelling out a background context, but with
recognizing the dynamic praxis at work in feelings of structure, and this is
the first step to imagining an antifederalist culture.

The myriad disasters of colonization can by and large be traced to its
organizational programs, what I have defined as a colonial modernity concerned with regulating what was, to Europe, a "back" hemisphere. The colonialism of British North America can be read as one long and concerted
effort to develop a suitable institutional structure that might manage disruptive groups and serial human resources, two challenges aptly captured in
that favored elite metaphor of the Hydra head, a monstrously fused mass
that is simultaneously hideously dispersed. The late emergence of an imperial crisis in the mid-eighteenth century gave the most cohesive shape yet
to an imperial program that more or less smoothly became American federalism, with the Revolution serving as another episode in the larger conflict.
An antifederalism took shape, in fits and starts, at the same time, though at
a profound disadvantage given its reactive position and institutional weaknesses. Only with the Shawnees' attempts to forge a pan-American confederation was a serious challenge mounted; otherwise most of the antifederalist projects were never far removed from their adversaries, as with the
Paxton Boys, who twisted a movement for local power into racist violence
and calls for a more militarized state; one sees the Confederate States of
America taking shape from their ignorance, crimes, and inconsistencies.
The result, by century's end, was the establishment of an institution Thomas
Paine first called "the United States of America," as if to suggest the U and
the S somehow trump the accidental A. The institutional appropriation of
nationalism should not persuade us that the culmination of colonialism was
nationalism: no amount of railing at nationalism changes the fact that the
institutional scheme of the Constitution recognized the need to appropriate
and use the group dimensions of nationalism. Institution dictated nation,
and institution dictates nation. If we take seriously the belief that the catas-
trophes of the present have strong roots in the past, we may be moved to
return to the brief possibility of a creative antifederalism.

Notes

Preface

1. Raymond Williams, *The Country and the City* (New York: Oxford University Press, 1973), 2.

2. Structural analysis from below is discussed in Ed White, "The Value of Conspiracy" (*American Literary History* 14, 1 [2002]: 1–31); nationalism is the subject of Ed White, "Early America Nations as Imagined Communities" (*American Quarterly* 56, 1 [2004]: 49–81); periodization is discussed in Michael Drexler and Ed White, "Colonial Histories" (*American Literary History*, forthcoming); Native Americans and the culture of colonization are treated in Ed White, "Captaine Smith, Colonial Novelist" (*American Literature* 75, 3 [2003]: 487–513); the question of literary agency is treated in Ed White, "The Ourang-Outang Situation" (*College Literature* 30, 3 [2003]: 88–108); and related questions of literary history are treated in Ed White and Michael Drexler, "Literary Histories," in *Companion to Early American Fiction*, ed. Shirley Samuels (Cambridge: Blackwell, 2004).

1. Divides

1. The closest thing to an overview of these insurrections is to be found in Richard Maxwell Brown, "Back Country Rebellions and the Homestead Ethic in America, 1740–1799," in *Tradition, Conflict, and Modernization: Perspectives on the American Revolution*, ed. Richard Maxwell Brown and Don E. Fehrenbacher (New York: Academic, 1977), which seeks to determine patterns across nine white yeomen's insurrections. For Metacom's War, a.k.a. King Philip's War, see the literature review in Jill Lepore, *The Name of War: King Philip's War and the Origins of American Identity*

(New York: Knopf, 1998). For Bacon's Rebellion, see Kathleen M. Brown, *Good Wives, Nasty Wenches, and Anxious Patriarchs: Gender, Race, and Power in Colonial Virginia* (Chapel Hill: University of North Carolina Press, 1996), and see the documents in *The Old Dominion in the Seventeenth Century: A Documentary History of Virginia, 1606–1689*, ed. Warren M. Billings (Chapel Hill: University of North Carolina Press, 1975), which includes documents for the Plant-Cutter Riots as well. For the Jersey riots, see Brendan McConville, *These Daring Disturbers of the Public Peace: The Struggle for Property and Power in Early New Jersey* (Ithaca, NY: Cornell University Press, 1999); for an overview of New York's conflicts, Sun Bok Kim, *Landlord and Tenant in Colonial New York: Manorial Society, 1664–1775* (Chapel Hill: University of North Carolina Press, 1978) is a useful starting point. On Pontiac's Rebellion, see Gregory Evans Dowd, *War under Heaven: Pontiac, the Indian Nations, and the British Empire* (Baltimore: Johns Hopkins University Press, 2002); Dowd's *A Spirited Resistance: The North American Indian Struggle for Unity, 1745–1815* (Baltimore: Johns Hopkins University Press, 1992) and Colin G. Calloway, *The American Revolution in Indian Country: Crisis and Diversity in Native American Communities* (New York: Cambridge University Press, 1995) offer overviews of important Native American uprisings. The literature on the North Carolina Regulation is growing; see, for example, Marjoleine Kars, *Breaking Loose Together: The Regulator Rebellion in Prerevolutionary North Carolina* (Chapel Hill: University of North Carolina Press, 2002) and A. Roger Ekirch, *"Poor Carolina": Politics and Society in Colonial North Carolina, 1729–1776* (Chapel Hill: University of North Carolina Press, 1981). For overviews of the South Carolina Regulation and the Yamassee War, see Tom Hatley, *The Dividing Paths: Cherokees and South Carolinians through the Era of Revolution* (New York: Oxford University Press, 1993). On the Massachusetts Regulation, see *In Debt to Shays: The Bicentennial of an Agrarian Rebellion*, ed. Robert A. Gross (Charlottesville, University Press of Virginia, 1993) and Leonard L. Richards, *Shays's Rebellion: The American Revolution's Final Battle* (Philadelphia: University of Pennsylvania Press, 2002). The standard history of the Whiskey Rebellion remains Thomas P. Slaughter, *The Whiskey Rebellion: Frontier Epilogue to the American Revolution* (New York: Oxford University Press, 1986). On conflicts in Vermont, see Michael A. Bellesiles, *Revolutionary Outlaws: Ethan Allen and the Struggle for Independence on the Early American Frontier* (Charlottesville: University Press of Virginia, 1993) and Peter S. Onuf, *The Origins of the Federal Republic: Jurisdictional Controversies in the United States, 1775–1787* (Philadelphia: University of Pennsylvania Press, 1983). The local context of the Paxton Riots is discussed in more detail in chapter 3, and Little Turtle's War and the Fries Rebellion will be discussed in my forthcoming *Rural Insurrections and the Early American Novel*.

I have followed Ronald P. Formisano in using the label "Massachusetts Regulation" to refer to the Shaysite Rebellion ("Teaching Shays/the Regulation," *Uncommon Sense* 106 [Winter 1998]: 24, 26–35), but use "Paxton Riots" to refer to what some Connecticut contemporaries called the Pennsylvania Regulation. The interconnectedness of yeomen insurrections under the "Regulation" label remains to be explored.

   2. Mary Beth Norton, et al., *A People and a Nation: A History of the United States*, 3rd ed., vol. 1 (Boston: Houghton Mifflin, 1990), 111–12; Gary B. Nash, *The*

Urban Crucible: The Northern Seaports and the Origins of the American Revolution, abridged ed. (Cambridge, MA: Harvard University Press, 1986), 157.

3. Charles Sellers, et al., *A Synopsis of American History*, 6th ed., vol. 1 (Boston: Houghton Mifflin, 1985), 33–34.

4. Ranajit Guha, "The Prose of Counter-Insurgency," in *Subaltern Studies 2: Writings on South Asian History and Society*, ed. R. Guha (Delhi: Oxford University Press, 1983), 27.

5. Allan Kulikoff, *From British Peasants to Colonial American Farmers* (Chapel Hill: University of North Carolina Press, 2000), 5–6.

6. I'm thinking here of the "image" studies of the 1950s and 1960s, including Leo Marx, *The Machine in the Garden: Technology and the Pastoral Ideal in America* (New York: Oxford University Press, 1964); Henry Nash Smith, *Virgin Land: The American West as Symbol and Myth* (New York: Vintage, 1957); and the important later feminist revisions like Myra Jehlen's *American Incarnation: The Individual, the Nation, and the Continent* (Cambridge, MA: Harvard University Press, 1986) and Annette Kolodny's, *The Land before Her: Fantasy and Experience of the American Frontiers, 1630–1860* (Chapel Hill: University of North Carolina Press, 1984).

7. Vernon Louis Parrington, *Main Currents in American Thought: An Interpretation of American Literature from the Beginnings to 1920*, vol. 1 (New York: Harcourt, Brace and Co., 1927), 177.

8. Nancy Armstrong and Leonard Tennenhouse, *The Imaginary Puritan: Literature, Intellectual Labor, and the Origins of Personal Life* (Berkeley and Los Angeles: University of California Press, 1992), 19–21, 205. "[I]f Foucault's historical model requires Anderson's transnational narrative to carry it from one historical moment to another," they write, "then Anderson requires Foucault" (21).

9. Jay Fliegelman, *Declaring Independence: Jefferson, Natural Language, and the Culture of Performance* (Stanford, Stanford University Press, 1993), 1, 3. Michael Warner, *The Letters of the Republic: Publication and the Public Sphere in Eighteenth-Century America* (Cambridge, MA: Harvard University Press, 1990), ix.

10. Nash, *Urban Crucible*, ix.

11. Paul Gilroy, *The Black Atlantic: Modernity and Double Consciousness* (Cambridge, MA: Harvard University Press, 1993); Enrique Dussel, *The Invention of the Americas: Eclipse of "the Other" and the Myth of Modernity*, trans. Michael D. Barber (New York: Continuum, 1995).

12. Michael Warner, "What's Colonial about Colonial America?" in *Possible Pasts*, ed. R. B. St. George (2002), 57.

13. Bernard Bailyn, *The Ideological Origins of the American Revolution* (Cambridge, MA: Harvard University Press, 1967); Gordon Wood, *The Creation of the American Republic, 1776–1787* (Chapel Hill: University of North Carolina Press, 1969) and *The Radicalism of the American Revolution* (New York: Knopf, 1992); and J. G. A. Pocock, *The Machiavellian Moment: Florentine Political Thought and the Atlantic Republican Tradition* (Princeton: Princeton University Press, 1975). The following pages also cite Bailyn's "Political Experience and Enlightenment Ideas in Eighteenth-Century America," in *The Craft of American History: Selected Essays*, ed. A. S. Eisenstadt (New York: Harper, 1966); "Central Themes of the American Revolution: An Interpretation," in *Essays on the American Revolution*, ed. Stephen G. Kurtz and

James H. Hutson (Chapel Hill: University of North Carolina Press, 1973); and Bernard Bailyn's interview with A. Roger Ekirch, "Sometimes an Art, Never a Science, Always a Craft: A Conversation with Bernard Bailyn," *William and Mary Quarterly* 51, 4 (1994): 625–58.

14. Shalhope's essays played an important role in the disciplinary definition of the synthesis: see Robert Shalhope, "Toward a Republican Synthesis: The Emergence of an Understanding of Republicanism in American Historiography," *William and Mary Quarterly* 29 (1972): 49–80, and "Republicanism and Early American Historiography," *William and Mary Quarterly* 39 (1982): 334–56. This quote is from the later essay, 334–35.

15. The secondary historiography on the Progressives is immense, but a useful introduction are the essays by Morey Rothberg ("John Franklin Jameson and the Creation of *The American Revolution Considered as a Social Movement*") and Alfred Young ("American Historians Confront *The Transforming Hand of Revolution*") in *The Transforming Hand of Revolution*, ed. Ronald Hoffman and Peter J. Albert (Charlottesville: University Press of Virginia, 1995), a collection focusing on J. Franklin Jameson's *The American Revolution Considered as a Social Movement*.

16. Gordon Wood, "Rhetoric and Reality in the American Revolution," in *In Search of Early America: The William and Mary Quarterly, 1943–1993*, ed. Michael McGiffert (Richmond, VA: William Byrd Press, 1993), 57. The essay originally appeared in 1966, and was later voted one of the eleven most influential essays to appear in the first fifty years of *The William and Mary Quarterly*.

17. Ibid, 64.

18. For a more focused account of nationalism in the North American colonial concept, and an engagement with Benedict Anderson's work, see my "Early American Nations as Imagined Communities," *American Quarterly* 56, 1 (March 2004): 49–81.

19. The essays in the roundtable included Joyce Appleby, "The Radical Recreation of the American Republic," *William and Mary Quarterly* 51, 4 (1994), 679–83; Barbara Clark Smith, "The Radical Recreation of the American Republic," ibid., 684–92; and Michael Zuckerman, "Rhetoric, Reality, and the Revolution: The Genteel Radicalism of Gordon Wood," ibid., 693–702. Quotations are taken from 684, 694, and 697. See also Wood's angry and often sarcastic response, "Equality and Social Conflict in the American Revolution," ibid., 703–16.

20. Warner, *Letters* 67, 187n60.

21. Other major works include Robert A. Ferguson, *Law and Letters in American Culture* (Cambridge, MA: Harvard University Press, 1984); Cathy Davidson, *Revolution and the Word* (New York: Oxford University Press, 1986); Robert A. Ferguson, "'We Hold These Truths': Strategies of Control in the Literature of the Founders," in *Reconstructing American Literary History*, ed. Sacvan Bercovitch (Cambridge, MA: Harvard University Press, 1986); Albert Furtwangler, *American Silhouettes: Rhetorical Identities of the Founders* (New Haven, CT: Yale University Press, 1987); Mark R. Patterson, *Authority, Autonomy, and Representation in American Literature, 1776–1865* (Princeton: Princeton University Press, 1988); Kenneth Cmiel, *Democratic Eloquence: The Fight over Popular Speech in Nineteenth-Century America* (New York: William Morrow, 1990); Warner's *Letters of the Republic*; Larzer Ziff, *Writing in the New Nation: Prose, Print, and Politics in the Early United States* (New Haven, CT:

Yale University Press, 1991); Thomas Gustafson, *Representative Words: Politics, Literature, and the American Language, 1776–1865* (New York: Cambridge University Press, 1992); Michael P. Kramer, *Imagining Language in America: From the Revolution to the Civil War* (Princeton: Princeton University Press, 1992); Fliegelman's *Declaring Independence*; Michael T. Gilmore, "The Literature of the Revolutionary and Early National Periods," in *The Cambridge History of American Literature*, ed. Sacvan Bercovitch (New York: Cambridge University Press, 1994); Alessandro Portelli, *The Text and the Voice: Writing, Speaking, and Democracy in American Literature* (New York: Columbia University Press, 1994); Terence Martin, *Parables of Possibility: The American Need for Beginnings* (New York: Columbia University Press, 1995); Philip H. Round, "The Discursive Origins of the American Revolution: The Case of Nathaniel Rogers, Merchant of Boston" (*Early American Literature* 30, 3 [1995]: 233–63); Christopher Looby, *Voicing America: Language, Literary Form, and the Origins of the United States* (Chicago: University of Chicago Press, 1996); Christopher Grasso, *A Speaking Aristocracy: Transforming Public Discourse in Eighteenth-Century Connecticut* (Chapel Hill: University of North Carolina Press, 1999); and Bruce Burgett, *Sentimental Bodies: Sex, Gender, and Citizenship in the Early Republic* (Princeton: Princeton University Press, 1998).

22. Barrington Moore Jr., *Social Origins of Dictatorship and Democracy: Lord and Peasant in the Making of the Modern World* (Boston: Beacon, 1966), 453.

23. Theda Skocpol, "A Critical Review of Barrington Moore's *Social Origins of Dictatorship and Democracy*," *Politics and Society* 4, 1 (1973): 6. Skocpol's major disagreements with Moore focused on his undeveloped theory of the state and neglect of the importance of intersocietal influences (e.g., modularity, external constraints). For a general introduction to Moore's work, and some overview of the reception of *Social Origins*, see Dennis Smith, *Barrington Moore, Jr.: A Critical Appraisal* (Armonk, NY: M. E. Sharpe, 1983).

24. See J. Franklin Jameson, *The American Revolution Considered as a Social Movement* (Princeton: Princeton University Press, 1967), especially chapter 2, "The Revolution and the Land." Jameson's work will be discussed in greater detail in the next chapter.

25. White, "Value of Conspiracy Theory": 1–31.

26. Jean-Paul Sartre, *Critique of Dialectical Reason*, vol. 1: *Theory of Practical Ensembles*, trans. Alan Sheridan-Smith (New York: Verso, 1991), 69.

27. Antonio Gramsci, *Prison Notebooks*, trans. Joseph A. Buttigieg and Antonio Callari, ed. J. Buttigieg (New York: Columbia University Press, 1992), 1: 100.

28. The passage is taken from the Supreme Court decision *Chisholm v. Georgia*, reprinted in *The Founders' Constitution*, vol. 5, *Amendments I–XII*, ed. Philip B. Kurland and Ralph Lerner (Indianapolis: Liberty Fund, 2000), 422. For more on the case, see Peter Irons, *A People's History of the Supreme Court* (New York: Viking, 1999), 92–95.

29. Looby, *Voicing America*, 20.

30. See Geoffrey Seed, *James Wilson* (Millwood, NY: KTO Press, 1978), a hagiography that nonetheless opens a chapter on "James Wilson's enterprise in the extension of settlement" with the observation that Wilson's "unsavory reputation in business sometimes affected adversely his credibility in other spheres" (160).

31. David Waldstreicher, *In the Midst of Perpetual Fêtes: The Making of American Nationalism, 1776–1820* (Chapel Hill: University of North Carolina Press, 1997), 219.

32. Jeffrey L. Pasley, "1800 as a Revolution in Political Culture: Newspapers, Celebrations, Voting, and Democratization in the Early Republic," in *The Revolution of 1800: Democracy, Race, and the New Republic*, ed. James Horn, Jan Ellen Lewis, and Peter S. Onuf (Charlottesville: University of Virginia Press, 2002), 133.

33. Roland Barthes, *Mythologies*, trans. Annette Lavers (New York: Hill and Wang, 1972), 131, 123.

34. Ibid, 28.

35. John Adams and Benjamin Rush, *The Spur of Fame: Dialogues of John Adams and Benjamin Rush, 1805–1813*, ed. John A. Schutz and Douglass Adair (Indianapolis: Liberty Fund, 1966), 31, 32, 55.

36. Quoted in Jack P. Greene, *Pursuits of Happiness: The Social Development of Early Modern British Colonies and the Formation of American Culture* (Chapel Hill: University of North Carolina Press, 1988), 170.

37. Jack [P.] Greene, *Imperatives, Behaviors, Identities: Essays in Early American Cultural History* (Charlottesville: University Press of Virginia, 1992), 7.

38. See *Historical Statistics of the United States: Two Centuries of the Census, 1790–1990*, ed. Donald B. Dodd (Westport: Greenwood, 1993), and John J. McCusker and Russell R. Menard, *The Economy of British North America, 1607–1789* (Chapel Hill: University of North Carolina Press, 1995), 202–3.

39. Figures from Nash, *Urban Crucible*, 1, 22, 66, 110, and 201, and from Edgar P. Richardson, "The Athens of America, 1800–1825," in *Philadelphia: A 300-Year History*, ed. Russell F. Weigley, Nicholas B. Wainwright, and Edwin Wolf (New York: Norton, 1982), 218.

40. Dodd, *Historical Statistics*.

41. James T. Lemon, *The Best Poor Man's Country: A Geographical Study of Early Southeastern Pennsylvania* (Baltimore: Johns Hopkins University Press, 1972), 14.

42. Edward Connery Lathem, *Chronological Tables of American Newspapers, 1690–1820, Being a Tabular Guide to Holdings of Newspapers Published in America through the Year 1820* (Barre, MA: American Antiquarian Society, 1972).

43. Gary Nash, *Freedom by Degrees: Emancipation in Pennsylvania and its Aftermath* (New York: Oxford University Press, 1991), 7.

44. On these questions, the essays in *A History of the Book in America*, vol. 1, *The Colonial Book in the Atlantic World*, ed. Hugh Amory and David D. Hall (New York: Cambridge University Press, 2000), offer an invaluable starting point.

2. Seriality

1. Carl A. Brasseaux, *The Founding of New Acadia: The Beginnings of Acadian Life in Louisiana, 1765–1803* (Baton Rouge: Louisiana State University Press, 1987), 24–25.

2. *The Statutes at Large of Pennsylvania from 1682 to 1801*, vol. 5, 1744–1759, ed. William Stanley Ray ([n.p.], 1898), 215.

3. Brasseaux, 49, 53.

4. *Colonial Origins of the American Constitution: A Documentary History*, ed. Donald S. Lutz (Indianapolis: Liberty Fund, 1998), 366. A year later, William Brad-

ford would similarly lament the dispersal of the Plymouth settlers; see *Of Plymouth Plantation, 1620–1647* (New York: Modern Library, 1981), 369 and chapter 23.

5. *Captain John Smith: A Selection of His Writings*, ed. Karen Ordahl Kupperman (Chapel Hill: University of North Carolina Press, 1988), 257, 142, 147.

6. Benedict Anderson, *Imagined Communities: Reflections on the Origin and Spread of Nationalism*, rev. ed (New York: Verso, 1991), 35. Anderson uses the concept of seriality more explicitly in *The Spectre of Comparisons: Nationalism, Southeast Asia, and the World* (New York: Verso, 1998), chapter 1, "Nationalism, Identity, and the Logic of Seriality."

7. Warner, *Letters of the Republic*, xiii (emphasis in original) and 40.

8. Sartre, *Critique*, vol. 1: 348, 279.

9. Iris Marion Young, "Gender as Seriality: Thinking about Women as a Social Collective," in *Feminist Interpretations of Jean-Paul Sartre*, ed. Julien S. Murphy (University Park: Pennsylvania State University Press, 1999), 222, 26. Of course, this is not an exhaustive account of identity politics, and there may be different group or institutionalized senses of identity that may in turn provide a deeper "psychological sense." For this reason, an account of community identity—say, of the eighteenth-century Delawares—would have to track serial, fused, and organizational dimensions in tandem.

10. See, for example, Sartre's *Being and Nothingness: An Essay on Phenomenological Ontology*, trans. Hazel E. Barnes (New York: Philosophical Library, 1956), 5. He would develop this idea further in *The Family Idiot: Gustave Flaubert, 1821–1857*, trans. Carol Cosman (Chicago: University of Chicago Press, 1981), 1: 11–12.

11. David Hardiman, *The Coming of the Devi: Adivasi Assertion in Western India* (Delhi: Oxford University Press, 1995). "Viewed in a long-term perspective the Devi movement thus represented only a stage in the self-assertion of the adivasis of South Gujarat. It represented, however, a most important element in this process, for it forged a remarkable change in consciousness amongst large numbers of adivasis and paved the way for wholly new forms of political organization" (216). See chapter 2, "Origins and Transformations of the Devi," for an account of the transmission and creative modification of the movement, and for a map of the movement of "the devi."

12. J. Hector St. John de Crèvecoeur, *Letters from an American Farmer and Sketches of Eighteenth-Century America*, ed. Albert E. Stone (New York: Penguin, 1986), 72, 43.

13. See for instance the summary of "The Jeffersonian Vision" in Nash, *Urban Crucible*: "The central actor in the Jeffersonians' social and political drama was neither merchant nor banker but the independent yeoman farmer—self-reliant, secure in person and possessions, enterprising and yet filled with concern for the public good. Such people exemplified the qualities essential to republican citizenship" (305). A similar portrait is sketched in *Synopsis of American History*: "Despite a flourishing overseas commerce...the country as a whole remained wedded to the vision of a simple, unprogressive, democratic utopia, dominated by self-sufficient and, therefore, independent and virtuous farmers" (97–98).

14. Marx, *Machine in the Garden*, 108, 110.

15. Warner, *Letters*, 40, xiii, emphasis in original.

16. The most comprehensive discussion of proprietary relations, legal and practical, is William Shepherd, *History of Proprietary Government in Pennsylvania* (New York: Columbia University Press, 1896). Chapter 6 of Beverley W. Bond Jr., *The Quit-Rent System in the American Colonies* (New Haven, CT: Yale University Press, 1919) offers a useful survey of quit-rent administration.

17. Shepherd, *History*, 16–17.

18. Mary M. Schweitzer, *Custom and Contract: Household, Government, and the Economy in Colonial Pennsylvania* (New York: Columbia University Press, 1987), 96.

19. Ibid, 96. James Lemon writes: "Agricultural villages did not materialize and farmsteads were dispersed. Indiscriminate settlement after 1700 led to irregular holdings, and farms definitely became the decision-making units as the few feudal ties were loosened" (*Best Poor Man's Country*, 102). Shepherd notes that Penn also planned "manors" (the proprietary "tenths") into his property grids, but these never functioned as political-administrative units as they did in the colony of New York (47). Rather, they became isolated proprietary outposts where overseers spent much of their time "fighting off squatters and trespassers" (Schweitzer, 90).

20. Gary [B.] Nash, *Quakers and Politics: Pennsylvania, 1681–1726*, new ed. (Boston: Northeastern University Press, 1993), 73–85.

21. Alan Tully, *William Penn's Legacy: Politics and Social Structure in Provincial Pennsylvania, 1726–1755* (Baltimore: Johns Hopkins University Press, 1977), 4.

22. Ibid, 5. Schweitzer mentions another obstacle to land management: before his death, a financially distressed William Penn had mortgaged the entire colony in 1705, and "until his heirs paid the mortgage off in the 1720s, even his agents could not legally grant title" (97).

23. Tully, 20.

24. Schweitzer, 89.

25. On the Scots-Irish, see Wayland Fuller Dunaway, *A History of Pennsylvania* (New York: Prentice Hall, 1935), 29–30, and James G. Leyburn, *The Scotch-Irish: A Social History* (Chapel Hill: University of North Carolina Press, 1962), 160–64. For German immigration, see especially Aaron Spencer Fogleman, *Hopeful Journeys: German Immigration, Settlement, and Political Culture in Colonial America, 1717–1775* (Philadelphia: University of Pennsylvania Press, 1996), 23–28 and 42–65, which locates the first migration crest from 1727 to 1732. Sally Schwartz, *"A Mixed Multitude": The Struggle for Toleration in Colonial Pennsylvania* (New York: New York University Press, 1987) also provides an overview, in chapter 4.

26. Ranajit Guha, *Elementary Aspects of Peasant Insurgency in Colonial India* (Delhi: Oxford University Press, 1983), 333.

27. *Pennsylvania Archives*, Second Series, 19 volumes, ed. John B. Linn and William Henry Egle (Philadelphia: Joseph Severns, 1874–1890), 7: 65, 7: 127, and 7: 96–97.

28. Ibid, 7: 104–5, 7: 98.

29. For a more detailed account of Jameson's career, see Rothberg, "John Franklin Jameson . . . ," 1–26.

30. Jameson, *American Revolution Considered as a Social Movement*. Further citations are given parenthetically in the text.

31. Lemon, *Best Poor Man's Country*, xiv, 1.

32. Grantland Rice, "Crèvecoeur and the Politics of Authorship in Republican America," *Early American Literature* 28, 2 (1993): 102, 104.

33. For overviews of the Delawares' dispersal, see James H. Merrell, *Into the American Woods: Negotiators on the Pennsylvania Frontier* (New York: W. W. Norton, 1999); Anthony F. C. Wallace, *King of the Delawares: Teedyuscung, 1700–1763* (Syracuse, NY: Syracuse University Press, 1990); and C. A. Weslager, *The Delaware Indians: A History* (New Brunswick, NJ: Rutgers University Press, 1972).

34. Shekellamy, also called Onkiswathetami, Swatana, Takashwangaroras, and Ungquaterughiathe, was born French, captured by the Iroquois, and raised as an Oneida, although he may have had affiliation with the Cayugas too. He became one of the chief Iroquois agents with Pennsylvania authorities, by virtue of his position supervising the Shawnees and Delawares, and was a participant in the minor treaties from the late 1720s to the 1740s. I follow the Pennsylvania records, which generally use the name Shekellamy, variously spelled Shikillima, Chicalamy, and Shickallemy. For more on his career, see *The History and Culture of Iroquois Diplomacy: An Interdisciplinary Guide to the Treaties of the Six Nations and Their League*, ed. Francis Jennings (Syracuse, NY: Syracuse University Press, 1985).

35. *Minutes of the Provincial Council of Pennsylvania, from the Organization to the Termination of the Proprietary Government*, 10 vols., ed. Samuel Hazard (Philadelphia: J. Severns, 1851–1852), 4: 649. Further treaty and council citations in this section of the text are given parenthetically.

36. Ibid, 3: 321.

37. Ibid, 3: 164.

38. Ibid, 3: 159.

39. Ibid, 2: 758–59.

40. Ibid, 3: 152.

41. Ibid, 2: 757.

42. Ibid, 3: 158.

43. Ibid, 3: 159.

44. Ibid, 3: 152.

45. Ibid, 6: 760.

46. Ibid, 6: 761.

47. Ibid.

48. Young, "Gender as Seriality," 201–11.

49. Schweitzer, *Custom and Contract*, 21.

50. *Minutes of the Provincial Council of Pennsylvania*, 4: 579.

51. Jennings, *History and Culture of Iroquois Diplomacy*, 124.

3. Fusion

1. Webb, "William Webb's Account of His Journey to the Conoys," *Pennsylvania Magazine of History and Biography* 34, 2 (1910): 252.

2. Quoted in Edward Countryman, *A People in Revolution: The American Revolution and Political Society in New York, 1760–1790* (New York: Norton, 1981), 165.

3. Sartre, *Critique*, 345, 368.

4. See Peter Linebaugh and Marcus Rediker, *The Many-Headed Hydra: Sailors, Slaves, Commoners, and the Hidden History of the Revolutionary Atlantic* (Boston: Beacon, 2000).

5. Well documented in Richard N. Rosenfeld's eccentric *American Aurora: A Democratic Republican Returns. The Suppressed History of Our Nation's Beginnings and the Heroic Newspaper that Tried to Report It* (New York: St. Martin's, 1997), chapters 3 and 4.

6. Fredric Jameson, *Marxism and Form: Twentieth-Century Dialectical Theories of Literature* (Princeton: Princeton University Press, 1971), 257, 268.

7. Sartre, *"What Is Literature?" and Other Essays*, trans. Bernard Frechtman, Jeffrey Mehlman, and John MacCombie (Cambridge, MA: Harvard University Press, 1988), 67–68.

8. Linebaugh and Rediker, *Many-Headed Hydra*, 3.

9. Armstrong and Tennenhouse, *Imaginary Puritan*, 204.

10. Archibald Loudon, *A Selection, of Some of the Most Interesting Narratives, of Outrages, Committed by the Indians, in Their Wars, with the White People* (Lewisburg, PA: Wennawoods, 1996), originally published in two volumes in Carlisle, PA (1808, 1811).

11. The Caughnawaga or Kahnawake were Mohawks associated with the French in the late seventeenth century; many were Roman Catholic, and most lived in the region south of Montréal. See William N. Fenton and Elisabeth Tooker, "Mohawk," in *Handbook of North American Indians*, ed. Bruce G. Trigger, vol. 15: *Northeast* (Washington: Smithsonian, 1978), 469–71, and John Demos, *The Unredeemed Captive: A Family Story from Early America* (New York: Knopf, 1994), chapter 6.

12. I cite the most accessible contemporary edition of Smith's narrative, from *American Captivity Narratives*, ed. Gordon M. Sayre (Boston: Houghton Mifflin, 2000); this anthology reprints the 1808 Loudon edition. Little has been written about Smith, but see Wilbur S. Nye, *James Smith: Early Cumberland Valley Patriot* (Carlisle: Cumberland County Historical Society, 1969). Slotkin briefly discusses Smith in ways that emphasize continuities with the Puritan tradition summarized by Armstrong and Tennenhouse: "Thus the captive of Puritan tradition becomes, in Smith's account, a combative, self-willed hero, deriving power, values, and independence of mind from intimacy with the Indians" (Richard Slotkin, *Regeneration through Violence: The Mythology of the American Frontier, 1600–1860* [Middletown, CT: Wesleyan University Press, 1973], 330). I will be taking issue with this emphasis on the "self-willed" individual.

13. Richard White, *The Middle Ground: Indians, Empires, and Republics in the Great Lakes Region, 1650–1815* (New York: Cambridge University Press, 1991), 327n25.

14. Mary Rowlandson, "The Sovereignty and Goodness of God," in *Puritans among the Indians: Accounts of Captivity and Redemption, 1676–1724*, ed. Alden T. Vaughan and Edward W. Clark (Cambridge, MA: Harvard University Press, 1981), 36.

15. Gordon Sayre has written about how white colonials commonly conflated beavers and Indians in a complicated naturalist ethnography. Although the comparison of Indian to beaver could dehumanize the former, making Indians just another form of wildlife, accounts of senseless and wasteful hunting of the beaver could implicitly challenge the mindlessness of white colonialism. With Smith's end-of-the-

century narrative, we see this interplay between Indian and beaver playing out in a new direction; the ethnographic parallel is made more explicit in an attempt to reform—to Indianize—white society. See Sayre, *"Les Sauvages Américains": Representations of Native Americans in French and English Colonial Literature* (Chapel Hill, University of North Carolina Press, 1997), chapter 5.

16. Eleanor M. Webster, "Insurrection at Fort Loudon in 1765: Rebellion or Preservation of Peace?" *Western Pennsylvania Historical Magazine* 47, 2 (1964): 129. Relatively little has been written about the Black-Boys, but see Nye, *James Smith*, and especially Rhea S. Klenovich, "James Smith and the Black Boys: Rebellion on the Pennsylvania Frontier, 1763–1769," *Cumberland County History* 8 (1991), which stresses the improvisational institutions (including pass and bail systems) established in the backcountry in the wake of the group actions.

17. Franklin, *The Papers of Benjamin Franklin*, vol. 12 (New Haven, CT: Yale University Press, 1968), 172–73.

18. James Smith, *A Treatise of the Mode and Manner of Indian War* (Paris, KY: Joel Lyle, 1812). See especially the diagrams on pages 14 and 16.

19. James Smith, *Remarkable Occurrences Lately Discovered among the People Called Shakers, of a Treasonous & Barbarous Nature, or, Shakerism Developed* (Abington, VA: John G. Ustick, 1811), 16.

20. Dowd, *A Spirited Resistance*, 27. I have also drawn upon: White's *The Middle Ground*; Eric Hinderaker, *Elusive Empires: Constructing Colonialism in the Ohio Valley, 1673–1800* (New York: Cambridge University Press, 1997); Charles E. Hunter, "The Delaware Nativist Revival of the Mid-Eighteenth Century," *Ethnohistory* 18 (1971); Anthony F. C. Wallace, "New Religions among the Delaware Indians, 1600–1900," *Southwestern Journal of Anthropology* 12 (1956); Anthony F. C. Wallace, "Revitalization Movements," *American Anthropologist* 58 (1956); and John Sugden, *Tecumseh: A Life* (New York: Henry Holt, 1997), 111–214.

21. Dowd, *Spirited*, 29–40.

22. See Anthony F. C. Wallace, *The Death and Rebirth of the Seneca* (New York: Vintage, 1972).

23. Quoted in Hunter, "Delaware Nativist Revival," 44.

24. Kenny, "Journal of James Kenny, 1761–63," ed. John W. Jordan, *Pennsylvania Magazine of History and Biography* 37 (1913): 1–47, 152–201.

25. Quoted in Wallace, "New Religions," 6.

26. On tutelary beings, see Ives Goddard, "Delaware," in Trigger, ed., *Handbook*, vol. 15, 219–20; for kinship and political phatries, see 224–26 in that volume. Concern with "species" classifications may also indicate the pressures of contact with the Shawnees, in which the basic subgroups were associated with animal figures; see Charles Callender, "Shawnee," in Trigger, ibid., 623–24.

27. Hinderaker, 154. Richard White summarizes a similar account of the shift from isolated manitous to the fused group in Miami tradition, where manitous were organized in a single lodge: "The animals of this revelation have all the marks of the other-than-human beings, or manitous, of earlier Algonquian accounts, but they are now united into a single powerful lodge or society. As before, they bestow power, but this power, being the sum of their individual powers, is far greater than that of the older visions" (*Middle Ground*, 218).

28. For Rudé's work, see "George Rudé: A Bibliography" in *History from Below: Studies in Popular Protest and Popular Ideology*, ed. Frederick Krantz (New York: Blackwell, 1988); for Thompson, see especially "The Moral Economy of the English Crowd in the Eighteenth Century" in Thompson's *Customs in Common* (New York: New Press, 1993).

29. Jesse Lemisch, "Jack Tar in the Streets: Merchant Seamen in the Politics of Revolutionary America," *William and Mary Quarterly* 25, 3 (1968): 371–407; Pauline Maier, *From Resistance to Revolution: Colonial Radicals and the Development of American Opposition to Britain, 1765–1776* (New York: Norton, 1972); Edward Countryman, *The American Revolution* (New York: Hill and Wang, 1985). See also the contributions by Countryman, Kay, Hoerder, and Hoffman in *The American Revolution: Explorations in the History of American Radicalism*, ed. Alfred F. Young (DeKalb: Northern Illinois University Press, 1976).

30. Thomas P. Slaughter, "Crowds in Eighteenth-Century America: Reflections and New Directions," *Pennsylvania Magazine of History and Biography* 115, 1 (1991): 3–34. Slaughter includes a thorough bibliography of several decades of crowd studies.

31. Wood, *Creation of the American Republic*, 363; Lemisch, "Jack Tar," 407.

32. My discussion of Guha focuses on two works: *Elementary Aspects of Peasant Insurgency in Colonial India* and "The Prose of Counter-Insurgency" (1–42). See also "On Some Aspects of the Historiography of Colonial India," in *Subaltern Studies 1: Writings on South Asian History and Society*, ed. R. Guha (Delhi: Oxford University Press, 1982), 1–8. Guha taught for almost two decades (from 1959 to 1970, and from 1971 to 1980) in England, where he must have encountered forms of British history from below. These were decisively reworked, though, within the Indian context.

33. "Prose," 10–11.

34. Ibid., 22.

35. The most authoritative work on the Paxton actions is Brooke Hindle, "The March of the Paxton Boys," *William and Mary Quarterly* 3, 4 (1946): 461–86. See also Peter A. Butzin, "Politics, Presbyterians and the Paxton Riots, 1763–64," *Journal of Pennsylvania History* 51, 1 (1973): 70–84; Frank J. Cavaioli, "A Profile of the Paxton Boys: Murderers of the Conestoga Indians," *Journal of the Lancaster County Historical Society* 87, 3 (1983): 74–96; James E. Crowley, "The Paxton Disturbance and Ideas of Order in Pennsylvania Politics," *Pennsylvania History* 37 (1970): 317–39; Hubertis Cummings, "The Paxton Killings," *Journal of Presbyterian History* (1966), 219–43; George W. Franz, *Paxton: A Study of Community Structure and Mobility in the Colonial Pennsylvania Backcountry* (New York: Garland, 1989); *The Paxton Riots and the Frontier Theory*, ed. Wilbur R. Jacobs (Chicago: Rand McNally, 1967); James Kirby Martin, "The Return of the Paxton Boys and the Historical State of the Pennsylvania Frontier, 1764–1774," *Pennsylvania History* 38, 2 (1971): 117–33; James P. Myers Jr., "The Rev. Thomas Barton's Authorship of *The Conduct of the Paxton Men, Impartially Represented* (1764)," *Pennsylvania History* 61, 2 (1994): 155–84; David Sloan, "Protest in Pre-Revolutionary America: The Paxton Example," *Indiana Social Studies Quarterly* 27, 3 (1974/75): 29–37; David Sloan, "'A Time of Sifting and Winnowing': The Paxton Riots and Quaker Non-Violence in Pennsylvania," *Quaker History* 66, 1 (1977): 3–22; Alden T. Vaughan, "Frontier Banditti and the Indians:

The Paxton Boys' Legacy, 1763–1775," *Pennsylvania History* 51, 1 (1984): 1–29; William S. Hanna, *Benjamin Franklin and Proprietary Politics* (Stanford: Stanford University Press, 1964); James H. Hutson, *Pennsylvania Politics, 1746–1770: The Movement for Royal Government and Its Consequences* (Princeton: Princeton University Press, 1972); Francis Jennings, *Empire of Fortune: Crowns, Colonies, and Tribes in the Seven Years' War in America* (New York: Norton, 1988); Lorett Treese, *The Storm Gathering: The Penn Family and the American Revolution* (University Park: Pennsylvania State University Press, 1992); R. M. Brown, "Back Country Rebellions", 73–99; Elisha P. Douglass, *Rebels and Democrats: The Struggle for Equal Political Rights and Majority Rule during the American Revolution* (Chicago: Quadrangle, 1965), 219–27; J.C.D. Clark, *The Language of Liberty, 1660–1832: Political Discourse and Social Dynamics in the Anglo-American World* (New York: Cambridge University Press, 1994); and the introduction to *The Paxton Papers*, ed. John R. Dunbar (The Hague: M. Nijhoff, 1957).

36. *Elementary Aspects*, 333 and 11.

37. These categories correspond to chapters 2, 3, 4, 5, 6, and 7 of *Elementary Aspects*.

38. See "Lists of Pennsylvania Settlers Murdered, Scalped, and Taken Prisoners by Indians, 1755–1756," *Pennsylvania Magazine of History and Biography* 32, 3 (1908): 309–19. The list, found in the Conrad Weiser Papers, continues for pages, including the names of those "captivated."

39. Franz, *Paxton*, 51–52.

40. *Minutes of the Provincial Council*, 6: 729.

41. Ibid, 6: 741.

42. Ibid, 7: 87, 7: 93.

43. John F. Watson, *Annals of Philadelphia and Pennsylvania, in the Olden Time: Being a Collection of Memoirs, Anecdotes, and Incidents of the City and Its Inhabitants and of the Earliest Settlements of the Inland Part of Pennsylvania, from the Days of the Founders* (Philadelphia: J. B. Lippincott, 1870), 2: 164–65. I have found acknowledgment of this event in neither the Assembly records nor the Minutes of the Provincial Council. Watson's account contains little detail, although it cites two eyewitnesses interviewed by Watson. The most detailed account—still rather sketchy—is William Smith's *A Brief View of the Conduct of Pennsylvania for the Year 1755* (London: R. Griffiths, 1756) which describes the parade of bodies in a paragraph-long postscript. It should be kept in mind, though, that Smith was an antagonist of the Quaker-allied Germans. The most detailed account of the 1755 actions, with emphasis upon their ethnic context, can be found in Sally Schwartz, *"A Mixed Multitude": The Struggle for Toleration in Colonial Pennsylvania* (New York: New York University Press, 1987), chapters 6 and 7, esp. 214–16.

44. Smith, ibid, xx.

45. Waldstreicher, *In the Midst of Perpetual Fêtes*, 7.

46. This view of revolutionary demonstrations as rehearsals hinting at potential violence is well developed in Maier's important *From Resistance to Revolution*.

47. *Minutes of the Provincial Council*, 7: 242.

48. The Moffit-M'Mullen depositions appear in ibid, 7: 282–83; see also the November 1756 letter of William Johnson, a frontier trader (7: 341–42); a second-hand

account of a "Woman who once belonged to John Fraser"—either an indentured servant or a slave—who gave information to Col. Adam Stephen (7: 381–82); the spy report by one George McSwaine (7: 395); diplomat Conrad Weiser's November 1756 report (7: 431); and the accounts given by two Indian prisoners, Wauntaupenny and Succomabe, in May 1757 (7: 531). James Smith's captivity narrative refers to this same moment, as does Mary Jemison's. See also "The Narrative of Marie Le Roy and Barbara Leininger, for Three Years Captive Among the Indians," translated from the German by Edmund de Schweinitz, *Pennsylvania Magazine of History and Biography* 29, 4 (1905): 407–20. This German-language captivity tale concludes with brief references to forty other captives.

    49. Anderson, *Imagined Communities*.

    50. See Hutson, "Investigation," 10–18.

    51. For these episodes, see Fred Anderson, *Crucible of War: The Seven Years' War and the Fate of Empire in British North America, 1754–1766* (New York: Vintage, 2000), chapters 47, 64, and 65.

    52. Alison Olson, "The Pamphlet War over the Paxton Riots," *Pennsylvania Magazine of History and Biography* 123, 1–2 (1999): 31.

    53. Ibid, 31–32.

    54. *Paxton Papers*, ed. Dunbar, 113. Subsequent citations from the pamphlet war are from this edition, and are given parenthetically in the text.

    55. Amélie Oksenberg Rorty, *Mind in Action: Essays in the Philosophy of Mind* (Boston: Beacon, 1988).

    56. For recent examples, see Francis Jennings, *Benjamin Franklin, Politician* (New York: Norton, 1996), 165, and H. W. Brands, *The First American: The Life and Times of Benjamin Franklin* (New York: Doubleday, 2000), 350–52. Writes Brands, "A man of reason, [Franklin] saw reason being challenged by the darkest, bloodiest forces of unreason" (351).

    57. Norman Gottwald, *The Tribes of Yahweh: A Sociology of the Religion of Liberated Israel, 1250–1050 B.C.E.* (Maryknoll, NY: Orbis, 1979), 120–23.

4. Institution

    1. Thomas Pownall, *A Topographical Description of the Dominions of the United States of America . . .* , ed. Lois Mulkearn (Pittsburgh, PA: University of Pittsburgh Press, 1949), 103.

    2. The work was revised for republication in the mid-1780s, but was never published in Pownall's lifetime; a scholarly edition appeared in 1949. I cite this edition, as the changes between the two editions are not significant for my purposes.

    3. Martin Brückner, "Contested Sources of the Self: Native American Geographies and the Journals of Lewis and Clark," in *The Construction and Contestation of American Cultures and Identities in the Early National Period*, ed. Udo J. Hebel (Heidelberg: Universitätsverlag, 1999), 29–30.

    4. Antonio Gramsci, *Selections from the Prison Notebooks*, ed. and trans. Quintin Hoare and Geoffrey Nowell Smith (New York: International, 1971), 125–26.

    5. On "institutional proliferation," see my "Value of Conspiracy Theory," 24–26.

6. Cornelius Castoriadis, "Modern Capitalism and Revolution," in *Political and Social Writings*, vol. 2: *1955–1960: From the Workers' Struggle Against Bureaucracy to Revolution in the Age of Modern Capitalism*, ed. David Ames Curtis (Minneapolis: University of Minnesota Press, 1988), 273.

7. Sartre, *Critique*, 678–710.

8. Here I combine the definitions from Capitaine De Jeney's *The Partisan: or, the Art of Making War in Detachment* (a book Washington owned) and Johann Ewald's *Treatise on Partisan Warfare*; Ewald served in the American war in the Hessian *jägers*. See Mark V. Kwasny, *Washington's Partisan War, 1775–1783* (Kent, OH: Kent State University Press, 1996), xii–xiii.

9. Washington, *Writings* (New York: Library of America, 1997), 208.

10. Ibid, 398, emphasis added.

11. Gramsci, *Selections*, 138–39.

12. See John Keane, *Tom Paine: A Political Life* (Boston: Little, Brown, and Co., 1995), 424–28; Jack Fruchtman Jr., *Thomas Paine: Apostle of Freedom* (New York: Four Walls Eight Windows, 1994), 355–62; and Eric Foner, *Tom Paine and Revolutionary America* (New York: Oxford University Press, 1976), 249–52. Also illuminating is the chapter on Paine in Isaac Kramnick, *Republicanism and Bourgeois Radicalism: Political Ideology in Late-Eighteenth-Century England and America* (Ithaca, NY: Cornell University Press, 1990).

13. Thomas Paine, *Collected Writings* (New York: Library of America, 1995), 397. Further parenthetical citations refer to this edition, but see the version in *The Complete Writings of Thomas Paine*, ed. Philip S. Foner (New York: Citadel, 1945), which includes Paine's prefatory condemnation of the Babeuf conspiracy (1: 607–8).

14. *Complete Writings of Thomas Paine*, 2: 249.

15. Ibid, 2: 426–27.

16. Ibid, 2: 1048.

17. James Holstun, *A Rational Millennium: Puritan Utopias of Seventeenth-Century England and America* (New York: Oxford, 1987), 120. For a brief history of the "praying towns," see James Axtell, *The Invasion Within: The Contest of Cultures in Colonial North America* (New York: Oxford University Press, 1985), 139–78.

18. David Brainerd, *The Life and Diary of David Brainerd*, ed. Jonathan Edwards (Grand Rapids: Baker Book House, 1989), 156n5. I cite this edition, rather than the Yale scholarly edition of Edwards' 1749 *Life and Diary*, as the 1989 edition includes Brainerd's two-part journal, written for the Scottish Honorable Society for Propagating Christian Knowledge, and covering the period from June 1745 to June 1746.

19. "Sinners in the Hands of an Angry God," *A Jonathan Edwards Reader*, ed. John E. Smith, Harry S. Stout, and Kenneth P. Minkema (New Haven, CT: Yale University Press, 1995), 97.

20. Norman Pettit, "Editor's Introduction," *The Works of Jonathan Edwards*, vol. 7: *The Life of David Brainerd* (New Haven, CT: Yale University Press, 1985), 2.

21. *Minutes of the Provincial Council*, 3: 311–12.

22. The third treaty also has Sassoonan speaking for the Brandywine Delaware, who were also in attendance. Weslager, in *The Delaware Indians*, identifies three main enclaves of Delawares from the 1710s to the 1740s: the Unami-Delaware on the

Tulpehocken River northwest of Philadelphia; the Brandywines, southwest of Philadelphia; and the "Delaware in the Forks," at the fork of the Lehigh and Delaware
Rivers, due north of Philadelphia (174–79). Migrations in the 1740s, partially under
the direction of the Six Nations, merged and/or scattered some of these groupings
(192–93).

23. Jennings, *Empire of Fortune*, 273n52.

24. See, for example, *Minutes of the Provincial Council*, 3: 313 and 3: 364.

25. Cadwallader Colden, *A History of the Five Indian Nations Depending on the
Province of New York in America* (Ithaca, NY: Cornell University Press, 1958), xvii,
xx–xxi.

26. Paul A. W. Wallace, *Indians in Pennsylvania*, ed. William A. Hunter, 2nd ed.
(Harrisburg: Pennsylvania Historical and Museum Commission, 1981), offers a con-
cise general introduction to Native American migrations and settlements throughout
the colonial period. See also Charles A. Hanna, *The Wilderness Trail, or the Ventures
and Adventures of the Pennsylvania Traders on the Allegheny Path*, 2 vols. (Lewisburg, PA:
Wennawoods, 1995), a meanly bigoted work of 1911 but one nonetheless sensitive
to Native American migrations. The standard reference on Pennsylvania's Native
Americans is *Handbook of North American Indians*, vol. 15: *Northeast*, which includes
essays on the Delawares, Nanticokes, Susquehannocks, Wyandots, Eries, Shawnees,
Miamis, and the Iroquois Six Nations. See also Merrell, *Into the American Woods*.

27. Weslager, *Delaware Indians*, 33.

28. A.F.C. Wallace, *King of the Delawares*, 9.

29. *Minutes of the Provincial Council*, 3: 326. See Weslager, *Delaware Indians*, 33–
37, and Goddard, "Delaware," in *Handbook*, 214–16, 235–38. There is a common
conflation of second-order anthropological groupings based ostensibly on language
differences and geopolitical groupings, but in fact grounded in the speculative
classification of early missionaries; see *King of the Delawares*, 10–12. For instance,
there is a common confusion between the "Munsee" division of the Delawares (supposedly a linguistic and regional division), and the political grouping of the "Minisinks." Native synonymy confounds but also illuminates the matter; the self-
designation of the Delawares, *Lenape* [original person] became a contested term among
Delaware subgroups, leading to such terms as Lenni Lenape [original, original person];
see Goddard, 235–36.

30. Callender, "Shawnee," in *Handbook*, 617. Callender is quick to add that
after contact this cohesion was progressively undermined, and Gregory Dowd
stresses sharp divisions among the Shawnee (*A Spirited Resistance* [Baltimore: Johns
Hopkins, 1992], 66–71). Nonetheless, by Dowd's account the Shawnee remained
cohesive enough to challenge the Iroquois, profoundly frustrate the government of
Pennsylvania, militarize the Delaware, and constitute with the Cherokee a major
driving force in an unprecedented pan-Indian movement stretching from the Great
Lakes to the Gulf of Mexico.

31. *Indians in Pennsylvania*, 111–14; *King of the Delawares*, 49; Christian F. Feest,
"Nanticoke and Neighboring Tribes," in *Handbook*, 240–52; and C. A. Weslager,
The Nanticoke Indians: Past and Present (Newark: University of Delaware Press, 1983),
148–77.

32. *Indians in Pennsylvania*, 114–17.

33. Laurence M. Hauptman, "Refugee Havens: The Iroquois Villages of the Eighteenth Century," in *American Indian Environments: Ecological Issues in Native American History*, ed. Christopher Vecsey and Robert W. Venables (Syracuse, NY: Syracuse University Press, 1980), 128–39.

34. On Conestoga, see *Indians in Pennsylvania*, 104, 131, 134, 177. Wallace is ambivalent about whether the Conestogas were a sociopolitical cluster or, anthropologically, remnants of Susquehannocks. On Gnadenhütten, see *King of the Delawares*, 39–42. For Shamokin and Logstown, see *Wilderness Trail*, 1: 192–96, 352–61.

35. The Five Nations inconsistently became the Six Nations in white colonial terminology in the 1720s and early 1730s. It's worth noting that Pennsylvanians rarely used the term "Iroquois," a word of French provenance; the first use of that name that I find in the Pennsylvania documents occurs in June 1743.

36. The term "Mingo," of Delaware origin, may be familiar as Fenimore Cooper's pejorative for the Iroquois.

37. *Minutes*, 3: 100.

38. Ibid, 3: 403.

39. The following summary of the Six Nations' particularity draws on Daniel K. Richter, *The Ordeal of the Longhouse: The Peoples of the Iroquois League in the Era of European Colonization* (Chapel Hill: University of North Carolina Press, 1992); Jennings, *Empire of Fortune*; and Julian P. Boyd, "Indian Affairs in Pennsylvania," in *Indian Treaties Printed by Benjamin Franklin, 1736–1762*, ed. Boyd (Philadelphia: Historical Society of Pennsylvania, 1938).

40. See *Death and Rebirth of the Seneca*.

41. For an overview of "the Indian trade" in Pennsylvania, see Stephen H. Cutcliffe, "Colonial Indian Policy as a Measure of Rising Imperialism: New York and Pennsylvania, 1700–1755," *Western Pennsylvania Historical Magazine* 64 (1981): 237–68.

42. Paul Wallace, *Conrad Weiser, 1696–1760: Friend of Colonist and Mohawk* (Lewisburg, PA: Wennawood, 1996), 44.

43. Ibid, 41–42.

44. I have not been able to determine the conventional names for these nations, although Onachkaryagoes may be a Seneca rendition of Onguiara, a "Neutral" subgroup called Niagagarega by the French. But that it's unclear to whom these names refer is significant in itself, since the names denoted unknown entities to the colonials.

45. *Minutes of the Provincial Council*, 3: 447–48.

46. Ibid, 4: 83–84.

47. Ibid, 4: 564–65.

48. Ibid, 4: 732.

49. Ibid, 4: 771 and 5: 307–10.

50. Ibid, 4: 562, 4: 782, and 5: 311.

51. On the Walking Purchase, see *King of the Delawares*, 18–31, and *Empire of Fortune*, chapter 17 and appendix B.

52. *Minutes of the Provincial Council* 4: 579–80.

53. Ibid, 4: 735.

54. Ibid, 5: 8–9.

55. I cite the text found in Benjamin Franklin, *Writings* (New York: Library of America, 1987), which is followed by Franklin's essay on "Reasons and Motives for the Albany Plan of Union" (383–401).

56. Delaware and Georgia were not included. After the first three years, the apportionment of delegates was to be determined proportionally by the colonies' respective financial contributions.

57. *Empire of Fortune*, 101, emphasis in original.

58. The major texts advocating influence are Donald A. Grinde, *The Iroquois and the Founding of the American Nation* ([n.p.]: Indian Historian Press, 1977); Bruce E. Johansen, *Forgotten Founders: Benjamin Franklin, the Iroquois, and the Rationale for the American Revolution* (Ipswich, MA: Gambit, 1982); Grinde and Johansen, *Exemplar of Liberty: Native America and the Evolution of Democracy* (Los Angeles: American Indian Studies Center, 1991); and *Exiled in the Land of the Free: Democracy, Indian Nations, and the U. S. Constitution*, ed. Oren R. Lyons and John C. Mohawk (Santa Fe, NM: Clear Light, 1992). For a more recent and comprehensive bibliography, see the roundtable debate in *William and Mary Quarterly* 53, 3 (1996).

59. *Indian Roots of American Democracy*, ed. José Barreiro (Ithaca, NY: Akwe:kon, 1992), 3.

60. Grinde, *Iroquois*, 94; Johansen, *Forgotten*, 32.

61. Grinde and Johansen, *Exemplar*, 72.

62. See, e.g.: Grinde, *Iroquois*, 30–31; Johansen, *Forgotten*, 59–62; Grinde and Johansen, *Exemplar*, 93–96.

63. Johansen, *Forgotten*, xvi.

64. Grinde, *Iroquois*, 94, 13.

65. Grinde and Johansen note that while Franklin "quoted anecdotes and discussed matters relating to the Delawares and Susquehannas, when he turned to the question of diplomacy and political structure of American Indians, he focused on the Iroquois" (*Exemplar*, 199). The two authors discuss Tammany, a Delaware chief of the late seventeenth century who became an important folkloric figure for eighteenth-century Euro-Americans, but they stress his symbolic value and do not discuss specific influences of the Delawares (169–78). Other scattered references to the Delawares or Shawnees cast them as Iroquois dependents and/or tributaries.

66. Philip A. Levy, "Exemplars of Taking Liberties: The Iroquois Influence Thesis and the Problem of Evidence," *William and Mary Quarterly* 53, 3 (1996), 598–99.

67. Ibid, 592.

68. Jennings, *Benjamin Franklin*, 86.

69. Franklin, *Writings*, 444.

70. Adams, *Political Ideas of the American Revolution: Brittanic-American Contribution to the Problem of Imperial Organization, 1765–1775* (Durham, NC: Trinity College Press, 1922), 15–16.

71. Kramnick, *Republicanism and Bourgeois Radicalism*, 6.

72. *Minutes of the Provincial Council*, 3: 448.

73. Ibid, 3: 448.

74. Wittgenstein uses this expression to describe relatively indeterminate categories and goes on to suggest that conceptual "kinship" comes from use and deter-

mines the clarity or fuzziness of the concept. See *Philosophical Investigations*, ed. G. E. M. Anscombe (New York: Macmillan, 1958), §§ 67–77.

75. *Minutes of the Provincial Council*, 5: 495–96.

76. Franklin, *Writings*, 401.

77. Boyd, "Indian Affairs," xxix. Boyd's essay valuably chronicles the shift in influence from New York to Pennsylvania and back again; see xli–xlv.

78. *King of the Delawares*, 69–72, 77, 80–82.

79. Ibid, 76–77.

80. Ibid, 93.

81. Jefferson is quoted in Stanley Elkins and Eric McKitrick, *The Age of Federalism: The Early American Republic, 1788–1800* (New York: Oxford University Press, 1993), 753. The Publius quote is from *The Debate on the Constitution: Federalist and Anti-federalist Speeches, Articles, and Letters during the Struggle over Ratification*, 2 vols. (New York: Library of America, 1993), 1: 411. Further references to the *Federalist Papers* are taken from this edition and will be cited parenthetically, with volume number.

82. Wood, *Creation of the American Republic*, 562.

83. See Albert Furtwangler, *The Authority of Publius: A Reading of the Federalist Papers* (Ithaca, NY: Cornell University Press, 1984), chapters 1 and 2. The criticism on *Federalist No. 10*, let alone the *Federalist Papers*, is immense, and I have relied heavily on Furtwangler's analysis, which makes a strong case against the classic attribution of papers to Madison, Hamilton, or Jay, insisting that a more useful approach would be to think of Publius—several authors experiencing various influences in a collaborative project—as the author figure united by a complex compromising outlook and affect.

84. Ibid, 133.

85. Saul Cornell, *The Other Founders: Anti-Federalism and the Dissenting Tradition in America, 1788–1828* (Chapel Hill: University of North Carolina Press, 1999), 22; Jackson Turner Main, *The Antifederalists: Critics of the Constitution, 1781–1788* (Chicago: Quadrangle, 1961).

86. The standard histories are Leland D. Baldwin, *Whiskey Rebels: The Story of a Frontier Uprising*, rev. ed. (Pittsburgh, PA: University of Pittsburgh Press, 1968), and, more recently, Slaughter's *The Whiskey Rebellion*.

87. Alexander Hamilton, *Writings* (New York: Library of America, 2001), 832–33. The federal expedition to suppress the Whiskey Rebellion will be addressed in detail in the sequel to this work.

88. Anderson, *Imagined Communities*.

Conclusion

1. For provenance information, see *The Papers of Benjamin Franklin*, ed. Leonard W. Labaree, Helen C. Boatfield, Helene H. Fineman, and James H. Hutson, vol. 9 (New Haven, CT: Yale University Press, 1966), 47–59. Citations of the text are from this volume.

2. Here, and with the other quotation from page 67, Franklin cites Bostonian William Clarke's "Observations on the late and present Conduct of the French."

3. The pamphlet does not appear, for instance, in the Library of America collection of Franklin's works.

4. Franklin, *Writings* (New York: Library of America, 1987), 1392.

5. Franklin, *Writings*, 374. Franklin explained the embarrassing comment as a semantic confusion whereby "Boers herding together" became "herd of boars"—he'd meant the Dutch, not pigs! The context of these remarks clarifies the clarification: Franklin proceeded to complain about the small numbers of "purely white People in the World" in comparison to the "black or tawny" peoples, which included "the Germans" with the exception of the Saxons (374).

6. Louis K. Wechsler, *Benjamin Franklin: American and World Educator* (Boston: Twayne, 1976), 161, 160.

7. Max Weber, *The Protestant Ethic and the Spirit of Capitalism*, trans. Talcott Parsons (New York: Scribner's, 1958), 51, 54, 52.

8. Russell B. Nye, "Introduction," in *Autobiography and Other Writings*, by Benjamin Franklin (Boston: Houghton, 1958), xix; Michael Warner, *Letters of the Republic*, 75–77.

9. Herbert Leibowitz, *Fabricating Lives: Explorations in American Autobiography* (New York: Knopf, 1989), 66.

10. *Writings*, 1191.

11. Walter Benjamin, "Theses on the Philosophy of History," in *Illuminations*, trans. Harry Zohn (New York: Schocken, 1968), 257.

12. Carl Van Doren, *Benjamin Franklin* (New York: Viking, 1938), 115.

13. Michael Zuckerman, "Doing Good while Doing Well: Benevolence and Self-Interest in Franklin's *Autobiography*," in J. A. Leo Lemay, ed., *The Oldest Revolutionary: Essays on Benjamin Franklin* (Philadelphia: University of Pennsylvania Press, 1976), 447–48.

14. R. Jackson Wilson, "Introduction," in *The Autobiography of Benjamin Franklin* (New York: Modern Library, 1981), xi.

15. Labaree et al., "Introduction," in *Autobiography of Benjamin Franklin*, 23–24.

16. A few illustrations: *The English Literatures of America*, ed. Myra Jehlen and Michael Warner (New York: Routledge, 1997), reproduces part 1, the "Plan of Conduct" from part 2, and a lone paragraph on smallpox from part 3; *The Literatures of Colonial America*, ed. Susan Castillo and Ivy Schweitzer (Malden, MA: Blackwell, 2001), reprints part 2; *The Heath Anthology of American Literature*, ed. Paul Lauter et al. (Boston: Houghton Mifflin, 2002), reprints parts 1 and 2 and a few pages of part 3.

17. Franklin, *Writings*, 1392.

18. Frederick Engels, "Revolution and Counter-Revolution in Germany," in *Karl Marx, Frederick Engels: Collected Works*, vol. 11 (New York: International, 1979), 9.

19. The few paragraphs of part 4 were probably written in the winter of 1789–90, months before Franklin's death, and seem to be extending the narrative of part 3 without formulating a new line of presentation. P. M. Zall's attempted reconstruction of the composition process of part 1 argues that interpolations may have been made until the fall of 1775, but still maintains that most of the text was probably written in 1771; see Zall, "A Portrait of the Autobiographer as an Old Artificer," in Lemay et al., *The Oldest Revolutionary*, 56–57. See also Lemay and Zall, "Introduction," in

The Autobiography of Benjamin Franklin: A Genetic Text (Knoxville: University of Tennessee Press, 1981), xxi. I've used Lemay and Zall's notes on the "genetic text," but citations from the *Autobiography* refer to the Library of America edition, which reproduces the genetic text.

20. In the spring of 1788, the rural counties had sent petitions, signed by over five thousand farmers, pleading that the legislature oppose the new constitution, and Antifederalists were mobilizing for a September convention in Harrisburg; meanwhile, urban Federalists were preparing to capitalize on their victory by repealing Pennsylvania's state constitution, the most democratic of the revolutionary constitutions. See Robert L. Brunhouse, *The Counter-Revolution in Pennsylvania, 1776–1790* (Harrisburg: Pennsylvania Historical Commission, 1942), 212–14.

21. See Van Doren, *Benjamin Franklin*, 132, and Ormond Seavey, *Becoming Benjamin Franklin: The Autobiography and the Life* (University Park: Pennsylvania State University Press, 1988), 156–57. Even the most detailed account of Franklin and the Hemphill trial, Merton A. Christensen's "Franklin on the Hemphill Trial: Deism Versus Presbyterian Orthodoxy" (*William and Mary Quarterly* 10 [1953]: 422–40), is primarily concerned with clarification of Franklin's theological beliefs.

22. Franklin wrote "A Dialogue between Two Presbyterians," "Observations on the Proceeding against Mr. Hemphill," and "A Defense of Mr. Hemphill's Observations," dated 10 April, 17 July, and 30 October 1735, respectively, by the editors of his collected works. A fourth pamphlet, "A Letter to a Friend in the Country" (25 September 1735) was probably written by Hemphill, although Franklin likely wrote its preface and may even have revised it. Given this last pamphlet's strong parallels, in some regards, with other writings of Franklin, I am assuming that its passage on Philadelphia, cited below, was authored by Franklin.

23. Franklin, *The Papers of Benjamin Franklin*, vol. 2 (New Haven, CT: Yale University Press, 1960), 30.

24. Ibid, 104–5.

25. Ibid, 84.

26. Ibid, 74–75.

27. Ibid, 48.

28. Franklin, *Writings*, 439–40.

29. Immobile, but not immobilized. Franklin's account misleads, insofar as it repeats the cliché that Quakers were manacled by "one of their Principles, that no kind of War was lawful" (1416). Francis Jennings has made a strong case, in reference to the second war, that the Quaker Assembly was not averse to a strong defense but was determined to resist the strengthening of the Proprietary executive branch and the weakening of the legislature; see *Empire of Fortune*, especially chapter 17.

30. The Quakers, hardly a newly fused ideological group, might seem the obvious exception here, though in the context at issue—a state militarization abstractly at odds with an obvious religious principle—the general lesson holds.

31. Franklin, *Writings*, 1361; Van Doren, *Benjamin Franklin*, 75. See, more recently, H. W. Brands, *The First American: The Life and Times of Benjamin Franklin* (New York: Doubleday, 2000), 92–93.

32. Franklin, *Writings*, prints these under the titles "Rules for a Club Formerly Established in Philadelphia" and the "Proposals and Queries to be Asked the Junto," following the texts if not the titles of Labaree's Yale edition of the *Papers*. For a brief discussion of provenance, see *The Papers of Benjamin Franklin*, vol. 1 (New Haven, CT: Yale University Press, 1959), 255–56.

33. David Leven, *Cotton Mather: The Young Life of the Lord's Remembrancer, 1663–1703* (Cambridge, MA: Harvard University Press, 1978), 75, 172–73.

34. *Writings*, 1092.

35. Cotton Mather, *Bonifacius: An Essay Upon the Good*, ed. David Levin (Cambridge, MA: Belknap-Harvard, 1966), 133.

36. Ibid, 133–34.

37. Franklin, *Writings*, 1092.

38. Ibid, 1092–93.

39. Citations from Mather, *Bonifacius*, 206–7, and Franklin, *Writings*, 136–37.

40. Warner, *Letters*, 90.

41. Franklin, *The Papers of Benjamin Franklin*, vol. 3 (New Haven, CT: Yale University Press, 1961), 198–99.

42. Ibid, 200–201.

43. Ibid, 216, 238.

44. Ibid, 215–16.

45. *Writings*, 1140–41.

46. On Franklin's interest in the Susquehannah Company, see Thomas P. Abernethy, *Western Lands and the American Revolution* (New York: D. Appleton-Century, 1937), 15.

47. Ibid.

48. Robert F. Oaks, "The Impact of British Western Policy on the Coming of the American Revolution in Pennsylvania," in *Pennsylvania Magazine of History and Biography* 101, 2 (1977), 171–72.

49. "Observations Concerning the Increase of Mankind, Peopling of Countries, &c." appeared in 1751, just as Franklin's land speculation was beginning.

50. Abernethy, *Western*, 25.

51. Franklin, *Papers*, 5: 456–63.

52. Franklin, *Papers*, 6: 468.

53. *Writings*, 805.

54. Vernon Parrington, *Main Currents in American Thought: An Interpretation of American Literature from the Beginnings to 1920* (New York: Harcourt, Brace and Co., 1927–30), 177.

55. Franklin, *Papers*, vol. 3, 216, emphasis added.

56. Van Doren, *Benjamin Franklin*, 756. Bailyn states that Franklin's speech was reprinted "in almost every state, a total of 36 times before mid-February 1788" (*The Debate on the Constitution: Federalist and Antifederalist Speeches, Articles, and Letters during the Struggle over Ratification*, ed. Bernard Bailyn [New York: Library of America, 1993], 1: 1138).

57. James Madison, *Notes of Debate in the Federal Convention of 1787 Reported by James Madison* (Athens: Ohio University Press, 1966), 654.

58. Ibid., 656.

59. *Minutes of the Provincial Council,* 5: 676. For Scarouady's broader analysis of imperial politics, see his comments throughout the treaty, 5: 665–86.

60. Ibid, 5: 680.

61. Peter Sloterdijk, *Critique of Cynical Reason,* trans. Michael Eldred (Minneapolis: University of Minnesota Press, 1987), 15, 11.

62. Ibid, 20.

Index

235

Ed White is associate professor of English at the University of Florida in Gainesville.